Domestic Violence and Protecting Children

by the same author

Domestic Violence and Child Protection
Directions for Good Practice
Edited by Cathy Humphreys and Nicky Stanley
ISBN 978 1 84310 276 2
eISBN 978 1 84642 476 2

of related interest

Practical Guide to Child Protection
The Challenges, Pitfalls and Practical Solutions
Joanna Nicolas
ISBN 978 1 84905 586 4
eISBN 978 1 78450 032 0

Challenging Child Protection
New Directions in Safeguarding Children
Edited by Lorraine Waterhouse and Janice McGhee
ISBN 978 1 84905 395 2
eISBN 978 0 85700 760 5

The Common-Sense Guide to Improving the Safeguarding of Children
Three Steps to Make a Real Difference
Terry McCarthy
ISBN 978 1 84905 621 2
eISBN 978 1 78450 092 4

Social Work with Troubled Families
A Critical Introduction
Edited by Keith Davies
ISBN 978 1 84905 549 9
eISBN 978 0 85700 974 6

Engaging with Perpetrators of Domestic Violence
Practical Techniques for Early Intervention
Kate Iwi and Chris Newman
ISBN 978 1 84905 380 8
eISBN 978 0 85700 738 4

Eradicating Child Maltreatment
Evidence-Based Approaches to Prevention and Intervention Across Services
Edited by Arnon Bentovim and Jenny Gray
Foreword by Harriet Ward
ISBN 978 1 84905 449 2
eISBN 978 0 85700 823 7

Domestic Violence and Protecting Children

New Thinking and Approaches

Edited by Nicky Stanley and
Cathy Humphreys

Jessica Kingsley *Publishers*
London and Philadelphia

Contains public sector information licensed under the Open Government Licence v3.0.

First published in 2015
by Jessica Kingsley Publishers
73 Collier Street
London N1 9BE, UK
and
400 Market Street, Suite 400
Philadelphia, PA 19106, USA

www.jkp.com

Library of Congress Cataloging in Publication Data
Domestic violence and protecting children : new thinking and approaches / edited by Nicky Stanley and
Cathy Humphreys.
     pages cm
  Includes bibliographical references.
  ISBN 978-1-84905-485-0 (alk. paper)
 1. Child welfare--Great Britain. 2. Child welfare. 3. Family violence--Great Britain.
4. Family violence.
5. Child abuse--Great Britain. 6. Child abuse. 7. Social work with children--Great Britain. 8. Social work
with children. I. Stanley, Nicky, 1955- II. Humphreys, Catherine.
  HV751.A6D663 2015
  362.760941--dc23
                              2015008797

British Library Cataloguing in Publication Data
A CIP catalogue record for this book is available from the British Library

ISBN 978 1 84905 485 0
eISBN 978 0 85700 875 6

Printed and bound in Great Britain

For our grown-up children: Rachel, Jack and Tom and Nicky

CONTENTS

Introduction: Domestic Violence and Protecting Children:
The Changing Landscape   13
Nicky Stanley, Professor of Social Work, University of Central Lancashire, and
Cathy Humphreys, Professor of Social Work, University of Melbourne

Part One: Children's and Young People's Perspectives

1. Children's Views of Safety and Adversity When Living
with Domestic Violence   18
Anita Morris, Manager of Social Work, Western Health, Melbourne,
Cathy Humphreys, and Kelsey Hegarty, Professor, Primary Care Research Unit,
University of Melbourne

2. Traversing the Generational Gap: Young People's Views
on Intervention and Prevention of Teenage Intimate
Partner Violence   34
Per Moum Hellevik, PhD candidate, Norwegian Centre for Violence and
Traumatic Stress Studies, University of Oslo, Carolina Överlien, Assistant
Professor, Stockholm University, Christine Barter, NSPCC Senior Research
fellow, School for Policy Studies, University of Bristol, Marsha Wood, Research
Associate, School of Policy Studies, University of Bristol, Nadia Aghtaie,
Lecturer, School of Policy Studies, University of Bristol, Cath Larkins,
Codirector, Centre for Children's and Young People's Participation, University
of Central Lancashire, and Nicky Stanley

Part Two: Prevention and Intervention for Children and Young People

3. School-based Prevention and the Disclosure of
Domestic Violence: A Can of Worms?   50
Jane Ellis, Senior Lecturer in Social Policy, Anglia Ruskin University,
Soo Downe, Professor of Midwifery Studies, University of Central Lancashire,
Nicola Farrelly, Research Fellow, School of Social Work, University of Central
Lancashire, Sandra Hollinghurst, Senior Lecturer in Health Economics,
University of Bristol, and Nicky Stanley

4. Advocacy for Children and Young People Experiencing
    Domestic Violence   63
    *Joanne Westwood, Senior Lecturer, School of Applied Social Science, University
    of Stirling, and Cath Larkins*

5. Children Who Are Violent to Their Parents
    Need Protection Too   81
    *Paula Wilcox, Reader in Criminology, University of Brighton, and
    Michelle Pooley, Community Engagement and Domestic Violence Practitioner,
    Brighton and Hove City Council*

6. Forced Marriage *Is* a Child Protection Matter   97
    *Zahra Alijah, Lecturer in Education, University of Manchester, and
    Khatidja Chantler, Reader, School of Social Work, University of Central
    Lancashire*

Part Three: Interventions for Mothers and Children

7. More Than a Mirage? Safe Contact for Children and Young
    People Who Have Been Exposed to Domestic Violence   112
    *Lorraine Radford, Professor of Social Policy and Social Work, University
    of Central Lancashire, and Marianne Hester, Chair in Gender Violence and
    International Policy, University of Bristol*

8. Supporting the Relationship Between Mothers and Children
    in the Aftermath of Domestic Violence   130
    *Cathy Humphreys, Ravi K. Thiara, Director, Centre for the Study of Safety and
    Well-Being, University of Warwick, Cathy Sharp, Director, Research for Real,
    and Jocelyn Jones, Director, Mindful Practice Ltd*

9. Infant-led Practice: Responding to Infants and Their
    Mothers (and Fathers) in the Aftermath of
    Domestic Violence   148
    Wendy Bunston, Associate Lecturer, La Trobe University, Melbourne

Part Four: Working with Abusive Fathers

10. Focusing on Fathering in the Context of Domestic Abuse:
    Children's and Fathers' Perspectives   166
    *Stephanie Holt, Assistant Professor, School of Social Work and Social Policy,
    Trinity College, Dublin*

11. Expanding Understandings of Success: Domestic Violence
    Perpetrator Programmes, Children and Fathering   182
    Sue Alderson, Senior Lecturer in Social Work, University of Seychelles,
    Liz Kelly, Director, Child and Woman Abuse Studies Unit, London
    Metropolitan University, and Nicole Westmarland, Professor of Criminology,
    Durham University

12. Reshaping the Child Protection Response to Domestic
    Violence Through Collaborative Working   196
    Neil Blacklock, Development Director, Respect, and Ruth Phillips, Doctoral
    Candidate, Child and Woman Abuse Studies Unit, London Metropolitan
    University

Part Five: Interagency Work

13. Working Together, Working Apart: General Practice
    Professionals' Perspectives on Interagency Collaboration in
    Relation to Children Experiencing Domestic Violence   214
    Eszter Szilassy, Research Associate, School of Social and Community Medicine,
    University of Bristol, Jessica Drinkwater, Aacademic General Practitioner,
    University of Leeds, Marianne Hester, Chair in Gender, Violence and
    International Policy, University of Bristol, Cath Larkins, Nicky Stanley,
    William Turner, Senior Lecturer, School for Policy Studies, University of
    Bristol, and Gene Feder, Professor of Primary Care, University of Bristol

14. Moving Towards Integrated Domestic Violence Services for
    Children and Families   232
    Nicky Stanley

    Conclusion: New Challenges and Developments in
    Responding to Children Experiencing Domestic Violence   249
    Cathy Humphreys and Nicky Stanley

    CONTRIBUTOR PROFILES   253

    SUBJECT INDEX   261

    AUTHOR INDEX   269

LIST OF TABLES

Table 4.1   Ages of children and young people referred to
HARV in evaluation period   67

Table 4.2   Demographic information for evaluation participants   69

Table 4.3   Length of time KIDVA cases opened years 2 and 3   75

Table 4.4   Reason for KIDVA case closures   77

Table 13.1   Research participants   216

LIST OF FIGURES

Figure 7.1 The 'three planets model' of agency responses to children and domestic violence 115

Figure 7.2 Coercive control and mothering 122

Figure 8.1 The iceberg exercise from a mothers' group: 'Through the eyes of a mother' 141

Figure 8.2 The iceberg exercise from a mothers' group: 'Through the eyes of a child' 141

Figure 11.1 Example of feelings from research book 191

Figure 12.1 Children subject to child protection plans by category of abuse 198

Figure 12.2 Reductions in domestic violence related child removals as a proportion of all removals after implementation of the Safe and Together Model™ in Florida, US 207

INTRODUCTION

Domestic Violence and Protecting Children

The Changing Landscape

Nicky Stanley and Cathy Humphreys

'Why doesn't she leave?' has been a much-debated question that domestic violence organisations have spoken out on strongly by describing the substantial personal and structural barriers that stand in the way of women escaping relationships of violence and abuse. It is a question rarely asked of children, however, as they often have little or no choice about leaving abusive perpetrators of domestic violence. Their lives are not necessarily improved by separation as they are frequently 'ordered' to have ongoing contact with fathers who have been abusive and may continue to be so post-separation. Moreover, separation can inflict a range of changes and losses on children and young people that they have not consented to.

The protection, safety and well-being of children affected by domestic violence continue to be a significant and complex social problem. One in four children experiences domestic violence of which five per cent is reported to be chronic and severe (Radford *et al.* 2011). The detrimental impact on children's health (Riviara *et al.* 2007) and well-being (Kitzmann *et al.* 2003) is uncontested. However, effective interventions are proving difficult to find and sustain although our understanding of domestic violence has developed and the sector abounds with creativity, commitment and concern for the lives of those affected by domestic violence.

In compiling this book, we wanted to capture some of the changes and innovations in the field that have emerged since we last collaborated to produce *Domestic Violence and Child Protection: Directions for Good Practice* in 2006. We had originally intended to publish a second edition of that book but there were so many new themes and developments to report that we decided that this would be an entirely new and original collection.

However, as in our earlier book, we have taken a broad understanding of 'protecting children' which goes well beyond statutory intervention as the primary source of safety and protection. Whilst recognising the significance of the mother–child relationship as the foundation for safety and protection for most children living with domestic violence, we have structured the book to begin with the voices of children to highlight their perspective and to counterbalance the tendency for children and their needs to be marginalised.

One major change that has occurred in this field is that domestic violence is now conceptualised in increasingly diverse forms. This recognition of variety and complexity testifies to the increasing confidence of the domestic violence sector and is reflected in both research and practice. In addition to addressing children's and young people's experiences of domestic violence in their parents' relationships, this volume includes chapters on violence and abuse in young people's intimate relationships including online as well as offline abuse, child to parent violence and forced marriage. Hearteningly, we have been able to include much more evidence on interventions aiming to support children and parents who have experienced domestic violence. These include prevention programmes delivered in schools, advocacy for children and young people, a schools-based intervention targeting forced marriage, interventions for infants and programmes that work to repair the mother–child relationship in the aftermath of domestic violence.

In 2006, including a section in our book on work with perpetrators felt like an innovative step, whilst in 2015 it seems a necessary part of any attempt to explore the service response to children's experience of domestic violence. In 2006, children's perspectives were rarely integrated into research on interventions for perpetrators of domestic abuse, whereas the section on perpetrators in this book presents a wealth of material on children's views of their fathers' fathering and on their involvement in services aiming to change their fathers' behaviour.

There are also new players in this field. Health, mental health services, education and drug and alcohol services are now more actively involved in multi-agency interventions. They bring increased opportunities for information sharing, the assessment and management of risk and a wider range of interventions. However, the complexity of managing confidentiality and the costs of collaboration set challenges which require constant negotiation and attention. Multi-agency working is an unpredictable and time-consuming process, but proving to be better than the alternative of single agency working. The continuation of multi-agency working, even in times of austerity and government cuts, provides testimony to the recognised value of working together.

The feminist discourse which has continued to advocate a gendered analysis of domestic violence and has spearheaded the social movement to address violence against women and their children has also shifted focus since 2006. Intersectionality has helped to reflect and construct the diversity of voices and experiences that are impacted by domestic violence (Laing and Humphreys 2013). The issues of poverty, age, disability, 'race' and ethnicity enhance the articulation of gender and domestic violence in ways that are more inclusive than earlier conceptions (McKibbin *et al.* 2015; Carbin and Edenheim 2013). Again, we have attempted to reflect this attention to diversity within the different chapters in this edited collection.

However, some aspects remain unchanged. Child contact continues to provide a context where domestic violence can be perpetuated and where the child or young person can be particularly isolated and exposed. Child protection social work still struggles to respond to families in ways that are not punitive or threatening. However, evidence presented in this book indicates that engaging more fully with abusive fathers, listening to children and providing them and their parents with appropriate services that address prevention and intervention may represent routes towards relinquishing negative approaches that make families wary of seeking support.

Some of the new and diverse forms of harm for children and young people identified here call attention to service gaps and shortfalls. Having uncovered the extent and nature of online and offline abuse in young people's intimate relationships, we need to identify appropriate forms of help for those who disclose such experiences. Schools are currently struggling to respond to the policy guidance in respect of forced marriage. Practitioners are requesting training and support to enable them to respond to child to parent violence.

Our knowledge base is expanding. Extensive research programmes exploring all aspects of children and young people's experiences of domestic violence as well as strategies to support their safety and well-being are pointing to new directions for policy and practice. Each chapter in this book draws on research studies to inform the authors' arguments and ideas. In devising a structure which organises the different aspects of our knowledge we have created a number of subsections for the book: (1) children's and young people's perspectives; (2) prevention and intervention for children and young people; (3) interventions for mothers and children; (4) working with abusive fathers; (5) interagency work.

Editing this collection has given us an idea of the measure of progress in this field over the last ten years. We find that whilst many challenges remain, new and imaginative interventions are emerging, diversity is increasing, the evidence base has developed and a wider range of actors are now engaged in protecting children from domestic violence. Children and young people who experience domestic violence have moved centre stage. This book aims to ensure that they stay there.

References

Carbin, M. and Endenheim, S. (2013) 'The intersectional turn in feminist theory: a dream of a common language?' *European Journal of Women's Studies 20*, 233–248.

Kitzmann, K., Gaylord, N., Holt, A. and Kenny, E. (2003) 'Child witnesses to domestic violence: a meta-analytic review.' *Journal of Consulting and Clinical Psychology 71*, 339–352.

Laing, L. and Humphreys, C. (2013) *Social Work and Domestic Violence: Critical and Reflective Practice.* London: Sage Publications.

McKibbin, G., Humphreys, C., Hamilton, B., Kellett, C. and Duncan, R. (2015) 'The intersectional turn in feminist theory: a response to Carbin and Edenheim (2013).' *European Journal of Women's Studies 22*, 99–103.

Radford, L., Corral, S., Bradley, C., Fisher, H. *et al.* (2011) *Child Cruelty in the UK 2011: An NSPCC Study into Childhood Abuse and Neglect over the Last 30 Years.* London: National Society for the Prevention of Cruelty to Children.

Rivara, F. P., Anderson, M. L., Fishman, P., Bonomi A. *et al.* (2007) 'Intimate partner violence and health care costs and utilization for children living in the home.' *Pediatrics 120*, 1270–1277.

PART ONE

Children's and Young People's Perspectives

CHAPTER 1

Children's Views of Safety and Adversity When Living with Domestic Violence

Anita Morris, Cathy Humphreys and Kelsey Hegarty

Introduction

> He held her down when she was like three months old, held a knife to her. He wouldn't have killed his own kid, but he was just trying to scare Mum. (Michelle, 16, talking about her younger sister and her stepfather)

In 1924, a paediatrician, Dr Ira Wile, wrote of children raised in a 'brawling home' (Wile 1924, p.474). Nearly a century later, there are still too many children and young people like Michelle who grow up in homes where there is domestic violence. Figures can convey the magnitude of the problem: one in four children in the UK and Australia has experienced domestic violence by 18 years of age (Indermaur 2001; Radford *et al.* 2011). Prevalence rates in the United States are similar (Finkelhor *et al.* 2009), whilst indigenous Australian young people and children in developing countries experience domestic violence at much higher rates (Indermaur 2001; Kishor and Johnson 2004).

Despite so many children and young people growing up in households marred by violence, opportunities for these children to talk about their experiences and to receive the support they need are limited (Murray and Powell 2012; Wilcox 2007). Yet studies that have directly sought children's perspectives have shown that children want to be able to talk to someone and will seek out the support of trusted adults and peers when it is safe to do so. Moreover, where such support is available, it is known to be of benefit to children's safety and well-being (Buckley, Holt and Whelan 2007; McGee 2000; Mullender *et al.* 2002).

This chapter draws on the findings of a qualitative Australian study known as the SARAH project, which involved interviews and focus groups with children and their mothers from a primary care population. All the participants had experienced domestic violence although no children were living with the violent father or stepfather at the time of the interviews. However, some of the younger children had regular, usually court-ordered, contact with their biological father. The SARAH project aimed to bring to light the experiences of children drawn from a primary care population, a group of children often hidden from view. It provided children and their mothers with an opportunity to talk about children's understandings of safety and resilience in the context of domestic violence.

Following a brief historical overview of research with children, the main part of this chapter reveals children's perspectives according to themes of vulnerability, danger, safety and agency experienced in the context of domestic violence. The lived experiences of four families who participated in the SARAH project are used to highlight facets of each theme and provide the basis for the implications for practice.

Background

Research interest in the plight of children who experience domestic violence gained momentum in the 1990s (Graham-Bermann and Levendosky 1998; Stanley 1997; Jaffe, Wolfe and Wilson 1990) following a time of service expansion for women experiencing domestic violence (Walby 1990). Through this context, it was noted that women who were escaping violent partners brought their children with them to the shelters (Mullender and Morley 1994). As researchers began to understand better the predicament of women experiencing domestic violence, they also sought to know more about the children (Kelly 1994). However, as questions about children's experience of domestic violence increased, concerns began to be raised about the ethics of researching children's experiences without consulting them directly (Peled 2001). Principles founded in the United Nations Convention on the Rights of the Child (1989) and supported by an emerging literature on the 'sociology of childhood' which understood children as social agents (Qvortrup 2005) provided the foundations for changes in research practice.

The concerns expressed by some of those researching in the domestic violence field included the criticisms that mainly adult perceptions and adult interpretations were sought; that researchers relied on refuge or child protection samples rather than understanding the broader group of children who experience domestic violence; and finally that there was a heavy dependency on quantitative studies (Edleson 1999).

Heeding the call for more qualitative research and broader sampling of children, the SARAH project was designed as a health-based study that reflected the new milieu of domestic violence research with children (Morris, Hegarty and Humphreys 2012). Such studies consider more closely the ethical nature of the research, the safety of participants and researchers, and look for ways to increase children's participation and collaboration in the research (Eriksson and Näsman 2010; Mudaly and Goddard 2009; Överlien 2012).

The SARAH project

To better understand children's safety in the context of domestic violence, the study took a child-centred approach (Mudaly and Goddard 2009) informed by a theoretical framework of ethics of care (Groenhout 2004) and dialogical ethics (Koehn 1998). These theories provided an empathic and relational lens through which to consider children's moral reasoning and decision making.

The study recruited participants from two general practice clinics and from a larger primary care study (WEAVE) of women who had experienced domestic violence (Hegarty *et al.* 2013). A total of 23 children and 18 mothers participated in semi-structured interviews and focus groups. The children ranged in age from eight years to 24 years old.

Mothers in the SARAH project voluntarily completed an expression-of-interest pamphlet in the waiting room of the clinic or were contacted via a safe phone number following their participation in WEAVE (Hegarty *et al.* 2013). Mothers consented to their child's participation, whilst children were able to assent (Alderson and Morrow 2011). This process of consent and assent affirmed the mother's role in deciding what was safe and appropriate for her child, whilst asserting the child's right to agree or disagree to participate in the research. All mothers participated in an initial risk-assessment interview so that the researcher could confirm that it was safe for a family to participate.

The researcher developed protocols for distress, disclosure and researcher safety (Morris *et al.* 2012). Child-friendly methods were employed including: the option to have a support person in the interview; an activity book to record responses to interview questions; and having toys, activities and refreshments available (Mudaly and Goddard 2009).

A hermeneutic phenomenological (Laverty 2003) approach was taken to analyse the data. This is an approach that focuses on the essence and interpretation of participants' experiences, leading ultimately to practical understanding. Mothers' perspectives on their children's experiences provided a family context and gave insight into the mother–child relationship both during the domestic violence and post-separation.

Perspectives on vulnerability and danger

> Cruel, evil, disgusting…he's just not a nice person. (Tahlia, 19, describing her father, Rodney)

This section highlights the experiences of children from two families whose stories of adversity reflect those of the majority of participant families in the SARAH project. Not only did these families experience adversity when living with domestic violence, but significant vulnerability and danger remained present for children and their mothers in the post-separation environment.

> I hated seeing Mum getting hurt. I remember one time Mum was in my room, reading a book to me…and Dad came in, he was just spitting on her and Mum just wasn't paying attention and then Dad went and got a cane stool, and…went to throw it at us, so I like kind of jumped towards Mum to try and stop it hitting her. But he still threw it anyway, didn't stop him. I think it hit both of us. (Tahlia, 19)

The persistent attempts by Tahlia's father, Rodney, to intrude on and harm Tahlia and her mother, Opal, were typical of the dangerous events children spoke of during their interviews. Tahlia, her older half-sister and their mother experienced 15 years of severe violence perpetrated by Rodney. They spoke of trying to have a safe and 'normal' home life despite many failed attempts by them and the police to keep Rodney from the home. The impact of his violence was far-reaching and included chronic physical and psychological injuries to mother and daughter, disruption of Tahlia's schooling contributing to Tahlia's ultimate disengagement from school, an inability to maintain employment and general isolation from family and friends.

Tahlia had witnessed her father injuring and abusing her mother and damaging household goods and furniture. On different occasions, Tahlia and her sister had hidden in a wardrobe and sought refuge with friends and neighbours. Simple life events that other families might take for granted could trigger violence:

> One year we put the Christmas tree in a different spot and that was it. Christmas presents were up the backyard and he went nuts. He threw them up the backyard because we put the Christmas tree in a different spot and he didn't like it. (Tahlia, 19)

Rodney's violence led to him being removed from the home and child protection services became involved. This too was a distressing experience:

> Once we split up and I had [child protection services] coming here randomly making sure that I was doing everything right – and I do. I cooked my meals, the house was clean, the kids were well looked after, because he caused me that trouble but he left for 12 months, [he] didn't have to answer any questions to [child protection services] or anything but I had to go to court to prove that I could keep my kids safe from him or else they were going to take them off me. (Opal, mother)

At the time of her interview, Opal reported that the court had granted a life-long intervention order. Despite reprieve from the regular intrusion, confrontation and violence, the scars of the violence were not easily erased. Mirroring her parents' relationship, Tahlia talked about how in early adolescence she had experienced violence in her own intimate relationship that included verbal abuse, physical violence, isolation and sexual infidelity. Her understanding of the violence was intertwined with feelings of love for the perpetrator:

> He wasn't a very nice person, but I still stayed with him because I loved him. And there was one time that he thought I'd lied to him, so he held me down and burnt me with a cigarette lighter. But I loved him so I still stayed with him. There'll always be that special...part [struggles with this word] in my heart for him, so I guess I can kind of tell how Mum feels except she was with Dad for a lot longer than I was with my ex-boyfriend. (Tahlia, 19)

Tahlia's narrative conveys her negative opinion of her father and her ex-partner, whilst at the same time she grapples with her feelings of obligation and love (see Chapter 10). Tahlia and her family's experiences demonstrated how severe violence over many years led to other vulnerabilities which were exacerbated by ineffective formal responses. At the time of their interviews, the danger had ebbed, Tahlia had become a mother and her stepsister was said to be enjoying a professional career and a stable partner. Opal was appreciative of a small job she had started.

These small gains are worthy of celebration, but the vulnerabilities remained as Opal described her own and Tahlia's ongoing battles with depression. They talked about trying now to build a 'normal' family life. However, the overriding theme in their narrative was one of a lack of agency for both mother and child.

Like Tahlia and her family, eight-year-old Linda, her mother Joyce, younger brother Mitchell and older stepsister Amelia experienced severe domestic violence perpetrated by Linda's father. An example is provided by Amelia:

> We decided that it'd be fun to sleep out on the trampoline, but mum's ex had all his friends over and he decided it would be great if he started smashing chairs and stuff and getting an axe out and chopping everything up and it was just really ridiculous and so we both got really scared and went back inside. I was just really disappointed and rather embarrassed... He does, he did stuff like that all the time. He was just...stupid. (Amelia, 15)

Joyce and her ex-partner's separation was preceded by a particularly brutal episode of violence that involved dragging her along the ground by her hair whilst in the company of friends and their children. The violence was subsequently mirrored in the behaviour of Linda's stepbrothers towards her when she stayed at her father's home:

> [Eight-year-old stepbrother] has been dragging me by the hair, [six-year-old stepbrother] has been kicking me up the bum. I don't retaliate to them otherwise I get into trouble. [Father's new partner] always says I'm the one who makes them cry. He [stepbrother] stamps his feet then he punches me in the stomach. I'm even going to be talking to my chaplain at school. You ask to go home and Dad says 'no', because I'm here for him. (Linda, 8)

In Linda's world there are two vastly different environments: the safe one she shares with her mother and siblings and the unsafe one she experiences when she goes to her father's home every second weekend for court-ordered access. In this environment, Linda's need for safety is quashed by the violence and control her father has modelled and which is now perpetuated by her young stepbrothers. Recognising that this feels unsafe, Linda has tried to assert herself and negotiate with her father to let her go home. However, her agency, and with it her safety, is thwarted when he responds that she is 'here for him'. The response reflects his own interpretation of the court's decision; that he has a right to have his daughter staying over. The court orders can be seen to endorse his sense of entitlement to put his own rights ahead of Linda's rights and her need to feel safe.

Linda's lack of agency in this context can only be countered by her plan to seek outside support from the school chaplain. Though her mother Joyce has tried to address the issue of the stepbrother's violence by talking to her ex-partner, Linda is aware that this was unsuccessful as Joyce also lacks agency in the relationship with her ex-partner. Linda spoke of feeling 'shy' on the days that she went to her father's house because she was preparing for the way she would be treated when she was there. Linda fears the behaviour of her stepbrothers who have also threatened to kill her two-year-old brother:

> When my stepbrothers were saying to Mitchell that they were threatening to kill him...Dad said 'Don't worry, he's gonna be safe 'cause if they do, they're gonna get a kick up the arse' and he's never going to buy them anything again. Mitchell always gets to go home whenever he wants because they always threaten him. (Linda, 8)

In the weeks following the final physical assault which led to their separation, Joyce received death threats from her ex-partner. Joyce now lives with a chronic disability as a result of the injuries she received. When her symptoms flare up, she and the children are once again victims of Linda's father's violence as the children need to assume caring responsibilities and schooling and household routines are disrupted:

> So I've gotta break it up [housework] over several days and just do a little bit each day, otherwise I'm gone for a week and then the kids aren't at school and you know, Amelia is helping me in and out of bed...and helping me walk and stuff like that. It's just horrible. So yeah...he really did me over that time. (Joyce, mother)

At the time of their interviews, the family was facing eviction from their home. Joyce was struggling financially and Amelia was experiencing anxiety and depression. These burdens were apparent, despite them presenting themselves as an 'upbeat' family who laughed, played and smiled during their interviews at the family home. Joyce was optimistic that she could secure temporary housing, she sought help from charities to put food on the table, and Amelia was learning a new language. Their resistance to adversity was admirable yet the impact of violence had left a lasting mark on the family.

Children's agency and negotiating safety

In contrast to the ongoing danger and vulnerability experienced by Talia, Amelia and Linda, this section introduces three children whose family contexts enabled them to experience a sense of agency. The term 'agency' is used to describe the child's 'capacity to act, interact and influence the shape of their childhood' (Neale and Flowerdew 2007, p.28). Agency is mediated by the child's familial and social context (Lieten 2008). The child's voice is an expression of agency, conveying their 'intentions, hopes, grievances and expectations' (Pufall and Unsworth 2004, p.8). For Max, Peter and Zoe, whose stories appear in this section, having agency meant that they could negotiate their safety in relationships.

Agency was facilitated by family contexts in which the children were able to have physical distance from the perpetrator, there was modelling of safety in relationships by older siblings and trusted adults, and the children had a sense of co-constructing family resiliency. Interestingly, children who could experience agency spoke of no less harrowing past experiences of violence and abuse than those in the previous section who remained unsafe. However, in each of the families described in this section, the critical factors noted above that facilitated agency were evident.

Max the eldest and Peter the youngest child were from a family of three boys. Their father's violence escalated from subtle psychological abuse towards their mother, Lorraine, when the boys were young, to more severe abuse as Max reached adolescence. The escalation occurred as the parental relationship broke down over their father's relationship with another woman who was pregnant with his child. Over many months, Lorraine endured harassment, damage to property, verbal abuse and threats. As the eldest child, Max wanted information from his parents to make sense of what was happening:

> I did sense…when things were going badly, I did kinda sense that as a kid. Then I just wanted to deal with it. I don't like being lied to or anything like that, or not told… And you know the only reason or I suppose the fact that when they broke up that they told us, that was only because I kind of enquired and said 'Come on what's going on?' Like you know I could sense it. (Max, 24)

Max and Peter recognised caring and supportive roles for themselves and each other in managing the situation:

> I ended up kinda being the in-between communicator and the mediator… She [mother] was definitely aware of how we felt because she wanted us, to kinda have the best, you know kinda do it the best possible way. I think everyone, um us three brothers, we were more concerned about her, I think… Not saying that I was more concerned about her than she was with me, it was more just I was less concerned about myself and more concerned about my mum. (Max, 24)

> Really my oldest brother…I think he bore the brunt of, the feelings from Mum, and like the conflict between the two. Even though I was eight I tried to help her in any way. (Peter, 18)

Despite the upheaval of court processes and relocation, Lorraine made the decision to move overseas, away from the abuse and back near her family of origin. The relocation gave Max and Peter opportunities to build relationships with trusted adults in their lives to further support them individually and as a family unit. The modelling of safety in these relationships was apparent:

> My grandma was very helpful. She was a support for Mum and for us. (Peter, 18)

> I suppose something, probably interesting that I realised…is my [relationship with my] girlfriend's dad. Um, I can talk to him about quite a lot of stuff. I suppose he's kind of a pseudo father in a way, in some ways, so…which is good. (Max, 24)

Compared with these supportive relationships, Max shared insights about the emotional distance he experiences in the relationship with his father:

> I don't really see him as a dad, like I see him as a dad, but I don't know. I think he lost, not the right, and not really respect, but something. I don't see him as a full dad… When my dad says something I just take it with a pinch of salt. But I just think that's because of our relationship. Um, he's a bit of distance away from it. And I just think he's kind of out of touch. (Max, 24)

In contrast, Peter has a closer relationship with his father. He spoke with pride about his family's resilience:

> How close our family is together…and that after what we have been through, that we're still, well us kids with Dad and his family are still quite close and our immediate family here…are still quite close as well. Um, so I'm quite proud that that relationship has been able to…hold up, in that way. (Peter, 18)

Peter and his brother Max had agency to negotiate their safety in relationships. Both young men had experienced physical distance from their father, whereas Max described a sense of emotional distance as well. The distance created space to appraise both the parental relationship and their own relationships with their father. They acknowledged positive parenting models of safety in relationships with others such as their maternal grandmother and Max's girlfriend's father. Finally, they both acknowledged a role in co-constructing family resiliency in their thoughts about their immediate family and expectations of their own intimate relationships:

> I want to be 100, 120 per cent sure that I want to get married... I wouldn't want to leave anything to chance because I've seen the effects. (Max, 24)

> I understand more the other side of a relationship and the way your actions can affect the other person. So, I think the relationships I've had, I've been a lot more conscientious... (Peter, 18)

Peter's and Max's reflections on relationships revealed moral reasoning from a caring and thoughtful stance in keeping with the principles of ethics of care (Groenhout 2004) and dialogical ethics (Koehn 1998).

Like Peter and Max, 11-year-old Zoe also experienced agency and was able to negotiate safety in her relationships. Zoe, the eldest of three children, had endured much danger and vulnerability in her early years. She was well aware of violence directed at her mother and herself. Leaving her mother unconscious and badly injured, her father Nigel abducted Zoe and her younger sister, Molly:

> When I was younger [sigh] um I remember being dragged out of the house over prickles and I fell on to the concrete and every time I just tried to get up he'd just drag me along again... (Zoe, 11)

Aged five and one at the time, Zoe and Molly were taken into the bush by their father, Nigel. They lived out of his truck for several weeks and Zoe cared for Molly during that time:

> We were in the truck with, with no toilets, no other you know hygienic stuff... And we were eating junk food for like, for three weeks... But me and Molly didn't know what was going on, so, so... And um she knew how to play games so we just played like 'cats and dogs' around on the back bed... We stopped at this area which had heaps of fires next to it. I'd look out and see that... something was wrong. But I wouldn't tell my sister because she wouldn't understand because she was one. But I'd just keep her close next to me. (Zoe, 11)

Like Peter and Max's mother, Lorraine, Zoe's mother, Penelope, made the decision to relocate back to her family of origin after the violent relationship ended. Zoe described her own impressions and fear of her father:

> I haven't been down there a lot to see 'em [paternal extended family] because he might be there or something.
>
> *Interviewer: What is it about your father that you don't want to be around him?*
>
> Um, well he's kinda a drug dealer. He likes to…smash, he smashes up this like white stuff and he sells it for money. So I guess that counts as a drug dealer… And the promises he makes to me never come true… And um…[sighs, thinking] and like, and things he's done to my mum, I just think what if I made him really mad, what would he do to me?
>
> *Interviewer: So what sort of things would you worry that he might do?*
>
> Um well, he has, he kinda bashed my mum when they broke up that night and like I, I'm worried that if I made him really, really mad he'd like, kinda bash me… (Zoe, 11)

Understandably, Zoe did not want to spend time with her father, despite court-ordered overnight access arrangements. Nigel's broader criminal history meant that access did not always occur due to time spent in prison and his transient lifestyle. However, over the years his parents maintained an interest in having their granddaughters to stay and would find ways to ensure that their father saw them at these times. Decision making about these arrangements was something that their mother, Penelope, felt was up to Zoe and Molly to negotiate for themselves:

> And Zoe goes 'No, I don't want to go, but ask Molly because she might want to go.' And so they'd [paternal grandparents] ask Molly, and Molly would look at Zoe… And she'd go [quoting Zoe] 'I'm not going Molly, however that's my decision. You go if you want to go.' And Molly would go 'Oh, no I'm happy, just staying here with my sisters.'
>
>   And, so…yeah she really did take a lead from Zoe and she trusted Zoe that she wasn't going to…lead her into any danger I suppose. And Zoe has taken on that role. I mean she's very protective of her sisters. (Penelope, mother)

What is interesting about this account is that it conveys a means of modelling safety in relationships which allows the girls an active choice about spending time with their father or paternal grandparents. Hence, Zoe and Molly were able to experience agency in their decision making. From the safe distance of her own home town, Penelope explained how her response to her partner's violence provided a template of assertion for her daughters to draw on:

> I think she [Zoe] saw that, at first, yes, Mum was scared. However, if she stuck to what she believed in, and she wasn't going to be pushed around, and she knew what was right, and all of a sudden he backed down.
>
> And I think she [Zoe] found that as well because she thought she had to go and see him and then once she stood up and said 'I'm not going there anymore', he backed down. So… it's quite amazing. So, I think she saw the fear I went through and she went through that fear. But then she saw the strength that I found, and she found that strength herself and now she knows that he can't, he, physically and mentally has no control over her. (Penelope, mother)

Through communication with her mother and her own experiences with her father, Zoe has learnt about relationships and trust. She now knows how to moderate her behaviour accordingly:

> I've realised that some people are just not who they think they are and you've just got to be careful who you say things around and who you are around. (Zoe, 11)

In contrast, Zoe spoke warmly of the support that she and her mother had received from close friends:

> I can definitely turn to one of my best friends' mum because she treats me like… I'm her daughter or something.
>
> I really do think that [family friend] really helped me…and Mum a lot. And, because she just took care of us, and same with Molly. She took care of all of us. (Zoe, 11)

Coupled with this significant informal support, Zoe also spoke about her new family unit: her sister Molly, their younger half-sister, her mother and her mother's new husband, whom Zoe and Molly refer to as 'Dad'. Zoe recalled a dream in which her sense of safety in the relationship with her new 'dad' was revealed:

> I've had this dream but I know it's not true. We were at my house in the pool and then all of a sudden Nigel [Zoe's father] has just come back in and he's asked for her [Zoe's mother's] forgiveness and she just went 'yes'. Then I got up and I said 'I'm staying here with Glen', which is my stepdad, he's like my real dad. I said 'I'm staying here with Dad, I'm not leaving with you guys.' And then Mum was like 'Yes, please come with us.' And I said 'No, I'm not going back there' and then I swam off to the other side to go with Dad. (Zoe, 11)

Zoe's recollection of her dream illustrates her sense of co-constructing a family unit with people like her 'dad' who she feels safe with and trusts. Her action, 'I swam off', also demonstrates that she feels she has agency to negotiate her own physical and emotional safety.

Children like Max, Peter and Zoe have all experienced the trauma of domestic violence, family separation and significant relocation. They each understand that their mothers experienced violence, abuse and fear. Zoe also spoke of her own direct experience of violence by her father towards her. However, these children have also witnessed the subsequent courage and strength of their mothers and they have been able to use this as a model to negotiate their own relationships with their fathers. They may have benefited from the physical distance between them and their fathers that gave them increased opportunities to negotiate contact on their own terms.

Implications for practice

Children who experience domestic violence want to feel safe (Buckley *et al.* 2007). However, knowing how best to support children to negotiate their safety in relationships requires the practitioner to have insight into key factors that can facilitate children's agency. Through children's voices, their vulnerability to the dangers posed by domestic violence was revealed and, for many, the ongoing 'absent presence' of the perpetrator of domestic violence was also identified (Thiara and Humphreys 2015). However, children's accounts also expressed their agency to negotiate their safety in the context of having experienced domestic violence. The previous section has highlighted critical factors that can facilitate children's agency: physical distance from the perpetrator; modelling of safety in relationships by older siblings and trusted adults; and children's sense of co-constructing family resiliency.

Drawing on these factors, practitioners can help families to communicate about children's agency to negotiate their safety. Practitioners can talk with mother and child together about when, with whom and where the child feels safe or unsafe, who provides support and whom they can trust. They can also encourage the modelling of safety in relationships by helping families rebuild their informal supports.

The physical space created when parents separate can be enhanced when the practitioner creates a dialogical space for mothers to consider the benefits to children. However, leaving may not always be the safest decision. Practitioners can create opportunities for children to reflect on their own and their family's safety and resilience to promote self-esteem and increase children's chances of experiencing their own positive intimate relationships into the future.

Acknowledgement

The SARAH Project received an Australian Research Council PhD scholarship grant which included funding and support from the industry partner, Berry Street, a large Australian not-for-profit children's welfare organisation.

References

Alderson, P. and Morrow, V. (2011) *The Ethics of Research with Children and Young People: A Practical Handbook.* London: Sage Publications.

Buckley, H., Holt, S. and Whelan, S. (2007) 'Listen to me! Children's experiences of domestic violence.' *Child Abuse Review 16*, 5, 296–310.

Edleson, J. (1999) 'Children's witnessing of adult domestic violence.' *Journal of Interpersonal Violence 14*, 8, 839–870.

Eriksson, M. and Näsman, E. (2010) 'Interviews with children exposed to violence.' *Children and Society 26*, 1, 63–70.

Finkelhor, D., Turner, H., Ormrod, R. and Hamby, S. (2009) 'Violence, abuse, and crime exposure in a national sample of children and youth.' *Pediatrics 124*, 5, 1411–1423.

Graham-Bermann, S. A. and Levendosky, A. (1998) 'Traumatic stress symptoms in children of battered women.' *Journal of Interpersonal Violence 13*, 1, 111–128.

Groenhout, R. (2004) *Connected Lives: Human Nature and an Ethics of Care.* Washington, DC: Rowman and Littlefield.

Hegarty, K., O'Doherty, L., Taft, A., Chondros, P. *et al.* (2013) 'Screening and counselling in the primary care setting for women who have experienced intimate partner violence (WEAVE): a cluster randomised controlled trial.' *Lancet 382*, 9888, 249–258.

Indermaur, D. (2001) 'Young Australians and domestic violence.' *Trends and Issues in Crime and Criminal Justice No. 195.* Issues paper. Canberra: Australian Institute of Criminology.

Kelly, L. (1994) *Evaluation of Hammersmith and Fulham Women's Aid Childwork Project, June 1993–June 1994.* London: Child Abuse Studies Unit, University of North London.

Kishor, S. and Johnson, K. (2004) *Profiling Domestic Violence: A Multi-Country Study.* Calverton, MD: ORC Macro.

Koehn, D. (1998) *Rethinking Feminist Ethics: Care, Trust and Empathy.* London: Routledge.

Laverty, S. (2003) 'Hermeneutic phenomenology and phenomenology: a comparison of historical and methodological considerations.' *International Journal of Qualitative Methods 2,* 3, 1–29.

Lieten, G. (2008) *Children, Structure and Agency: Realities across the Developing World (Vol. 16).* London: Routledge.

McGee, C. (2000) *Childhood Experiences of Domestic Violence.* London: Jessica Kingsley Publishers.

Morris, A., Hegarty, K. and Humphreys, C. (2012) 'Ethical and safe: research with children about domestic violence.' *Research Ethics 8,* 2, 125–139.

Mudaly, N. and Goddard, C. (2009) 'The ethics of involving children who have been abused in child abuse research.' *International Journal of Children's Rights 17,* 2, 261–281.

Mullender, A., Hague, G., Imam, U., Kelly, L., Malos, E. and Regan, L. (2002) *Children's Perspectives on Domestic Violence.* London: Sage.

Mullender, A. and Morley, R. (1994) *Children Living with Domestic Violence: Putting Men's Abuse of Women on the Child Care Agenda.* London: Whiting and Birch.

Murray, S. and Powell, A. (2012) *Domestic Violence: Public Policy in Australia.* Melbourne: Australian Scholarly Publishing.

Neale, B. and Flowerdew, J. (2007) 'New structures, new agency: the dynamics of child–parent relationships after divorce.' *International Journal of Children's Rights 15,* 1, 25–42.

Överlien, C. (2012) '"He didn't mean to hit mom, I think": positioning, agency and point in adolescents' narratives about domestic violence.' *Child and Family Social Work 19,* 2, 156–164.

Peled, E. (2001) 'Ethically Sound Research on Children's Exposure to Domestic Violence: A Proposal.' In S. Graham-Bermann and J. Edleson (eds) *Domestic Violence in the Lives of Children: The Future of Research, Intervention, and Social Policy.* Washington, DC: American Psychological Association.

Pufall, P. and Unsworth, R. (2004) *Rethinking Childhood.* New Brunswick, NJ: Rutgers University Press.

Qvortrup, J. (2005) *Studies in Modern Childhood: Society, Agency, Culture.* New York, NY: Palgrave Macmillan.

Radford, L., Corral, S., Bradley, C., Fisher, H. *et al.* (2011) *Child Abuse and Neglect in the UK Today.* London: National Society for the Prevention of Cruelty to Children.

Stanley, N. (1997) 'Domestic violence and child abuse: developing social work practice.' *Child and Family Social Work 2,* 3, 135–146.

Thiara, R. K. and Humphreys, C. (early access 2015) 'Absent presence: the ongoing impact of men's violence on the mother–child relationship.' *Child and Family Social Work,* DOI: 10.1111/cfs.12210.

UN General Assembly (1989) *Convention on the Rights of the Child.* Treaty Series. New York, NY: United Nations.

Walby, S. (1990) *Theorizing Patriarchy.* Oxford: Blackwell.

Wilcox, K. (2007) 'Supporting children living with violence at home: the need for nationwide "good practice".' *Australian Domestic and Family Violence Clearinghouse Newsletter 28,* 3–5.

Wile, I. (1924) 'Children and this clumsy world.' *The Survey 51,* 471–486.

CHAPTER 2

Traversing the Generational Gap

Young People's Views on Intervention and Prevention of Teenage Intimate Partner Violence

Per Moum Hellevik, Carolina Överlien, Christine Barter,
Marsha Wood, Nadia Aghtaie, Cath Larkins and Nicky Stanley

Introduction

Forming intimate relationships is an important part of personal development during adolescence (Conger *et al.* 2000; Furman and Shaffer 2003). For the majority of young people, intimate relationships provide positive and healthy experiences, but for some their relationships can involve physical and psychological violence, sexual abuse, control, isolation and so forth (Barter *et al.* 2009). Intimate partner violence (IPV) is recognised as a serious concern for public health and as a human rights violation (Abramsky *et al.* 2011; De Koker *et al.* 2014; Krug *et al.* 2002). Adults have been the main focus of research on IPV but increasing attention is being given to IPV among younger people and adolescents (De Koker *et al.* 2014).

Methodological and conceptual differences between studies, in addition to a lack of research on the subject, make it difficult to summarise prevalence rates of teenage IPV. Nevertheless, research has consistently uncovered violence and abuse in teenage intimate relationships (Leen *et al.* 2013). At the same time, there is an emergent awareness of the role of digital media in IPV, especially in young people's relationships (Alvarez 2012; Burke *et al.* 2011; Draucker and Martsolf 2010; Melander 2010; Zweig and Dank 2013). Behaviours such as threats, harassment, coercion, stalking and surveillance are some of the ways in which the digital media is used in addition to 'traditional' IPV.

In this chapter we will examine intervention and support seeking as well as prevention in relation to teenage IPV, with a specific focus on young people's own experiences, evaluations and views on the matter. Using the young people's responses to survey questions and their own voices as our starting point, we will address the following research questions: Who do young people with experiences of intimate partner violence seek support from? What are the barriers to seeking support? Who do young people see as the main providers of preventive initiatives when it comes to teenage IPV? How can these actors best help prevent teenage IPV?

The study – Safeguarding Teenage Intimate Relationships (STIR)

STIR was a European study funded by the European Union's Daphne programme that investigated face-to-face and digital experiences of IPV in young people's lives. Using a multi-method approach, the study was conducted using the same design in five countries – the UK, Norway, Italy, Bulgaria and Cyprus. A confidential survey was completed by 4564 young people between 14 and 17 years old, in a total of 45 schools in the five countries. Approximately equal numbers of girls and boys took part in the survey. All the survey findings in this chapter are based on the 3277 young people who reported having had some form of an intimate relationship. In addition, 100 interviews with young people aged between 13 and 18 years old were undertaken and 91 of these were included in the analysis. Interview participants were recruited through schools and settings such as youth camps and workshops for young people. Sixty-seven of them were girls, and 24 were boys. The interviews were semi-structured and followed an interview guide closely in order to allow for cross-cultural comparisons. Each country had a youth advisory group which provided advice on the language and concepts used in the survey. Furthermore, all participating countries held meetings discussing teenage IPV with key national experts within the field. Among the subjects discussed, prevention and intervention were central.

The survey data were analysed using SPSS, version 22. The interviews with the young people were analysed using a framework analysis (Srivastava and Hopwood 2009). Developed by Ritchie and Spencer (1994), framework analysis provides a systematic and transparent matrix-based method for analysing qualitative data and is suitable for cross-national comparative studies such as STIR. In the following section, we will outline our findings on the young people's responses to and views on intervention and the prevention of teenage IPV.

Intervention – support seeking and its barriers
Who do the young people reach out to?

Analysis of the survey data revealed consistent patterns in who young people reached out to when they experienced IPV. There were notable differences in whether they tried to work out their problems by themselves or whether they reached out to others for support. The survey data showed that of those who were or had been in a relationship, 58 per cent had experienced at least one form of teenage IPV, although rates varied between countries. Seventy-four per cent of respondents told someone about it, whilst 26 per cent did not. Friends were by far the most common group for young people to confide in across all forms of IPV. A total of 64 per cent chose to confide in a friend whilst only 17 per cent spoke to an adult. In line with previous studies (Barter *et al.* 2009; Jackson, Cram and Seymour 2000), we also found that more girls than boys, across all forms of violence, were willing to seek support from others. Of the girls, 75 per cent spoke to a friend about IPV, whilst only 54 per cent of the boys did the same. Eighteen per cent of girls and 15 per cent of boys spoke to an adult. Furthermore, we found differences in the young people's willingness to reach out to others based on the type of IPV they experienced. In total, 70 per cent of those who had experienced digital violence, 66 per cent of those who were victims of face-to-face physical/psychological violence and 56 per cent of those who experienced sexual violence told someone about it.

The finding that many victimised young people chose not to disclose their situation to anyone is a matter for concern. The importance of social support and how it improves psychological and physical well-being have been extensively researched (Thoits 2011). Cohen and Wills (1985), among others, have shown how social support protects against mental health problems in the face of adversity. Along the same lines, a lack of social support has been found to be one of the most important risk factors for post-traumatic stress reactions following traumatic events (Brewin, Andrews and

Valentine 2000). Also, not disclosing to adults such as teachers, who may be mandated reporters, could result in a continuation of the violence and a lost opportunity for change.

Barriers to seeking social support

Whilst the data from the survey told us something about who the young people spoke to about IPV, it did not contribute to our understanding about the reasoning for these choices. Through analysing the accounts provided in the interviews, we identified three main reasons for refraining from seeking support from others: (1) the violence was seen as a private issue; (2) a lack of trust in others; and (3) wanting to protect the perpetrator or the relationship. In line with theories of social support (Brewin *et al.* 2000; Thoits 2011), we understand these reasons as barriers to seeking social support.

1) INTIMATE PARTNER VIOLENCE AS A PRIVATE ISSUE

Most young people who felt that the violence was a private issue constructed this in two ways. On the one hand, they saw the violence as their own responsibility, and, on the other, the young people did not want to be a burden to others. Research has found that the need for autonomy in adolescence can be a barrier to seeking professional help (Wilson *et al.* 2002; Wilson and Deane 2012). Those who saw the violence as something they had to take care of themselves argued that they were at an age when they should be able to handle the issues on their own, that seeking help would be admitting that they were not able to handle their problems, or they simply stated that they liked to handle problems on their own. As an 18-year-old girl from Bulgaria said:

> I think that in order to build my character, I have to sit, think about the situation and cope alone. (Sophia, 18, Bulgaria)

In the interviews, both young men and young women from Bulgaria, more often than other nationalities, considered IPV as an issue that needed to be handled by the victim alone.

Some of the young people interviewed reasoned that others were likely to have issues of their own to deal with, or that the violence was not yet serious enough to bother others with:

> ...there are times when we'll have a huge fight and I won't tell anyone. I'll try to get over it by myself and I'll be a bit down ... And with my friends I will not show anything...I will just smile, make an effort to look OK because I don't want to burden others with my problems. I will only say something to someone when things are really, really bad and I am a mess. (Elena, 18, Cyprus)

The finding that young people may refrain from disclosure because they 'don't want to burden others with their problems' is in line with the findings of Thoresen *et al.* (2014). In an attempt to increase the understanding of social support and why young people might choose not to seek support during difficult times, these researchers investigated young people's barriers to seeking support after a terror attack (the Utøya massacre in Norway). They found that one of the most common barriers to seeking support from others was that the young people did not want to burden others with their problems, as they were thought to have enough to deal with in their own lives, and young people were afraid others would not understand.

2) A LACK OF TRUST

A lack of trust in the competence of adults and professionals was common in several of the young people, a finding consistent with other studies (Jackson 2002; Leavey, Rothi and Paul 2011). Some young people believed that adults gave inadequate advice because of a generational gap, stating that adults were 'old-fashioned', they overreacted and that they did not understand the issues today's teenagers face. This was particularly pertinent with regard to digital violence. Others felt that professionals such as school nurses or teachers either lacked the necessary knowledge about IPV or did not take it seriously enough. An 18-year-old Norwegian girl, who was taken to the school nurse by her friends because she could not stop crying, gave this example:

> *Interviewer: And what questions did she [the school nurse] ask?*
>
> Nina: Very few. I told her it was a boy, and then she said 'Oh, heartbreak, it'll pass. You'll have to remember to eat enough and sleep regularly and it will pass.' And I said 'Ok, then.'

When young people felt that they were not being taken seriously, they became unsure whether confidentiality would be respected. They were afraid that adults would carelessly share information about their situation. For some young people this lack of trust extended to their friends. They did not feel that they could trust their friends to be able to see the situation from their point of view. A lack of trust in friends was also a result of previous experience of gossip and rumours, experiences that made them cautious about sharing such personal and private information:

> Well, I wouldn't talk to my friends about something very personal because you know, we're young, we're only 17, and it's easy that something may 'slip', that someone may tell somebody else what you said and then everybody gossips about you. So I wouldn't turn to my friends. (Giorgos, 17, Cyprus)

The view that adults lack competence and knowledge, whilst other young people are inexperienced and may lack an ability to be discrete, meant that many young people avoided involving others in their problems. These findings emphasise the importance of responses to interpersonal violence. When reviewing literature on domestic violence victims and their support seeking from friends, Sylaska and Edwards (2014) concluded that seeking support was associated with psychological health benefits if the response to the disclosure was positive, whilst negative responses were associated with negative consequences for psychological health. Disclosing one's situation to someone who may respond negatively, or even place the blame on the victim, could be perceived as a risk too great to take.

3) PROTECTING THE RELATIONSHIP

Finally, some young people chose not to tell anyone about the violence because they wanted to protect either the perpetrator or the intimate relationship itself. There were different explanations offered. Some were worried about the consequences disclosure could have for the perpetrator, such as problems with their parents, or problems with having to quit school or sports as a punishment. For others, the violence was not sufficient to make them want to end the relationship. They were afraid that others, often parents, would force them to end the relationship if they found out about the violence. As Lise commented:

> ...I told him, when I was tired of getting all that crap, I told him that he should be careful, I have... 'I could tell the police about you', but I would never do it, but I told him to make him feel a bit afraid... to be a little mean, since I was so tired of him being so angry, but... he knows I would never do that to him. (Lise, 18, Norway)

There are several different reasons why victims of IPV stay in a violent relationship (Rhodes and McKenzie 1998). Feelings of care and love can be fundamental reasons for remaining in a relationship and/or protecting a perpetrator (Barter 2014; Eckstein 2011). Additionally, for adolescents, being in an intimate relationship can be very important both socially and individually (Brown 1999).

Prevention – responsibilities and respect
The school and the home as the main arenas for prevention

In all five countries, school was the most frequently mentioned arena where young people thought violence prevention work should take place. Young people suggested a number of ways in which schools could engage in preventive activities. They argued that school counsellors should involve young people in discussions on issues such as setting limits in intimate relationships and that the school nurse should be easily approachable and show an understanding of young people's realities. One 16-year-old girl from Cyprus said:

> Yes, they [the teachers/counsellors] need to...get into young people's way of thinking, tap into our psychology and with their manner show us that we're being listened to and that we're understood. (Kyrenia, 16, Cyprus)

A focus on schools as a site for prevention work was particularly emphasised by Norwegian young people. A 17-year-old girl forcefully stated as follows:

> The adults should talk to young people about these matters, to teach them what they should avoid, what they should watch out for. Do it in schools, have a huge conference, a huge meeting, and talk about it. (Petra, 17, Norway)

Similar views were shared by Tone, a 17-year-old Norwegian girl who thought that the school and teachers should not just inform and advise young people on these matters, they should also follow them on digital media and intervene if necessary. Tone had been harassed and threatened on Facebook by a former boyfriend. A teacher told her that he knew about the harassment. When she asked why he had not done anything if he knew about it, he answered that he was 'just a teacher', and that his understanding was that they should not have contact with their students on the internet. Tone strongly disagreed with his standpoint:

> The schools should talk about it more, take it more seriously. The teachers should be more involved. I got really depressed, I was like, why didn't you say something, you could have helped me, you could have done something for me. (Tone, 17, Norway)

Tone and several other young people argued that school prevention work should include stricter, hands-on policies such as not allowing the use of mobile phones and social networking sites during the school day.

The view that schools should take a more active role in preventing teenage IPV was shared by Davide from Italy. His views provide important insights into a teenager's need for privacy and reluctance to share intimate details with adults which can co-exist with wanting and appreciating information and advice:

> I don't think I would talk about my personal life to some counsellor in school, but I still believe that seminars and discussions in class would help. I remember we had one last year and it was really helpful. (Davide, 16, Italy)

Prevention work in schools should, according to the young people interviewed, be conducted by teachers, counsellors and school nurses (see Chapter 3). Young people highlighted a particular need for information about what is legal and permitted/appropriate behaviour on digital media. It is therefore important that any preventive work should include all forms of violence (Barter 2014).

However, the young people emphasised that the overall approach is important. Andrea from Cyprus noted that young people do not want to feel that they are being lectured or patronised or that someone is trying to impose on them a perception of what is 'right'. She argued that young people learn best through empathy and awareness and through being placed in the position of a person who is experiencing an unhealthy relationship.

> I believe that what will help teenagers is to put them in the position of a person who is not in a healthy relationship. When you put them in the position of someone, the emotions will be stronger. (Andrea, 17, Cyprus)

That way they can understand what abuse is and how it feels, without being lectured by adults. The message conveyed was that young people want information from and dialogue with adults, but this needed to be done in a non-judgemental way. Traversing the generation gap should be done with empathy and respect. A 15-year-old from the UK suggested that violence prevention work should take place regularly as part of the regular curriculum. As such, the preventive work could include not just information about warning signs and the potential risks of social media, but also issues such as gender equality:

> I think a good thing would be to add, like for an hour in high school, stuff like this to the curriculum... I think if you did this with the whole year about healthy relationships then the punishments for domestic violence and stuff, at least like an hour a week or even in assemblies and that would, maybe people who hadn't heard it was wrong would know it was wrong, and girls would be able to recognise it. (Lily, 15, UK)

Several young people regarded gender as an important aspect of prevention work, but this was not the case in all countries. In Cyprus, Norway and the UK, young people pointed out how differences between the genders need to be problematised when dealing with IPV, whilst in Italy and Bulgaria, gender was not identified as an important issue.

The home was considered another important setting for violence prevention initiatives. It was suggested that parents should teach their children appropriate behaviour as well as providing positive role models and even follow and protect them on digital media:

> I think parents should be good role models. If parents scream on the phone and post ugly messages, then you think it is OK, if they don't do it, it is a form of prevention. (Sofie, 16, Norway)

However, it was only in Norway that a wish for adults to take a more proactive role in young people's online lives was specifically mentioned.

Placing responsibility on young people themselves

In Bulgaria, most young people interviewed suggested that it was young people themselves who should prevent violence from happening. This view was shared to some extent by interviewees from all five countries. Young people stated that positive and negative experiences should be shared between friends and that it was important to learn from each other's mistakes. Peers were seen not only as responsible for passing on knowledge about how to prevent violence, they were also seen as having a role in physically preventing violence from taking place. Nikolaj from Bulgaria described a situation where he had to stop a friend from hitting his girlfriend whilst at a cafe:

> There are a lot of people who are stressed, and they blow off steam by being mean and hurtful to their partners. In this case it was very important to intervene and say that this is not OK, so that he could calm down. (Nikolaj, 18, Bulgaria)

Other young people felt that the only person who could prevent violence from occurring was the individual him/herself. For some, it was about choosing the right partner, leaving the partner if necessary, and standing up for oneself:

> [In my next relationship] I wouldn't descend to his level and if he tried to control me I would say to him: 'You have no right over me, you have no right to control me, you are not my husband.' Even if he was jealous I would say that it is my right to do what I want to do, I am a 17 year old girl, I am not 40! And no one can force me not to wear a short outfit or not to go out. (Maria, 17, Bulgaria)

Voices of resignation

Looking across the views articulated by young people in this study, there seemed to be a common understanding that prevention of IPV was indeed possible. Primary responsibility for preventive work was placed with adults, particularly with school staff and parents. However, there were a few divergent voices that could be interpreted as a form of resignation in the face of abusive behaviour. When asked what could prevent teenage intimate partner violence, one 13-year-old girl from the UK stated as follows:

Molly: If there was no Facebook…and like not, not being able to send a photo.

Interviewer: Yeah, but the technology's here now, isn't it? It's not going to go away.

Molly: Yeah. It's annoying.

Similarly, a Norwegian participant had difficulties in coming up with any suggestions on how to prevent digital violence. After contemplating the question from the interviewer, she commented thus:

I don't know how to stop it. I really don't understand how you will be able to stop it. It is so massive. (Pernille, 15, Norway)

Discussion

The findings from the qualitative interviews conducted for this study are complex. Many of the young people interviewed wanted more involvement from adults in preventing and responding to IPV, identifying schools and parents as potential sources of both information and support. However, when asked who they sought support from when victimised, the answer was clear: the large majority turn to peers rather than adults.

The finding that many young people who have experienced IPV have friends to turn to can be interpreted positively. Nevertheless, many of the young people acknowledged that peers often lacked sufficient knowledge in order to provide appropriate advice and help. For example, they often lacked knowledge about what help public services, such as the police and child protection services could provide. Additionally, the lack of experience that many adolescents have with intimate relationships can make it difficult to judge when things are really bad, or just ordinary aspects of an intimate relationship (Wekerle and Wolfe 1999). Finally, attitudes and behaviours among peers towards IPV seem to play an important part in young people's perpetration of IPV (Pepler 2012). Seeking support from peers therefore puts a great deal of responsibility on young people and those who experience IPV do not necessarily receive the proper support, or any support at all, by reaching out to peers. Furthermore, the finding that many young people tell no one about their difficult experiences emphasises the importance of adult involvement. Nevertheless, it is important that this is done empathetically, by adults reaching out to and being approachable for young people in need.

Schools are an arena where almost all children and adolescents spend a large part of their time. Additionally, school staff have experience and training in communicating with young people. As such, schools are highly suitable sites for violence prevention work (Stanley, Ellis and Bell 2010). Furthermore, in schools, the peer environment is readily accessible for prevention and intervention initiatives. Programmes such as Coaching Boys into Men (Miller *et al.* 2012) and Mentors in Violence Prevention (Katz, Heisterkamp and Fleming 2011) are examples of interventions that try to prevent teenage IPV by addressing peer attitudes and behaviours, especially in regard to gender. In extension of this, it is important to note that the young people in this study wanted schools to give them information on more general topics such as gender equality, as well as on IPV. This finding underlines the importance of prevention work that addresses the gendered dynamics of IPV. By including these topics in the regular curriculum, and not only in time-limited prevention programmes, schools could generate a general awareness of what constitutes healthy relationships. Such awareness raising could be beneficial for both students and school staff. However, schools should not be expected to take sole responsibility for such interventions. By including the wider community, and not focusing solely on school initiatives, greater results might be achieved (De Koker *et al.* 2014). Efforts should be made by all those delivering preventive work to ensure that it is creative, bottom-up, inclusive and based on respect.

Finally, whilst the young people participating in this study communicated a strong need for information from and dialogue with adults about IPV and healthy relationships, it is important to stress that they also have a right to receive it. Countries that have ratified the United Nations Convention of the Rights of the Child are legally obliged to provide educational measures to protect children and adolescents against all forms of violence and abuse, as well as giving them information aimed at the promotion of their social well-being and physical and mental health.

Conclusion

Across all the countries included in this research, the young people participating in the STIR study demonstrated high levels of engagement in discussing intervention and prevention in relation to teenage IPV. Most expressed optimistic views about the value of prevention work, but stressed that its implementation should make young people feel included. Although adults may be cautious about engaging in issues that can be perceived as personal and emotionally loaded, the message conveyed by a majority of the young people across all countries was nevertheless a desire for an increased adult presence in their lives. This included a greater presence in the school, home and online.

However, a lack of trust in adults and an expectation that they would be unable to comprehend fully the young person's situation emerged as a barrier that could prevent young people from accessing support from adults. Experienced peers represented an alternative source of help. Many young people in this study also felt that the violence and abuse they experienced were their own responsibility or that peers should prevent IPV from happening. The potentially severe and long-term consequences of IPV in young people's relationships mean that young people should not be left to manage this form of harm on their own. Rather, professionals and parents need to offer support that is both respectful and accessible to young people.

References

Abramsky, T., Watts, C., Garcia-Moreno, C., Devries, K. L. *et al.* (2011) 'What factors are associated with recent intimate partner violence? Findings from the WHO multi-country study on women's health and domestic violence.' *BMC Public Health 11*, 1, 1–17.

Alvarez, A. R. G. (2012) '"IH8U": Confronting cyberbullying and exploring the use of cybertools in teen dating relationships.' *Journal of Clinical Psychology 68*, 11, 1205–1215.

Barter, C. (2014) 'Responding to Sexual Violence in Girls' Intimate Relationships: The Role of Schools.' In J. Ellis and R. K. Thiara (eds) *Preventing Violence against Women and Girls. Educational Work with Children and Young People.* London: Policy Press.

Barter, C., McCarry, M., Berridge, D. and Evans, K. (2009) *Partner Exploitation and Violence in Teenage Intimate Relationships.* London: NSPCC.

Brewin, C. R., Andrews, B. and Valentine, J. D. (2000) 'Meta-analysis of risk factors for posttraumatic stress disorder in trauma-exposed adults.' *Journal of Consulting and Clinical Psychology 68*, 5, 748–766.

Brown, B. B. (1999) '"You're Going Out with Who?" Peer Group Influences on Adolescent Romantic Relationships.' In W. Furman, B. B. Brown and C. Feiring (eds) *The Development of Romantic Relationships in Adolescence.* New York, NY: Cambridge University Press.

Burke, S. C., Wallen, M., Vail-Smith, K. and Knox, D. (2011) 'Using technology to control intimate partners: an exploratory study of college undergraduates.' *Computers in Human Behavior 27*, 3, 1162–1167.

Cohen, S. and Wills, T. A. (1985) 'Stress, social support, and the buffering hypothesis.' *Psychological Bulletin 98*, 2, 310–357.

Conger, R. D., Cui, M., Bryant, C. M. and Elder Jr, G. H. (2000) 'Competence in early adult romantic relationships: a developmental perspective on family influences.' *Journal of Personality and Social Psychology 79*, 2, 224–237.

De Koker, P., Mathews, C., Zuch, M., Bastien, S. and Mason-Jones, A. J. (2014) 'A systematic review of interventions for preventing adolescent intimate partner violence.' *Journal of Adolescent Health 54*, 1, 3–13.

Draucker, C. B. and Martsolf, D. S. (2010) 'The role of electronic communication technology in adolescent dating violence.' *Journal of Child and Adolescent Psychiatric Nursing 23*, 3, 133–142.

Eckstein, J. (2011) 'Reasons for staying in intimately violent relationships: comparisons of men and women and messages communicated to self and others.' *Journal of Family Violence 26*, 1, 21–30.

Furman, W. and Shaffer, L. (2003) 'The Role of Romantic Relationships in Adolescent Development.' In P. Florsheim (ed.) *Adolescent Romantic Relations and Sexual Behavior: Theory, Research, and Practical Implications.* Mahwah, NJ: Lawrence Erlbaum.

Jackson, S. (2002) 'Abuse in dating relationships: young people's accounts of disclosure, non-disclosure, help-seeking and prevention education.' *New Zealand Journal of Psychology 31*, 2, 79–86.

Jackson, S., Cram, F. and Seymour, F. (2000) 'Violence and sexual coercion in high school students' dating relationships.' *Journal of Family Violence 15*, 1, 23–36.

Katz, J., Heisterkamp, H. A. and Fleming, W. M. (2011) 'The social justice roots of the mentors in violence prevention model and its application in a high school setting.' *Violence against Women 17*, 6, 684–702.

Krug, E. G., Mercy, J. A., Dahlberg, L. L. and Zwi, A. B. (2002) 'The world report on violence and health.' *Lancet 360*, 9339, 1083–1088.

Leavey, G., Rothi, D. and Paul, R. (2011) 'Trust, autonomy and relationships: the help-seeking preferences of young people in secondary level schools in London (UK).' *Journal of Adolescence 34*, 4, 685–693.

Leen, E., Sorbring, E., Mawer, M., Holdsworth, E., Helsing, B. and Bowen, E. (2013) 'Prevalence, dynamic risk factors and the efficacy of primary interventions for adolescent dating violence: an international review.' *Aggression and Violent Behavior 18*, 1, 159–174.

Melander, L. A. (2010) 'College students' perceptions of intimate partner cyber harassment.' *Cyberpsychology, Behavior, and Social Networking 13*, 3, 263–268.

Miller, E., Tancredi, D. J., McCauley, H. L., Decker, M. R. *et al.* (2012) '"Coaching boys into men": a cluster-randomised controlled trial of a dating violence prevention program.' *Journal of Adolescent Health 51*, 5, 431–438.

Pepler, D. (2012) 'The development of dating violence: what doesn't develop, what does develop, how does it develop, and what can we do about it?' *Prevention Science 13*, 4, 402–409.

Rhodes, N. R. and McKenzie, E. B. (1998) 'Why do battered women stay? Three decades of research.' *Aggression and Violent Behavior 3*, 4, 391–406.

Srivastava, P. and Hopwood, N. (2009) 'A practical iterative framework for qualitative data analysis.' *International Journal of Qualitative Methods 8*, 1, 77.

Stanley, N., Ellis, J. and Bell, J. (2010) Delivering Preventative Programmes in Schools: Identifying Gender Issues in C. Barter and D. Berridge (eds) *Children Behaving Badly? Peer Violence Between Children and Young People.* Chichester: John Wiley.

Sylaska, K. M. and Edwards, K. M. (2014) 'Disclosure of intimate partner violence to informal social support network members: a review of the literature.' *Trauma, Violence, & Abuse 15*, 1, 3–21.

Thoits, P. A. (2011) 'Mechanisms linking social ties and support to physical and mental health.' *Journal of Health and Social Behavior 52*, 2, 145–161.

Thoresen, S., Jensen, T. K., Wentzel-Larsen, T. and Dyb, G. (2014) 'Social support barriers and mental health in terrorist attack survivors.' *Journal of Affective Disorders 156*, 187–193.

Weisz, A. N. and Black, B. M. (2009) *Programme to Reduce Teen Dating Violence and Sexual Assault: Perspectives on What Works.* New York, NY: Columbia University Press.

Wekerle, C. and Wolfe, D. A. (1999) 'Dating violence in mid-adolescence: theory, significance, and emerging prevention initiatives.' *Clinical Psychology Review 19*, 4, 435–456.

Wilson, C. J. and Deane, F. P. (2012) 'Brief report: need for autonomy and other perceived barriers relating to adolescents' intentions to seek professional mental health care.' *Journal of Adolescence 35*, 1, 233–237.

Wilson, C. J., Rickwood, D., Ciarrochi, J. and Deane, F. P. (2002) 'Adolescent barriers to seeking professional psychological help for personal-emotional and suicidal problems.' Suicide Prevention Australia 9th Annual National Conference, June 2002. Available at http://ro.uow.edu.au/cgi/viewcontent.cgi?article=1539&context=hbspapers, accessed on 22 May 2015.

Zweig, J. and Dank, M. (2013) *Teen Dating Violence and Harassment in the Digital World: Implications for Prevention and Intervention.* Washington, DC: The Urban Institute.

PART TWO

Prevention and Intervention for Children and Young People

CHAPTER 3

School-based Prevention and the Disclosure of Domestic Violence

A Can of Worms?

Jane Ellis, Soo Downe, Nicola Farrelly, Sandra Hollinghurst and Nicky Stanley

> A can of worms: a situation that causes a lot of problems for you when you start to deal with it.[1]

Introduction

Work with children and young people to prevent domestic violence has emerged as a core aspect of policy and practice to end violence against women and girls. Governments in England, Wales, Scotland and Northern Ireland now incorporate primary prevention – stopping violence before it occurs – into their strategies, although approaches to this work and the extent of implementation in practice vary from nation to nation. The factors shaping the development and delivery of work in schools are myriad, ranging from government strategy to the views of individual teachers. Despite a commitment to prevention in the national domestic violence strategies for England, Personal, Social and Health Education (PSHE), the part of the school curriculum where the topic of domestic violence is usually located (Ellis 2004), is non-statutory. In this respect, England differs from the other UK countries.

At the local level, the academies and free schools programme in England is shifting the relationship between schools and local authorities (Friend 2014). This structural change is producing greater autonomy for schools but has also increased competition and fragmentation resulting

---

1 Cambridge Dictionaries Online, 2014.

in a situation where education is 'characterised by multiple sources of control and influence' (Woods 2011, p.51). This situation looks likely to amplify the already patchy picture of schools' engagement with preventive work on domestic violence (Ellis 2004; EVAW 2011; Stanley *et al.* 2015). Structured learning opportunities for children and young people are therefore far from universal. One factor often reported, both in research and anecdotally, which hinders the inclusion of such work in the curriculum, is teachers' anxieties about it eliciting increased disclosures of domestic violence (House of Commons Education Committee 2012; EVAW 2011). As Barry and Pearce have noted in relation to prevention work in schools: 'Early scoping told us that schools viewed the content and subject matter of planned interventions as a potential "can of worms"' (2014, p.171).

This chapter presents findings from the PEACH (Preventing Domestic Abuse for Children) study (Stanley *et al.* 2015) about the disclosure of domestic violence in young people's own relationship or that of their parents/carers in the context of primary prevention programmes. The PEACH study, a mixed knowledge review of primary prevention of domestic violence in the UK, incorporated a UK mapping study across 18 local authorities and a systematic review of the published and UK grey literature. The study also incorporated consultation with three groups representing education and media professionals and researchers and young people as well as individual interviews with international experts. Each component of the study generated data with regard to disclosure and threw light on the aims, content, delivery and outcomes of school-based prevention.

Aims and content of programmes

The likelihood that prevention initiatives might elicit disclosures of domestic violence is not an unreasonable cause of concern since analysis of the topics included in the content of prevention programmes revealed that disclosure and related themes are often directly discussed with children and young people. Mapping data showed that increased awareness and recognition of abuse was the most common topic in the 98 reported programmes but that a significant number, over a third of programmes, also addressed issues related to keeping safe and help-seeking. These included topics such as disclosure and safeguarding (37%), information on support services (40%), safety strategies (44%) and help-seeking (37%).

The review of published and grey literature identified similar content of programmes for both primary and secondary school aged students. Programme content aimed at supporting children/young people who had lived with, or who were living with, domestic violence was also evident in the review of the grey literature where coverage of help-seeking and information on support services was explicitly reported in 11 of the 18 reviewed programme evaluations. Twenty-five programmes, 19 from North America, were included in the systematic review and all of them included information on help-seeking and support services as an aspect of the programme content although use of such services was rarely a consideration in the evaluation of programme outcomes.

Ellis (2004) has noted that school-based work has two broad aims: first, to enable all children to learn how to conduct non-abusive, respectful relationships with the aim of reducing the incidence of domestic violence in the long term; and, second to provide support for children living with domestic violence in a potentially less stigmatising setting (Jaffe, Wolfe and Wilson 1990). Both these aims were evident in the programmes reviewed by the PEACH study but were also in some cases explicitly articulated. Three respondents to the mapping survey described young people disclosing domestic violence as an achievement of their programmes suggesting *this was indeed a specific aim in these cases.* One reported that the project had achieved 'increased disclosures of domestic abuse'. On the other hand, respondents were also asked to describe the challenges encountered in developing and delivering programmes. Two-thirds of the 39 comments received in response to a question about challenges related to either accessing or getting buy-in from schools. It is interesting to note, however, that no reports were made of schools' anxieties about disclosures although such concerns might have underpinned comments such as 'schools have such differing opinions on whether this is a valid or useful topic for their students' (respondent to PEACH mapping survey).

The young people's consultation group convened for the research identified that raising awareness of domestic violence so that young people could recognise it in their own relationships was a legitimate and important aim of any preventive intervention. However, they linked the two broad aims discussed earlier in noting that increasing young people's understanding and awareness of domestic violence could facilitate disclosure of personal experience:

...if you're being abused and...you might not realise it's abuse and you might not think it's that important, but if you see all these statistics on the TV and anywhere else where it's being advertised... you might feel more comfortable with it, thinking that it's something which you can have a say in because it's something that matters and it's not something which is just happening to you... but is something you can speak about openly... (Young People's Consultation Group 1)

This quote suggests that disclosure could be a positive outcome for a young person rather than a problem. Further, they went on to argue that young people needed to know that, once consultation group members acknowledged they were in an abusive relationship, services would be available to help them: 'it makes people aware but then they need the help afterwards' (Young People's Consultation Group 1). Group members commented that young people also needed to know the consequences of seeking help: 'I think that they should bring to light what actually happens after you call the people...' (Young People's Consultation Group 1). Participants in the young people's consultation group noted there was a fear that disclosure of domestic violence in their parents' relationship might lead to children being taken into care. We will return to this later in the chapter.

Level of disclosure

Despite the anxieties expressed through the comparison with a 'can of worms', there is little research evidence about the number of disclosures that can be attributed directly to children and young people being formally taught about domestic violence. Only one of the programmes included in the systematic review, that evaluated by Alexander, Macdonald and Paton (2005), made reference to the number of programme participants experiencing domestic violence in their parents' relationships. This was a small qualitative study in which a research question, answered anonymously, formed a 'specific invitation to disclose' (Alexander et al. 2005, p.190) with the responses used to create the categories of 'experiencing' and 'non-experiencing' domestic violence (2005, p.190). Thirty-two per cent of students in the study (n=81) were identified as 'experiencing', with this categorisation then being used to compare responses to young people's views of domestic abuse. Nonetheless, no data were presented on the number of young people who openly disclosed their experience of domestic violence during the programme.

Two evaluations included in the grey literature reviewed reported the number of disclosures recorded whilst the respective programme was running. The Zero Tolerance project had a helpline linked with the programme although no report of its use was provided; however, 44 per cent of the staff interviewed for this evaluation reported being aware of children/young people who had required support during the project and 'issues had arisen in all but two of the settings' (Reid Howie Associates 2001, p.30).[2] The Domestic Violence Awareness Raising programme evaluation was the only one where the number of disclosures occurring during the period of the programme was reported. In this case, '11 children/young people disclosed child abuse or domestic violence from a cohort of 532' (Ellis 2006, p.181). This ratio of approximately 1:48 is low in comparison to other research that suggests one in six children and young people experience domestic violence at some point in their childhood (Radford *et al.* 2012).

There was a considerable amount of discussion about disclosure at the three meetings of the education consultation group and the potential for teaching about domestic abuse 'to open the floodgates to disclosure' (Education Consultation Group 1), which was identified as a disincentive for some schools to deliver these interventions. However, there was substantial variation in the extent to which group members had found that delivering these interventions in schools prompted disclosures of domestic violence:

> When we did domestic abuse awareness in schools, I mean one lesson for an hour, we got nine disclosures from pupils from that. (Education Consultation Group 2)

> One of the things that's been quite remarkable about the programme over the years is that there's been very little disclosure... (Education Consultation Group 2)

Regardless of whether disclosures are quantified, they do occur and it is therefore imperative that programmes make provision to manage them.

---

2   Support for staff had also been made available and two who had experienced domestic violence had sought help.

The process of disclosure

Little is known about the factors which influence children's and young people's decisions to disclose as a consequence of taking part in domestic violence prevention programmes, nor is it understood whether disclosure varies across particular subgroups. There is, however, some evidence about disclosure of maltreatment which highlights that this is not a straightforward matter and that it is experienced as a difficult process for children and young people (Allnock and Miller 2013). The importance of creating a safe environment for these interventions was noted by Manship and Perry who concluded thus:

> A safe and confidential environment in which participants can reflect on their own experiences, their hopes and aspirations for the future and talk openly was felt to enable programmes to run more effectively and to encourage high levels of engagement. (Manship and Perry 2013, p.31)

Details of how such an environment can be created, and whether disclosures of domestic violence require the same conditions as disclosures of maltreatment, did not emerge from the PEACH study; however, the grey literature reviewed included an example that illuminates this issue. This was Ellis's (2006) evaluation which highlighted an initial activity in the programme addressing the need to respect boundaries within the group. This activity was undertaken with the intention of establishing a safe and respectful environment and was linked to discussion with children and young people about confidentiality and its limits in relation to safeguarding. Although a single example, this does not preclude the possibility that other programmes included similar material. For instance, the Shifting Boundaries programme in New York (Taylor *et al.* 2013) centred on developing young people's understanding and behaviour around the concept of boundaries – personal, social and legal.

Whilst teachers are an obvious group of professionals to whom children and young people might disclose, a key concern for the young people in the consultation group on disclosure was confidentiality. Whilst some teachers could be considered trustworthy, the young people participating in the consultation group expressed ambivalence about talking to them because they could not be sure that confidentiality would be maintained. A similar view was expressed in the education consultation group discussed below.

Managing disclosures

A key debate in the literature and among practitioners is who should deliver school-based initiatives – teachers or staff from external specialist organisations (Avery-Leaf and Cascardi 2002; Ellis and Thiara 2014; Jones 1991; Weisz and Black 2009). The study revealed, across all the data, that three models of staffing had been adopted: the first and least frequently implemented entailed teachers delivering the work on their own; the second most frequently identified model comprised partnership working between teachers and other professionals; the third approach involved initiatives delivered solely by staff from external specialist agencies. The mapping survey found that nearly half the interventions identified were delivered by multi-agency teams consisting of teachers working in partnership with specialist services, and such a model was advocated by those participating in the consultation groups and expert interviews. In these cases, teachers appeared to take a variety of different roles ranging from 'sitting in' as an observer to facilitating sessions. The latter often occurred in the context of programmes that had adopted a 'whole school' approach with the intention of embedding the issues into school culture and across the curriculum, with teachers delivering the work and schools taking greater ownership of the initiative.

The question of who should deliver programmes was discussed extensively in the education consultation group in relation to disclosures. Group members described using learning mentors both to offer confidential opportunities for children to disclose and to liaise with other agencies that might need to be involved in responding to a disclosure. Whilst children generally valued teachers as a trusted source of information, they might struggle to disclose to a teacher as they would fear losing control of what happened to the information they supplied, as highlighted by the young people in the consultation group. Learning mentors were seen to be accessible and non-threatening repositories for disclosures and it was noted that sometimes it was easier for children to disclose to school staff other than the form teacher, including playground assistants or art teachers. Other group members described disclosures being handled by the school's safeguarding team or officer, but difficulties in passing safeguarding referrals on to children's social services were identified and attributed to 'the huge barrier between education and social care [and] misunderstanding of what each sector does' (Education Consultation Group 1). It was agreed that school staff could be prepared for disclosures by being equipped with information about phonelines that children could call and contact details of relevant local agencies.

Group members argued that the teacher's role was primarily to signpost young people to appropriate sources of support rather than to act as a counsellor. Most programmes delivered by specialist domestic abuse organisations had direct links to support services within their own organisation which offered one-to-one or group therapeutic work which was 'felt to be a vitally important part of the programmes' (Manship and Perry 2012, p.32).

The grey literature reviewed revealed advantages and disadvantages in the three models of staffing. External staff brought knowledge and expertise about domestic violence and were confident about dealing with disclosures but some lacked skills in managing group dynamics (Fox *et al.* 2013). On the other hand, some school staff resisted teaching on domestic violence since they lacked confidence and competence, particularly in respect of dealing with disclosures (Fox, Hale and Gadd 2013). Examples of training for teachers to equip them to deliver programmes which had been provided by domestic violence specialists were found across the data. Training for staff emerged as an important aspect of programme delivery since the systematic review indicated that longer interventions delivered by appropriately trained and confident staff were likely to be more effective.

Staff training

The training available for staff varied from programme to programme according to the role that staff took in implementation. The mapping data showed that in almost two-thirds of cases all staff had received some type of training to deliver the initiative. No data on the content of training for staff were gathered from the mapping survey; as almost all of the programmes reported were led by external agencies, however, it is likely that staff from such organisations would have had training in dealing with disclosures.

The grey literature showed that training for school staff, whether supporting or delivering programmes, focused on increasing their knowledge of domestic violence and information on the programme content. Little information about the content of this training was available although data on the take-up of the training was given in two of the evaluations reviewed. Five of the eight schools involved in the Respect programme (Reid Howie Associates 2001) had sent 'the key member of the staff' to an in-service training session. Uptake of such training was inconsistent in the nine participating schools in the Domestic Violence Awareness Raising programme: in three schools, no staff took part in the training whilst in one primary school almost of all the staff (n=35) had completed it (Ellis 2006).

Ten of the programmes included in the review of the grey literature were delivered by teachers in partnership with staff from a specialist domestic violence organisation and two in partnership with staff from children's organisations; the latter were aimed at primary school children (Datta, Haddon and Shaw 2005; McElearney, Stephenson and Adamson 2011). In all of these instances, the teachers received training prior to the intervention from staff in the partner organisation or from colleagues who had undertaken training in order to train others to deliver the programme (DMSS 2012; Thiara and Ellis 2005). In all the evaluations reviewed, those staff who had received training mostly reported finding it positive and helpful, although there was no information on whether dealing with disclosures was included. Suggestions for changes in training were noted. For example, Reid Howie Associates (2001) reported that 97 per cent of staff thought that the training was 'OK' or 'better than OK' although about half said their understanding of the issues had not improved and some thought the teaching material needed better explanation. For most staff, the training was crucial to their being able to deliver or support a programme. However, ongoing support was also important since 'teachers who did not feel supported were likely to feel underconfident in using the materials and dealing with the issues' (Hester and Westmarland 2005, p.25). However, in the case of the ten programmes delivered by teachers themselves, ongoing support throughout the intervention was usually provided (see, for example, Reid Howie Associates 2001).

Outcomes of preventive interventions

The ultimate goal of preventive interventions is behaviour change, reflected in the increased use of randomised control trials in evaluations, particularly in North America where the public health model of violence prevention is dominant. However, in the UK, outcome measures, which were discussed in both the education and media consultation groups, were less clearly defined and many local programme evaluations were said just to 'skim the surface really' (Education Consultation Group 1). Although there was discussion of what outcomes could be used to measure the impact of school programmes, it was acknowledged that the types of impact likely to result from domestic violence prevention programmes were not formally recorded in schools. However, outcome measures related to help-seeking were felt to be relevant; these might include disclosures of domestic violence, use of a school helpline or an increase in referrals. It was suggested that students' 'actual knowledge of where to go' (Education Consultation Group 1) for help would be a meaningful outcome measure.

The systematic review found evidence of skewed data in studies suggesting that small groups of students, who were at higher risk of being perpetrators or victims of domestic violence at baseline, might have exerted a strong influence on the outcomes of interventions. This suggests that programmes aimed at children and young people may be more or less effective for certain subgroups, depending on how far these influences are identified and taken into account. It is likely that these subgroups include children and young people who are already experiencing abuse in their own intimate relationships or in their families. This reiterates the arguments reported above concerning the need for programmes delivered in schools to be linked to services that can respond to disclosures of domestic violence. These arguments are supported by the view expressed across the consultation groups and interviews that interventions should in the first instance be delivered to whole populations but then might need to be tailored for particular groups.

The qualitative and grey literature reviewed showed self-reports of students increasing their knowledge of domestic violence and help-seeking, as well as changes in attitude. Children and young people reported that they had discovered the importance of telling someone about domestic violence and they had also learnt who they could tell. This could simply be someone whom was trustworthy:

> If you are afraid you should tell a friend or a teacher. When you tell someone that you trust, they will help you out. They will talk to that person or they will talk to your parents if you don't want to. That's why it is important. (Belknap *et al.* 2013, p.66)

In addition, a more realistic approach to help-seeking was identified by Bell and Stanley (2006) who found that young people were more likely to describe turning to family members than professionals for help after participating in the programmes (however, quantitative data suggested this was not sustained at follow-up after one year).

Conclusion

Managing disclosures elicited by preventive interventions was identified as a potential source of concern for schools, and thus equipping staff to feel confident and competent in dealing with such disclosures emerges as a key issue in their design and implementation. The expertise to respond directly to disclosures might, however, reside in the specialist domestic violence sector or in a service already engaged in providing relationship support to young people such as schools counselling services or sexual health services. Despite this, the shift to safeguarding being 'everyone's responsibility', introduced following Every Child Matters (Chief Secretary to the Treasury 2003), combined with teachers' duty of care towards their students means that school staff require understanding and training to meet these obligations (Baginsky and Macpherson 2005). The research showed that teachers are well placed to deliver interventions in schools but that they require training and support from those with specialist knowledge and skills in working with domestic violence. This training could be provided at the level of teachers' qualifying education as well as at post-qualification level.

The evidence reviewed in the PEACH study consistently suggested the value of school-based programmes building close links with relevant support services or ensuring that they have in-house capacity to respond to children's and young people's disclosures of domestic violence in their own or their parents' relationships. In this respect, preventive interventions when co-delivered with specialist organisations might offer the possibility for school staff to increase their skills in dealing with disclosures and subsequently help improve the health and well-being of children and young people. Young people themselves emphasised that, regardless of who they disclosed to, they need the support to be confidential and to be informed about its availability at an early stage in a programme.

Acknowledgement

The PEACH study was funded by the National Institute for Health Research Public Health Research Programme. The views and opinions expressed are those of the authors and do not necessarily reflect those of the Public Health Research Programme, NIHR, NHS or the Department of Health.

References

Alexander, H., Macdonald, E. and Paton, S. (2005) 'Raising the issue of domestic abuse in school.' *Children and Society 19*, 3, 187–198.

Allnock, D. and Miller, P. (2013) *No One Noticed, No One Heard: A Study of Disclosures of Childhood Abuse.* London: NSPCC.

Avery-Leaf, S. and Cascardi, M. (2002) 'Dating Violence Education: Prevention and Early Intervention Strategies.' In P. Schewe (ed.) *Preventing Violence in Relationships: Interventions across the Life Span.* Washington, DC: American Psychological Association.

Baginsky, M. and Macpherson, P. (2005) 'Training teachers to safeguard children: developing a consistent approach.' *Child Abuse Review 14*, 5, 317–330.

Barry, M. and Pearce, J. (2014) 'Preventing Sexual Violence: The Role of the Voluntary Sector.' In J. Ellis and R. K. Thaira (eds) *Preventing Violence against Women and Girls: Educational Work with Children and Young People.* Bristol: Policy Press.

Belknap, R. A., Haglund, K., Felzer, H., Pruszynsk, J. and Schneider, J. (2013) 'A theater intervention to prevent teen dating violence for Mexican-American middle school students.' *Journal of Adolescent Health 53*, 1, 62–67.

Bell, J. and Stanley, N. (2006) 'Learning about domestic violence: young people's responses to a healthy relationships programme.' *Sex Education 6*, 3, 237–250.

Chief Secretary to the Treasury (2003) *Every Child Matters.* London: The Stationery Office.

Datta, J., Haddon, A. and Shaw, C. (2005) *An Evaluation of the Miss Dorothy Programme in Primary Schools. Executive Summary.* London: NCB.

DMSS Research & Consultancy (2012) *Tender's Healthy Relationship Education in Schools Funded by Comic Relief.* North Dalton: DMSS.

Ellis, J. (2004) *Preventing Violence against Women and Girls: A Study of Educational Programmes for Children and Young People.* London: Womankind Worldwide.

Ellis, J. (2006) *Children and the Prevention of Domestic Violence through School-Based Work.* Unpublished PhD Thesis. Coventry: University of Warwick.

Ellis, J. and Thiara, R. K. (eds) (2014) *Preventing Violence against Women and Girls: Educational Work with Children and Young People.* Bristol: Policy Press.

End Violence Against Women (EVAW) (2011) *A Different World is Possible: Promising Practices to Prevent Violence against Women and Girls.* London: EVAW.

Fox, C., Hale, B. and Gadd, D. (2013) 'Domestic abuse prevention education: listening to the views of young people.' *Sex Education: Sexuality, Society and Learning,* DOI: 10.1080/14681811.2013.816949.

Friend, P. (2014) 'What Did You Learn at School Today? Creating Effective Spaces for Domestic Violence Prevention.' In J. Ellis and R. K. Thiara (eds) *Preventing Violence against Women and Girls: Educational Work with Children and Young People.* Bristol: Policy Press.

Hester, M. and Westmarland, N. (2005) *Tackling Domestic Violence: Effective Interventions and Approaches.* London: Home Office.

House of Commons Education Committee (2012) *Children First: The Child Protection System in England. Further Written Evidence Submitted by Women's Aid Federation of England (Women's Aid).* HC 137. Available at www.publications.parliament.uk/pa/cm201213/cmselect/cmeduc/137/137vw66.htm, accessed on 31 March 2015.

Jaffe, P., Wolfe, D. and Wilson, S. (1990) *Children of Battered Women.* Newbury Park, CA: Sage.

Jones, L. (1991) 'The Minnesota School Curriculum Project: A Stateside Domestic Violence Project in Secondary Schools.' In B. Levy (ed.) *Dating Violence: Young Women in Danger.* Seattle, WA: The Seal Press.

Manship, S. and Perry, R. (2012) *An Evaluation of Domestic Abuse Programmes for Adolescents in Kent and Medway.* Kent: Canterbury Christchurch University.

McElearney, A., Stephenson, P. and Adamson, G. (2011) *Keeping Safe: The Development of Effective Preventative Education in Primary Schools in Northern Ireland: Exploring Practice, Policy and Research Implications.* Belfast: NSPCC.

Radford, L., Corral, S., Bradley, C., Fisher, H. *et al.* (2011) *Child Abuse and Neglect in the UK Today.* London: NSPCC.

Reid Howie Associates (2002) *Evaluation of the Zero Tolerance 'Respect' Pilot Project.* Edinburgh: Scottish Executive.

Stanley, N., Ellis, J., Farrelly, N., Hollinghurst, S., Bailey, S. and Downe, S. (2015) *Preventing Domestic Abuse for Children and Young People (PEACH): A Mixed Knowledge Scoping Review.* Public Health Research.

Taylor, B. G., Stein, N. D., Mumford, E. A. and Woods, D. (2013) 'Shifting boundaries: an experimental evaluation of a dating violence prevention program in middle schools.' *Prevention Science 14,* 64–76.

Thiara, R. K. and Ellis, J. (2005) *WDVF London-Wide Schools Domestic Violence Prevention Project.* London: Westminster Domestic Violence Forum.

Weisz, A. N. and Black, B. M. (2009) *Programme to Reduce Teen Dating Violence and Sexual Assault: Perspectives on What Works.* New York, NY: Columbia University Press.

Woods, P. (2011) *Transforming Education Policy: Shaping a Democratic Future.* Bristol: Policy Press.

CHAPTER 4

Advocacy for Children and Young People Experiencing Domestic Violence

Joanne Westwood and Cath Larkins

Introduction

This chapter reports on the evaluation of a children's independent domestic violence advocacy service (KIDVA) in the north-west of England which worked with children and young people aged between 11 and 25. The evaluation of the KIDVA provision used multiple methods to report on the processes involved in developing and delivering this unique provision and examined the benefits of the service for children and young people. We begin with a brief outline of policy and practice issues related to children and young people who experience domestic violence and then describe the methods used to capture their experiences and evaluate how advocacy was implemented. The evaluation data illustrate the range of services provided under the banner of advocacy and the role children and young people played in shaping the KIDVA services. Their involvement appeared crucial to the success of the service. The evaluation found that the current funding model for children and young people's advocacy should move away from a spot purchase approach, so as to ensure sustained and long-term availability and relationship building.

The policy context

Domestic violence has both short-term and long-term impacts on the well-being of children and young people who experience or witness it (Stanley 2011) and there is a growing awareness that young people may experience violence and abuse both in their parents' relationships and in their own interpersonal relationships (Barter and McCarry 2012; Barter *et al.* 2009). UK government (2013) guidance aimed at professionals working in child protection stipulates that children have a right to have their voices heard and are entitled to support in their own right and to advocacy to help them to express their views (p.10). This can be regarded as mirroring the universal provision in Article 12 of the 1989 United Nations Convention on the Rights of the Child (UN 1989) and the associated General Comment 12 that 'adequate time and resources' and support appropriate to their capacity should be provided so that they can confidently contribute their views on matters that affect them, including issues of violence (UNComRC 2009, para 134(e)). In the UK, individual advocacy is a well-recognised means of providing children with support, but access to advocacy for children who are not in alternative care is limited (Brady 2011). Despite specific national provision, children who are at risk in situations of violence usually lack the support that advocacy might provide in promoting their human right to be heard.

Statutory social work support is designed to safeguard children, ensure their immediate welfare and assess any future risk. Safeguarding interventions may, however, taper off once the victim and her children are out of immediate danger (Stanley *et al.* 2011). The needs and rights of children and young people to have a voice in the aftermath of domestic violence are marginalised at best and invisible at worst. Although services support victims with practical and legal issues, there is a general shortage of services for children and young people who experience domestic violence, with services tending to focus on supporting women and addressing the impact of the violence/abuse on parenting and mothers' abilities to continue to protect their children (Radford *et al.* 2011).

Hyndburn and Ribble Valley (HARV) is a specialist domestic violence organisation funded to deliver the KIDVA service. HARV recognised that children and young people were not able to access support to process their experiences of domestic violence independently from their mothers, nor were they provided with the opportunity to talk about the impact of the violence they had experienced. HARV's staff were also keen to provide support to assist children and young people to keep themselves safe and provide opportunities for them to develop strategies to manage their feelings, including those of torn loyalties and anger towards their mothers and the perpetrators (often fathers, stepfathers or their mothers' partners). Whilst these aspects of advocacy work may be leaning towards therapeutic interventions, it was clear to HARV that addressing these issues would enable young people to move forward and start to take decisions about what they themselves wanted. HARV had carried out some limited school-based work to raise awareness among pupils and to provide one-to-one support in school settings. It had also delivered holiday and weekend youth and play sessions which were funded on a short-term contract basis. The provision of three years' funding from Comic Relief allowed the organisation to develop these services and to appoint a full-time KIDVA worker to provide advocacy for children and young people.

Advocacy for children and young people

Advocacy involves 'speaking up for children and young people and ensuring their views and wishes are heard and acted upon by decision-makers' (DoH 2002). Although advocacy is commonly described as enabling 'voice' (Dalrymple 2005; Knight and Oliver 2007, p.418), advocacy must enable diverse forms of communication about wishes and views so as to be part of a wider process of seeking influence. Advocacy can include any social action on behalf of children which aims to redistribute power or reallocate resources (Melton 1987 in Boylan and Dalrymple 2011) and children may also advocate for themselves through embodied acts of resistance (Larkins 2014). Advocacy services can take various forms (Boylan and Dalrymple 2009), working with individuals or groups or through self-advocacy. Advocates can be informal, peer or formal, building short- or long-term relationships. They can be independent, contracted or spot purchased to provide advocacy to specific service users or services.

Advocacy services for children and young people who have experienced domestic violence are in their infancy. UK policy now recognises the impact of domestic violence on children and young people but has so far failed adequately to address the lack of services and resources available to mitigate these impacts.

The KIDVA service

The KIDVA service draws on the model of the Independent Domestic Violence Advisor (IDVA) service for adult survivors which HARV was already delivering. Some aspects of the service were in line with the National Standards for the Provision of Advocacy (DoH 2002) which apply to health and social care advocacy for children. The service aimed to support children and young people to articulate their concerns and worries about the effects of domestic violence on their lives in formal meetings and other settings and to ensure that children and young people had a say in how KIDVA and HARV services were developed and delivered (in line with National Advocacy Standards 1 and 2). KIDVA put children and young people in touch with other services and resources in their community and provided access to specialist black and ethnic minority workers where appropriate. The organisation had clear policies in relation to discrimination and worked to ensure that children and young people were treated equally (Standard 3). Children and young people could self-refer to the KIDVA service or be referred for one-to-one or group work. Referrals to KIDVA could come from the Multi-Agency Risk Assessment Conference (MARAC), an interagency forum dealing with high-risk domestic violence referrals (CAADA 2014), or from HARV's service for adult victims of domestic violence. Group and individual support was delivered by the KIDVA worker in a range of settings (Standard 4).

Children and young people aged between 11 and 25 who were experiencing domestic violence in their parents' relationships and/or their own intimate relationships were eligible for the KIDVA service. The original intention was to offer a service to children and young people for a maximum of three months with the aim of reducing risks of further violence. Referrals were followed up quickly and services were promoted to other agencies through the MARAC and other local networks (Standards 4, 5 and 6).

After a referral, the KIDVA worker contacted the child's or young person's school or contacted them directly to undertake an initial assessment. For all children and young people under the age of 14, consent for contact with the child was requested from the mother (or safe carer) before contact was made with the child. Some of the young people using the service were parents themselves and in these cases a delicate balance was negotiated to ensure that the aims of the advocacy intervention were clear whilst also recognising that the child of the young person might require protection in their own right. Confidentiality and the organisation's safeguarding policies were explained (Standard 7). The KIDVA worker then completed a safety plan with the child or young person at this initial meeting.

Children and young people retained the right to refuse to participate in the advocacy process (Standard 1). KIDVA only followed up information once they had met with the child/young person and gained their consent from them and (where appropriate) from the safe carer.

Referrals

In total, 198 children and young people were referred to the KIDVA worker across the three years of the evaluation.

Table 4.1 below shows that the ages of children and young people referred ranged between nine and 24 years with most in the 11–18 age range.

Table 4.1 Ages of children and young people referred to HARV in evaluation period			
Age ranges	Year 1	Year 2	Year 3
10 and under	0	13	0
11–18 years	13	36	73
18–25 years	14	25	24
Total	**27**	**74**	**97**

Children and young people using the service were able to choose from a range of activities/services shown below:

- One-to-one sessions: initial assessments, risk assessment and safety planning. Issue-based work included completing domestic violence safety plans, direct work on self-esteem/confidence, healthy relationships, power and control wheel, and explaining the MARAC processes. These took place in school/college and were arranged by the KIDVA worker through the nominated school liaison officer.

- Attendance at and support for meetings including explaining the process to them beforehand and providing transport if required. The advocate would speak on behalf of the young person at the meetings, or support them to express themselves and ensure that their views were raised.

- Court support included preparation and support for children and young people to attend court proceedings associated with domestic abuse.

- Communication with children and young people or with others on their behalf.

- Group activities were provided regularly, particularly during school holiday periods and in the evenings at community locations.

- Other activities included delivering regular Facebook sessions which provided information about activities and events, as well as enabling children and young people to contact their worker. The KIDVA worker also arranged police welfare checks and offered practical problem solving when necessary.

The KIDVA worker did not accept referrals which focused on child protection issues and worked closely with HARV's children's safeguarding worker to identify any child protection concerns and ensure referrals were made to children's social services.

The evaluation
Participants
The advocacy service was evaluated over three years using multiple methods. In year one, we carried out participatory focus groups with 12 children and young people and examined 12 anonymised case referral records. In year two, we conducted individual face-to-face interviews with nine young service users and telephone interviews with three HARV staff and ten stakeholders. In year three, we completed non-participant observation of 12 KIDVA service users during an outdoor activity programme. In each year, we also collected demographic and referral data from the organisation's case records. Demographic details of children and young people participating in the evaluation are given in Table 4.2.

Table 4.2 Demographic information for evaluation participants

Year	Method	No.	Age range	Gender	Ethnicity
1	Focus group	12	11–16	7 female 5 male	10 white British 2 South Asian British
2	Interviews	9	11–21	4 female 5 male	7 white British 2 Pakistani British
3	Non-participant observation	12	12–16	7 female 5 male	All white British

Ethics and consent

Relevant ethical approvals were obtained for the three years of the study. It was important to guarantee confidentiality and deal appropriately and safely with any disclosure made (Morris, Hegarty and Humphreys 2012). Consent was gained for all those children/young people participating in the study, and for the researchers to examine the case records kept by the organisation with a guarantee that no personal details would be seen by the researcher. Children and young people could choose to withdraw consent during the fieldwork period and we provided for this option in the consent form. Consent was also gathered from members of staff and stakeholders who participated in interviews.

Methods
Focus groups with children and young people

The first focus group session used draw/write techniques to obtain young people's own perspectives on what was good about the KIDVA service, what they got out of it and what could be improved. In the second session, the research team returned to the group with KIDVA's standards of service provision and outcomes to assess their relevance and to develop deeper understandings of the young people's experiences and perspectives. We also added further priority ranking cards, drawn from the National Advocacy Standards (DoH 2002) and Every Child Matters (HM Government 2004), as these seemed potential frameworks for analysis (Kelle 2005).

Interviews with children and young people

The interviews with children and young people were audio-recorded and transcribed. Analysis was undertaken by reading through the interview transcripts and drawing out the themes. Research shows that it is difficult for children and young people to talk about their experiences of domestic violence (Buckley, Holt and Whelan 2007) and so questions were focused on the support available, their relationship with the KIDVA service, the types of activities they got involved in and their relationships with important adults.

Non-participant observation – outdoor education

We video-recorded three sessions of outdoor activities during one weekend. Our study did not seek to measure the impact of the outdoor activities; rather our focus was on observing the interactions between KIDVA and the children and young people.

Children's and young people's experiences of the KIDVA service

The qualitative data and case recording showed that the young people consistently experienced a range of positive outcomes which they attributed to the service and they expressed an appreciation of how support had been delivered to them. Several themes emerged from this data related to service delivery: accessible and safe service; trust and confidentiality; feeling listened to and respected; KIDVA skills and outcomes; relationships and friendships; engaging in and enjoying a range of activities; and well-being, safety and security. We use these to structure the findings reported on the following pages.

An accessible and safe service

Focus group participants emphasised the KIDVA's worker's availability and accessibility: '[KIDVA's] been there when I've needed someone to talk to.' The advocate had enabled feelings of security: 'I'm secure that I've got someone there who listens' and 'you know when you're in danger that you can tell staff'. The service had also succeeded in creating a safe atmosphere: 'I know I'm safe here [at the service]' and 'I feel reassured here [at the service]'; 'You know you're not going to be physically and emotionally abused here because everyone's gone through similar things.'

Trust and confidentiality

Being able to trust their advocacy worker and the provision of private sessions were highly significant for these children and young people. These sessions often took some time to develop. The case records showed the KIDVA service working at building regular contact with the young person to develop a relationship. For example, one female interviewee aged 14 described receiving the KIDVA service for a few months. She had witnessed violence as a young child but had never been able to talk to her mum about it. On those occasions when the KIDVA visited young people in school, it was important that there was a private space available for them. The need for privacy was balanced by an understanding that confidentiality could be broken in extreme cases and those children or young people who discussed this understood that this would be done to protect and safeguard them from harm or danger: 'My friend doesn't always understand how important it is not to tell. But I can tell people [workers] here' and 'I can talk to my mum more. At home, I keep most of my stuff to myself and my best friend. She [KIDVA] will ask before she tells someone.' However, in the focus groups, two young people noted the importance of having a relatively high threshold for breaking confidentiality.

Feeling listened to and respected

Young people in focus groups described KIDVA workers showing them respect, listening to them and saw them as honest, faithful and trustworthy. They felt that workers took their ideas seriously: 'because they don't judge them [our ideas]. [They just say] "OK, that's a good idea".' The children and young people provided examples of how respect was demonstrated: 'They talk to you when you are upset and worried' and show 'care and encouragement'. They felt that rather than being told what to do, they were given advice or provided with a range of potential options which they could take or leave.

The KIDVA worker encouraged a sense of ownership and empowerment in relation to decisions. One participant noted difficulties in talking about past problems with her mum: 'I don't want to talk about what happened with my dad to my mum as I don't want to upset my mum.' The KIDVA worker provided an opportunity for this discussion to be initiated and helped this young person to process what had happened, to understand the importance of a healthy relationship and develop a closer relationship with her mum. For this male interviewee aged 11, having someone else to talk to was really helpful: 'I'm not keeping [it] to myself, I wouldn't be able to stop thinking about it. It was upsetting for me, 'cos it was quite bad.'

KIDVA skills

The workers were described as calm, happy, friendly and approachable. One interviewee said:

> We [the KIDVA worker and child/young person] will talk about whatever is on my mind, then go off the subject a bit and just like talk about general stuff and…erm have a bit of a laugh or whatever, and then go back. (Male, 21)

Similar comments about approachability and the KIDVA worker's ability to engage and build rapport were evident. A 14-year-old female described 'a friendly relationship – I can speak to her about anything, and she's professional but friendly'. The workers were described as 'a good laugh' and as having a 'good sense of humour'. Some focus group participants described the workers as like family or friends, but sometimes with a significant difference: 'You can say things to her that you can't say to your mum because you're scared.'

During the outdoor activities we observed the KIDVA worker using active listening skills and non-verbal encouragers to engage with children and young people's reluctance, anxiety and concerns about participating in the activities. At the start of the weekend, the children and young people were visibly nervous and silent, or talking quietly in small groups or pairs. On the first day, during the giant swing session, we noted them growing in confidence, relaxing into the activities and their environment. On the last day, when we observed them raft-building, they were willing participants expressing their excitement and interest in the activities, even when they were challenging or physically hard. As well as seeking affirmation from their peers, they were rewarded with praise from the KIDVA worker, the outdoor education facilitator and the support workers.

During these activities, the KIDVA worker demonstrated core advocacy skills in being able to support children and young people to be heard, to influence decisions that affected them and to develop and practice self-advocacy skills. Examples of self-advocacy also appeared in interviews where young people described making contact with the KIDVA worker when they felt that they needed to express themselves about a family issue. Having control over what and who they spoke to about their experiences was important. This male interviewee aged 21 wanted information about the sentencing of the perpetrator: 'I just asked [the KIDVA worker] if she could find out more information on it. A couple of days later she rang me up.' For this female interviewee aged 12, being able to take the initiative in contacting the KIDVA worker was important: 'She gives us her number, so we can ring her whenever we need to.'

Relationships and friendships

Making new friends, spending time with friends and learning about and being in positive and rewarding peer relationships were key for the young people in focus groups and those who were interviewed. In addition, some of the children and young people who were experiencing strained or difficult family relationships described these as having been repaired or improved as a result of their involvement with the KIDVA service:

> I asked her to tell my mum how I felt about my dad going away, and to ask my mum, as she was stressed out, to give me more time. [The KIDVA worker] spoke to her and now she does it, she spends more time with me. (Girl, aged 11–13 years)

Focus group participants also described increased opportunities to enjoy themselves, and the social and group activities appeared to have contributed to developing their social skills: 'I feel like I have gained new friends.' In several cases, the KIDVA worker had undertaken work with siblings and with other family members at the request of the child or young person. An 11-year-old boy described HARV as 'an organisation that helps with family problems'.

Engaging in and enjoying a range of activities

The KIDVA provision involved encouraging children and young people to engage with and actively participate in a programme of social activities. For some, this was the first time they had ever engaged in group social activities: 'never been to a youth club [before]'; '[I] get out and have fresh air [now].' Some of these activities took place in community settings and some involved outings to fun interesting places. These were seen by the children and young people as integral to their continued engagement with the service as well as providing opportunities for them to talk to the KIDVA workers about current issues or difficulties in their lives. Engagement in activities enabled them to develop social skills: 'coming here gives me confidence in socially interacting with others' and 'can talk to each other'. Group activities also encouraged 'confidence in what you are doing, choosing what is right and wrong'.

Well-being, safety and security

The feelings of safety, security, being listened to and supported within the service also had positive consequences for how children and young people felt in their daily lives. For some children and young people, having someone to talk to who was 'on their side' and understood them promoted their well-being by giving a 'sense of direction in life'. It also enabled some to manage difficult and conflicting feelings about and responses to their experiences of domestic violence: 'made home life more peaceful', 'to walk around school calmly without being anxious' and 'makes you feel as though you're not fighting the world with two hands'.

Young people participating in the focus groups said that the support they received from the KIDVA service made them feel safer: 'I feel more secure', '[the advocate] helped me not to be scared of Dad', '[We] feel safer at home', and 'if KIDVA weren't here I wouldn't be alive now'. Interviewees identified that one-to-one support had enabled them to 'deal with difficult situations'. For one young person, this was to 'get on with my brother more'; for another, it 'helped me with anger issues'. Two young people stated they were now better at safety planning.

Frequency, length and methods of contact between KIDVA and child/young person

Clearly, the KIDVA service succeeded in engaging children and young people through a diverse range of approaches. The evaluation aimed to identify the resources required for the service to be delivered and we therefore captured information on the length and pattern of interventions as well as on case closure. The length of contact between the KIDVA service and children and young people varied considerably, as shown in Table 4.3 which compares patterns of service delivery in the second and third years of the evaluation when the service was more established.

Table 4.3 Length of time KIDVA cases opened years 2 and 3		
Length of time case opened	Year 2	Year 3
Less than one month	11	15
1–3 months	43	63
3–6 months	8	16
7–12 months	12	3

In year 1, analysis of case files revealed that it was often taking several weeks for the KIDVA worker to set up appointments and complete initial meetings with children and young people. A comparison of service patterns in years 2 and 3 (when complete data were available) showed that in year 3 there was an increase in those cases open for less than six months and a decrease in cases open for more than seven months from 16 per cent to 3 per cent. This might be explained by the KIDVA service becoming more efficient at tracking and managing referrals. However, children and young people interviewed and those attending outdoor activities also appeared to value long-term relationships with the service. Interview participants talked about maintaining contact with the KIDVA service through the private Facebook group established and by phone and/or text messages as well as meetings being set up by a third party (school or mother). Long-term engagement was particularly important in supporting young people to engage with the service and enact their own decisions. This was evident in Tina's case described below:

Case Study: Tina

Tina was aged 19 and in an abusive relationship with the father of her son, aged two. The case had been open for eight months and was ongoing. At the outset of the intervention, Tina stated that she was in a relationship which was undermining her as a mother as well as damaging her self-confidence. Tina was supported by her parents who took care of her son, and helped Tina to manage her health condition; however, Tina felt she needed to address her relationship with Tony, her partner, by herself and wanted to do this without worrying her parents. Having access to KIDVA enabled Tina to express herself and understand her position as a parent with responsibilities as well as her rights to be safe in her personal relationship. Over time, Tina disclosed more about the extent and severity of domestic violence in the relationship. The risk assessment undertaken by the KIDVA service produced a score sufficiently high to warrant a MARAC referral, but Tina was initially resistant to being referred to the local MARAC as she was unsure about the process. Once it was explained and she understood the role of the MARAC, the referral went ahead because she realised she needed to put her child and her own interests first. Similarly, the KIDVA service was able to explain why a referral to children's services was important, given Tina's health condition and her need for support with her son.

The KIDVA worker made several attempts to contact Tina and rescheduled several appointments in the early weeks when Tina failed to arrive. The KIDVA worker demonstrated tenacity in her approach to working with Tina during the eight months the case was open.

By the end of the research period, it was clear from the case notes that Tina had found the strength to end the relationship with Tony; she had also stopped responding to his text messages. Earlier on in the relationship with Tony, Tina would have been unable to do this as she would have anticipated abuse if she did not immediately answer his texts. The confidence, self-esteem and strength took a while to build and involved the KIDVA service working alongside Tina, at her pace, and understanding the pressures Tina was experiencing throughout this time. Tina made the decision to end her relationship herself and in doing so protected herself and her son from further abuse – sending a clear message to his father that abusive behaviour was not acceptable. His relationship with his son was monitored thereafter through supervised contact and he was required to undergo assessment by children's social services.

Given the value of these longer-term KIDVA interventions, it is of concern that in the third year of the evaluation, as shown in Table 4.4, the most frequently recorded reason for case closure was the end of MARAC support. Once the request contained in the MARAC referral was met – for example, safety planning had been delivered – the KIDVA worker was required to close the case as there was no further funding available to continue the service.

Table 4.4 Reason for KIDVA case closures	
Reason for closure	**Number**
MARAC support ended	52
Work completed or support ended by mutual agreement	20
Client refuses support or disengaged	16
Worker or young person left the area/service	4
Other	4
Referred to outreach service	1
Total	97

The fact that KIDVA intervention ended at the same time as other services delivered via MARAC was a matter for concern, as together these services formed a safety plan. However, interviewees described how the private Facebook group established for those using the KIDVA service was used to arrange places to meet up with the KIDVA worker whilst their case was open. Additionally, once one-to-one sessions ceased, children and young people were referred to youth groups and activities which aimed to ensure that any difficulties which arose could be picked up and referred again if necessary – this was a very welcome measure for the participants interviewed. In some instances, this low-level monitoring of closed cases led to a further intervention such as referral to children's social services. Maintenance of long-term relationships is a key issue in the current economic climate when many universal services have been withdrawn or restricted, and this may be particularly damaging for children and young people exposed to domestic violence as their family circumstances are often fragile.

Discussion

For us as participatory researchers, it was important that the evaluation enabled children and young people to have a say in shaping the future of the KIDVA service, given the lack of control and influence they experienced in other areas of their lives. This study invited children and young people to contribute their ideas about the development of the service and these were fed into various aspects of delivery such as the service's use of social media contacts and implementation of their suggestions for group and outdoor activities including staffing the KIDVA Facebook page. The value young service users placed on youth group and outdoor activities also contributed to the decision to continue this aspect of the service, although resources only permitted intermittent activities. Throughout the evaluation, we also observed that children and young people were able to make active decisions about which aspects of the service they engaged with, shaping their experience of the KIDVA service to conform with their own individual wishes.

Contradictions were apparent between the benefits of long-term service provision where time to build relationships emerged as crucial and conceptions of advocacy as a time-limited service. In the case of this service, these contradictions were heightened by the fact that the external funding for the service was available for only three years. This echoes findings from the review of advocacy services by the Children's Commissioner for Wales (2012) which noted that children were more likely to access advocacy where long-term relationships existed. The KIDVA service demonstrates the value of relationship-based advocacy, where the advocate provides information and support over the long term about what abuse is, as well as facilitating access to other services so young person can make their own informed decisions about their relationships and safety.

HARV was successful in securing funding for one additional year of KIDVA provision and managed to continue delivering the service with a change of KIDVA worker. The key features of this service which might inform the development of similar advocacy services were: continuity in terms of KIDVA workers knowing what was going on in a child or young person's life; rapport and relationship building; a service that was focused on children and young people; clarity about the advocate's role and remit; and provision of activities with peers to reduce isolation.

References

Barter, C., McCarry, M., Berridge, D. and Evans, K. (2009) *Partner Exploitation and Violence in Teenage Intimate Relationships*. NSPCC. Available at www.nspcc.org.uk/preventing-abuse/research-and-resources/partner-exploitation-and-violence-in-teenage-intimate-relationships, accessed on 19 December 2014.

Barter, C. and McCarry, M. (2012) 'Love, Power and Control: Girls' Experiences of Partner Violence and Exploitation.' In N. Lombard and L. McMillan (eds) *Violence against Women: Current Theory and Practice in Domestic Abuse, Sexual Violence and Exploitation*. London: Jessica Kingsley Publishers.

Brady, L. (2011) *Where Is My Advocate? A Scoping Report on Advocacy Services for Children and Young People in England*. London: Office of the Children's Commissioner.

Boylan, J. and Dalrymple J. (2009) *Understanding Advocacy for Children and Young People*. London: Open University Press.

Boylan, J. and Dalrymple, J. (2011) 'Advocacy, social justice and children's rights.' *Practice: Social Work in Action 23*, 1, 19–30.

Buckley, H., Holt, S. and Whelan, S. (2007) 'Listen to me! Children's experiences of domestic violence.' *Child Abuse Review 16*, 296–310.

CAADA (2014) *Information about MARACs*. Available at www.caada.org.uk/marac/Information_about_MARACs.html, accessed on 19 December 2014.

Children's Commissioner for Wales (2012) *A Review of Independent Professional Advocacy Services for Looked-After Children and Young People, Care Leavers and Children in Need in Wales*. Swansea: CCfW. Available at http://dera.ioe.ac.uk/14666/1/283.pdf, accessed on 19 December 2014.

Dalrymple, J. (2005) 'Constructions of child and youth advocacy: emerging issues in advocacy practice.' *Children & Society 19*, 3–15DoH (2002) *National Standards for the Provision of Children's Advocacy Services*. Available at http://webarchive.nationalarchives.gov.uk/+/www.dh.gov.uk/en/Consultations/Responsestoconsultations/DH_4017049, accessed on 16 April 2015.

HM Government (2004) *Every Child Matters*. Available at www.gov.uk/government/publications/every-child-matters, accessed on 19 December 2014.

HM Government (2013) *Working Together to Safeguard Children: A Guide to Inter-Agency Working to Safeguard and Promote the Welfare of Children*. Available at www.gov.uk/government/uploads/system/uploads/attachment_data/file/281368/Working_together_to_safeguard_children.pdf, accessed on 19 December 2014.

Kelle, U. (2005) '"Emergence" vs. "forcing" of empirical data? A crucial problem of "Grounded Theory" reconsidered.' *Forum: Qualitative Social Research 6*, 2, Art. 27.

Knight, A. and Oliver, C. (2007) 'Advocacy for disabled children and young people: benefits and dilemmas.' *Child and Family Social Work 12*, 417–425.

Larkins, C. (2014) 'Enacting children's citizenship: developing understandings of how children enact themselves as citizens through actions and acts of citizenship.' *Childhood 21*, 1, 7–21.

Morris, A., Hegarty, K. and Humphreys, C. (2012) 'Ethical and safe: research with children about domestic violence.' *Research Ethics 8*, 2, 125–139.

Radford, L., Aitken, R., Miller, P., Ellis, J., Roberts, J. and Firkic, A. (2011) *Meeting the Needs of Children Living with Domestic Violence in London.* Project Report. London: NSPCC.

Stanley, N., Miller, P., Richardson Foster, H. and Thomson, G. (2011) 'A stop-start response: social services' interventions with children and families notified following domestic violence incidents.' *British Journal of Social Work 41*, 2, 296–313.

Stanley, N. (2011) *Children Experiencing Domestic Violence: A Research Review.* Dartington: Research in Practice.

UN (1989) *United Nations Convention on the Rights of the Child.* Committee on the Rights of the Child. Available at www.ohchr.org/en/professionalinterest/pages/crc.aspx, accessed on 19 December 2014.

UN Committee on the Rights of the Child (2009) General Comment No. 12 (2009) *The Right of the Child to Be Heard* CRC/C/GC/12, 1 July 2009.

CHAPTER 5

Children Who Are Violent to Their Parents Need Protection Too

Paula Wilcox and Michelle Pooley

> It's one of the biggest taboos in family life. It happens – we know that – but no-one talks about it. And there's really no-one to talk to about it – mothers (who are most often on the receiving end) don't tell their friends and there isn't the network of support organisations to help you deal with it the way there are for women battered by partners.[1]

Introduction

Child to Parent Violence and Abuse (CPV) is the most hidden and misunderstood of the various forms of family violence. The idea that parents/carers (in this chapter we will use the term 'parents' to denote parents or carers) who are responsible for children's welfare can become victims of abuse from their own child is an extremely challenging one. The issue is not only difficult for parents experiencing violence from their children, but also for policymakers, practitioners and the general public. Absent from national and European programmes on young people's violence and from programmes on violence against women until 2013, this form of domestic violence is not adequately addressed in Europe.

The Responding to Child to Parent Violence (RCPV) action research project, funded by the European Union's Daphne III programme, explored this issue within a European context from 2013 to 2015. The University of Brighton in partnership with the National Association XXI Rhodope Mountain Initiative in Bulgaria, Brighton and Hove City Council in England, the National University of Galway in Ireland, the University

---

1 Chamberlain, Parentline Plus, cited in Lewis 2009.

of Valencia in Spain and Åmål municipality in Sweden coordinated the project. At the start of the project in Bulgaria and Sweden, CPV had not been named or worked with in any way.

To date, research has predominantly focused upon exploring the possible causes of the onset of CPV by identifying the risk factors that may precipitate children and young people into becoming violent (Kennair and Mellor 2007; Routt and Anderson 2011). Most studies have been quantitative in nature. The small number of qualitative studies have focused solely on researching parents' perspectives, so the opinions, needs and voices of young people are lacking (Holt 2011), as are the voices of practitioners who told us that this study on RCPV was long overdue and much needed.

The chapter will argue that European policymakers are currently failing to grasp the difficulties faced in families where children are abusive and violent to their parents and that responses to CPV are fragmented; there is also an assumption that parenting programmes are sufficient to tackle CPV. Practitioners prioritise work with children who have been abused by parents, but we argue that, in order to protect children, it is necessary also to work with those who are abusive and violent towards their parents (some of whom will have been abused themselves). It is critical that practitioners are able to identify, listen to and work with children and parents experiencing CPV in a way that differs from that of traditional parenting programmes and we will discuss this below. This chapter draws on early findings from the RCPV action research project, in particular the English and Spanish literature reviewed and questionnaire data from England and Ireland. Future publications from the research will examine parents' and young people's views in depth. We first explain our research methodology, followed by an exploration of conceptual problems and the extent of CPV, highlighting the influence of stigma and shame. We then move on to look at practitioners' responses to CPV and discuss ideas on how practice and policy might be enhanced.

Research methods

The primary aims of the RCPV project were to research understandings and raise awareness of CPV, explore gendered approaches in interventions and capture good practice. As an action research project, each participating country examined its legal, social policy, attitudinal and cultural perspectives on CPV – this will be the subject of a future paper. An iterative approach was taken to enable each country to agree activities relevant to their needs and for the community partners together with their academic research colleagues to research the impact of implementing these activities. Overall, a mixed methods approach was taken.

We developed an evaluative framework for training, interventions and awareness-raising activities. Data collected relating to training and awareness raising included self-efficacy questionnaires (n=37 pre-training; n=47 post-training) and training evaluation questionnaires (n=74) which were implemented at two training sessions in Brighton and Hove (Break4Change n=27 and Non-Violent Resistance (NVR) n=25 in May 2013) and one training session in Galway (Break4Change n=22 in June 2013). Observations of the training and 20 qualitative interviews with practitioners were completed.

We researched the effect of two CPV interventions (Break4Change and NVR) that ran during the project's timeframe using quantitative evaluation questionnaires with practitioners, parents and young people. Follow-up qualitative interviews with parents and young people who had attended Break4Change and two focus groups with practitioners who facilitated the interventions were carried out. Data were also collected and compiled from historical records and films made of the Break4Change programme since its inception in 2009.

Defining child to parent violence

There is no universal definition of CPV in the international literature and the RCPV study found that services lack policy guidelines or standard definitions. Moreover, different contemporary family forms are frequently not considered:

> We don't have any specific definition or an agency definition of child to parent violence but I would say it is where a young person uses physical, psychological or other forms of violence or abuse in order to exert control over his or her parent. (Community safety worker, England)

Most of the professionals interviewed said that CPV is not the usual kind of boundary- or patience-testing behaviour all parents experience with their teenage children, but rather a more persistent pattern of emotional abuse and physical violence used over time which ends up controlling and dominating parents (Coogan 2012). The RCPV project recorded children as young as five years old being abusive to parents and carers but chose to focus on adolescent children since targeted CPV programmes work with this age group.

Definitions of CPV within North American research literature have tended to focus on a limited range of physical behaviours, such as hitting and kicking, ignoring psychological and other types of violence (Browne and Hamilton 1998; Paulson, Coombs and Landsverk 1990). Harbin and Madden, however, refer to 'actual physical assaults and verbal and non-verbal threats of physical harm' (1979, p.1288).

In Europe, the majority of work on CPV has been carried out in Spain and there the definition most widely drawn on is that of Aroca and colleagues:

> Child to parent violence is where the son/daughter acts intentionally and consciously with the desire to cause harm, injury and/or suffering to their parents, repeatedly over time, and with the immediate aim of gaining power, control and dominance over their victims to get what they want through psychological, economic and/or physical means. (Aroca, Bellver and Alba 2012, p.136)

In England and Ireland, the most commonly used definition of CPV is that of the Canadian researcher Barbara Cottrell: 'Parent abuse is any harmful act by a teenage child intended to gain power and control over a parent. The abuse can be physical, psychological or financial' (Cottrell 2003, p.1).

A different approach to capturing the notion of CPV is where it is self-defined: that is, adolescent/children's behaviour should be considered violent or abusive 'if others in the family feel threatened, intimidated or controlled by it and if they believe that they must adjust their own behaviour to accommodate threats or anticipation of violence' (Paterson *et al.* 2002, p.90). This approach has led some jurisdictions to adopt the term 'adolescent violence in the home' to cover the fact that sibling abuse by these young people may be just as common as abuse of the parent (Howard 2011).

CPV is not only about physical violence but includes behaviour which is more subtle, undermining and controlling of parents. These controlling behaviours are often precursors to the more physically violent aspects of this phenomenon. The full range of behaviours identified by the RCPV research programme included:

- Verbal abuse such as yelling, arguing, challenging, sarcastic and belittling comments, threats, name-calling and swearing.

- Physical abuse such as hitting, slapping, punching, kicking, shoving and pushing, breaking and throwing things, punching holes in walls, throwing things down the stairs, spitting, using weapons. Findings revealed significant rates of injury among parents (bruises, cuts, broken bones).

- Emotional abuse such as intimidation, controlling the running of the household, 'mind games', unrealistic demands, running away from home or staying out all night, lying, threats to hurt or kill, to run away, to commit suicide or hurt themselves, degrading the parent or other family members or withholding affection.

- Financial abuse such as stealing money or parent's belongings, selling family possessions, destroying the home or parents' belongings, demanding parents buy things they can't afford, incurring debts the parents must cover and so on.

- Sexual abuse was reported by a very small number of mothers who experienced this from their sons (n=2).

In England, CPV has been incorporated into the definition of domestic violence for those aged 16 and 17, thus locating CPV within the criminal justice system. In March 2013, the Home Office introduced a new official definition of domestic violence to be used across government. The definition of perpetrators was extended downwards to include young people aged 16 to 17 and the definition of domestic violence expanded to include coercive or controlling behaviour (Home Office 2013).

How this change in the age range of perpetrators of domestic violence will be implemented and will affect young people in practice is still not clear, and criminalising young people this early in their lives raises serious concerns. Although there are similarities between CPV and intimate partner violence, as highlighted by Gallagher (2007) and Wilcox (2012), it is important to distinguish between the two forms of violence as they differ in a number of important respects. The parent has a responsibility to parent, making the option of leaving the relationship even more complex. 'Victim' parents may not be physically bigger than the 'abusing' adolescent; however, they are on the face of it more powerful in terms of resources. Nevertheless, an adolescent who threatens to wreck the house or take life-threatening risks uses their positional power to take over control of their parents' house, thereby considerably changing the power dynamics.

The prevalence of CPV

Prevalence studies in existing international literature show great variability due to differences in the samples (populations) and the research methods used, which have been mainly quantitative in nature. A number of large-scale studies suggest that approximately 9 per cent to 14 per cent of parents are at some point physically assaulted by their adolescent children (Agnew and Huguley 1989; Cornell and Gelles 1982; Pagelow 1990; Paulson *et al.* 1990; Peek, Fischer and Kidwell 1985). In Japan, the prevalence rate was found to be 4 per cent (Honjo and Wakabayashi 1988), whilst in Australia the overall rate is estimated at approximately 9 per cent to 10 per cent (Gallagher 2004; Howard 2011).

In Europe, there is limited evidence and awareness of the problem in policy and practice fields. Researchers in Spain revealed that violence in the family by those who have not come of age now accounts for 10 per cent of the offences committed by this group (Registrados 200 casos de maltrato familiar por parte de menores, 2013). A clinical French study reported that the prevalence in France was 0.6 per cent (Laurent and Derry 1999). In the UK, research on patients reporting domestic violence in an emergency department at a local hospital reported that 6 per cent of the cases were cases of young people's violence against their parents (Smith *et al.* 1992). Family Lives (formerly Parentline Plus) reported that they receive approximately 95 calls per month from parents worried about the aggressive behaviour of their child towards them (Parentline Plus 2010). Hunter, Nixon and Parr's (2010) report examining family intervention projects (FIPs) found that 11 per cent of 256 families in receipt of FIP services (the majority of whom were single mothers) experienced this phenomenon.

A London study of CPV by Condry and Miles (2014) analysed all cases of adolescent to parent violence reported to the Metropolitan Police over one year (April 2009–March 2010) defined as constituting a criminal offence. Utilising a broad definition of violence to include threats, use of force and criminal damage (but excluding offences such as theft and handling), they found 1892 cases of violence from adolescents aged 13–19 years towards a parent; most involved violence against the person or criminal damage in the home. Adolescents reported to the police for CPV were overwhelmingly male (87.3%) and 77.5 per cent of reporting parents were female. Eight-six per cent of offences reported against mothers were perpetrated by their sons and 14 per cent by their daughters: 'Our findings reveal that adolescent to parent violence is a gendered phenomenon' (Condry and Miles 2014, p.1).

Within the RCPV England project, 65 practitioners working with CPV (reported via 52 quantitative questionnaires and 15 qualitative interviews) revealed significant levels of CPV on their caseloads:

> I have been working in this team for a year now and I think that out of the cases that I have had it, you know, somewhere up to a quarter, and that's not necessarily violence but abuse, abusive children towards the parents. (Family coach, England)

> 100 per cent would experience verbal abuse and controlling behaviour but physical violence I would say about 20 per cent to 30 per cent. This would be child to parent violence – this is what we hear about – there may be DV [domestic violence] also going on but we don't hear as much about that. (Youth justice worker, Ireland)

Since CPV is not a distinct category of harm measured by services, prevalence is likely to be higher than recorded statistics indicate. As Urra notes in relation to Spanish statistics: 'only one in eight parents dare to report CPV. If we add to this fact that you can only bring justice to those over 13 years, the number of cases would increase significantly' (Urra cited in Matey 2011).

Naming CPV and enabling discussion of this issue

Naming child to parent violence is complex. It is important to emphasise that if parents do disclose CPV, they rarely if ever use terms found in the literature such as 'child to parent violence' or 'parent abuse'; rather they talk about 'having problems in the family' or 'not being able to control their child'. This is critical as practitioners need to be aware that parents are loath to talk about their child's violence towards them and they may minimise or even deny that abuse is being used (Routt and Anderson 2015, pp.27 and 58). Further research elucidating the way in which the parent–child relationship shapes concepts of violence and abuse is key to ensuring programme frameworks that make sense to policymakers, practitioners and most importantly parents and children. If the words and language associated with this phenomenon become articulated within a popular discourse, then discussion will become easier for all.

Practitioners emphasised that whilst CPV remains unidentified as a specific category it will be difficult to prioritise this issue and for their organisation to monitor it. The interviews undertaken with practitioners confirmed that CPV is not considered a usual topic of conversation among family and friends. Although it is usual to talk about children's schooling, education, health and well-being, there is little if any discussion among parents of children's abusive and violent behaviour. As mentioned above, we found a lack of awareness of CPV to be a specific problem and, perhaps because of this, many practitioners share the same hesitancy as parents in raising CPV with families. In interviewing practitioners, we found that workers are not asking questions about this phenomenon: 'People really don't bring this up, we need to initiate conversations and bring it up ourselves' (Family worker, England).

Those in domestic violence organisations had a different perception of CPV which they encountered through women who were being supported in refuges:

> We were working more anyway say on parenting in general as an issue just in terms of supporting women – that is where we started to pull in our own refuge child care service more into outreach in particular because it was coming up so much there. And then as women began to talk more about children being abusive we began to see that there was even slightly more different focus and concern there. (Domestic violence worker, Ireland)

In addition to the organisational silence and the lack of an effective response to CPV, stigma and shame also contribute to the difficulties experienced in disclosing and asking about CPV, and so we will turn to look at this topic.

Stigma and CPV

A lack of appropriate parenting skills is often cited in parent abuse studies as a 'reason' for this abuse occurring, thus positioning mothers as 'failing parents' (Cottrell 2001 cited in Baker 2012, p.268). The stereotyping of the victim of CPV as a working-class mother was challenged by responses from the practitioners interviewed:

> The other thing for us was there was very interesting diversity in the backgrounds of the people who came. You had the single parents, you had parents who were the skilled professionals... they had this violence in common and I thought for me if nothing else happened, meeting each other and finding there wasn't just 'a type' who experienced this... (Social care worker, Republic of Ireland)

As in the case of domestic violence, the silence surrounding the issue of parent abuse (Hunter *et al.* 2010; Wilcox 2012) reflected in the low level of CPV reporting, can be attributed to the shame felt by victims for 'allowing' the violence to happen to them:

> I think a part of me 'managed' or coped or ignored for too long, but when it [child's violence] was affecting other people's families that's the point, if I'm honest, that's the point when I sought help. (Amy, mother, England)

Violence is not reported because it is seen as an indication of a personal failure as a mother and this feeling is reinforced by their child's abuse. This appeared to be particularly true for those mothers for whom domestic violence from a male partner was a historical or current factor; the sense of shame could be so powerful that some normalised the abuse:

> It is only really, really, really recently that I have had the real belief that it is not OK for him [son] to be violent towards me. Well I have not been giving him the message that it is not OK. Both of my children have learned that it's OK to be aggressive and violent towards your mother and I, I, I am ashamed but it is only really recently. (Amy, mother, England)

The shame and stigma of experiencing violence from your own child raises doubts as to one's skills as a 'good parent', as Cottrell has noted:

> They [parents] feel hopeless, helpless and in emotional turmoil because they are unable to control the situation and because of the possible physical danger. These are parents who have lost their leadership role in their families and are shocked that this could happen. (Cottrell 2005, p.57)

A sense of self-blame may be magnified by social and media messages about the need for parents, particularly mothers, to maintain control of their children (Hendrick 1997) or face punitive legal sanctions such as parenting orders (Holt 2008). It is important to note that it is not only mothers and parents but also young people who feel ashamed about their violence and abuse.

Criminalising children – a deficit model

The country reports produced by the study partners in Europe showed that CPV tends to be addressed through the criminal justice system. We now turn to look at how this can prove problematic when addressing CPV. Traditionally, domestic violence perpetrator interventions have tended to be mostly problem-focused, instructional, expert-led and focused on male abusers. They are often based on cognitive behavioural approaches (with an individual pathology perspective targeting individual characteristics or problems) and/or on feminist theory (focusing on the socio-cultural roots of domestic violence). Many of these interventions assume that abusers have deficits in knowledge and/or skills that contribute to abusive behaviour and thus they are in need of re-education. The resulting psycho-educational programmes focus on confronting abusers to recognise and admit their violence, take responsibility for their behaviour and learn new ways of dealing with anger and communication (Gondolf 2002).

The RCPV project practitioner interviews found that, when working with children, it is better not to focus on deficit or blame because this mirrors the very strategies that abusers use themselves. Some young people may also have complex personalities and a very fragile sense of self and they therefore do not respond well to criticism.

Similarly, children may be viewed as both 'sociopathic and dangerous' or as 'innocent victims'. Neither stereotype assists a child to make positive change. Furthermore, the findings of this project support previous research which highlights that some children who are abusing their parents have themselves grown up with other forms of family violence, have problems with drugs or alcohol, low self-esteem and high insecurity (Calvete *et al.* 2014; Cottrell and Monk 2004; Daly and Nancarrow 2009). For instance, as one practitioner has noted:

> I mean there is one mum that I wanted to refer to [domestic violence service] because she had, her child had been violent to her and his dad was violent to mum, they had split up, and I did want her to discuss that because she was saying, 'Oh, his behaviour is bringing up old feelings for me' and all of that stuff and I suggested that she try and work with Rise [domestic violence services] to address her feelings around it but she wasn't up for it. (Family worker, England)

It is not helpful to children when such problems are used as an excuse for their violence since they can come to believe that they have no control or choice about their behaviour. Rather, it is useful to acknowledge their past experiences in a supportive and understanding manner, whilst letting them know that even though they have witnessed or experienced abuse, they are not bound to repeat the behaviour. The message that they are capable of not repeating the violence or abuse is empowering and helps them feel supported to make positive changes:

> Q: How do you feel about taking part in the Break4Change programme?
>
> A: It helps people to change.
>
> Q: Do you feel that it helped you to change?
>
> A: Yeah.
>
> Q: I see, in what ways?
>
> A: I've learnt to control my anger. (Graham, 14)

If children are criminalised too early, we may be in danger of missing a unique opportunity to rewire through engaging with the effects of abusive behaviour. It is important to give a clear message that abusive and violent behaviour is wrong. Referring to the specific abusive and violent behaviour that a child uses is key and this facilitates an approach that separates the behaviour from who they are as a person.

Practitioners assert that it is not helpful for children to 'be labelled as "abusers" as this can have a downward spiral effect' (Break4Change 2013, p.11). When young people understand how their behaviour impacts on family members and they learn ways to be accountable, such as talking about it with their parent and taking action to repair the harm done (making amends), their sense of shame is reduced and they begin to feel better about themselves. This further reduces acts of abuse and violence.

Practitioners – awareness, training and support

The practitioners participating in this study felt they were lacking in knowledge and were under-skilled in respect of CPV as they had not received relevant training; almost all stressed the need for more awareness-raising and a programme of training on this issue:

> The training course was fantastic in raising my awareness of CPV and it has been really influential on my own work and so because of this awareness I am far more alert to it as an issue. I would say the rest of the team are possibly less likely to spot the existence of abuse to a parent or parents. (Community safety worker, England)

> I have worked with a number of cases where there has been CPV in the house, in the home and it is a very, very difficult thing for families to cope with and you know often it is as difficult for the young person to deal with as it is for the parents, there is a lot of regret, yeah, a lot of regret involved for the young people and it is a kind of learned behaviour that they want to get out of themselves. (Family coach, England)

Practitioners reported that parenting programmes such as Triple P[2] were seen as an inappropriate response to CPV. Triple P aims to enhance family protective factors and to reduce risk factors associated with severe behavioural and emotional problems in children. These programmes support common parenting difficulties but practitioners considered that specialist CPV interventions for children and/or parents were more effective for intervening in CPV. The family context was identified as vital for assessing the extent of CPV, as other forms of violence may be revealed, and non-violent interaction patterns between parents and adolescents could be explored.

---

2 See: www.triplep.net/glo-en/home

CPV interventions with children require an approach which names the behaviour, identifies whether a child is motivated to change and explores the gains and losses that a young person achieves through their abuse. The behaviours involved in CPV and domestic violence are similar, as are the feelings of shame, guilt and betrayal experienced. In both circumstances practitioners hear phrases like 'walking on egg shells' and 'Jekyll and Hyde'. Both forms of abuse are fundamentally about perpetrators exerting control. Abusers often claim to love their victims. Tackling CPV is about developing respect and respectful ways of behaving towards others; it is not about love. It is often quite clear that the children do love their parent but (for most) a close relationship is not possible whilst they use abusive behaviour (amazingly, some relationships remain affectionate despite the severe abuse of a parent). It was evident from the interviews completed with parents that they empathised with the way children felt and some relationships remained empathetic despite the severe abuse. Hope for change is needed by both parties; one mother had told her child: 'You might not feel like I understand but I am trying to understand and I think if we both want to make it better then we can' (Susan, England).

The issue of talking about children's violence and the complexity of not only defining CPV but understanding the family history and current context presents practitioners with challenges. These can only be surmounted with a programme of awareness raising, training and mentoring on CPV delivered in organisations where management practices support work in this field.

Conclusion

Although the forms of violence used by children against their parents can take many different forms and parents can feel as though their children are controlling them, it is crucial to remember that adolescents are still children who are struggling with many different emotional issues. Too often parents who experience CPV are referred to numerous parenting groups where they are treated as 'bad parents' and such approaches can constitute mother-blaming. This approach can reinforce the child or young person's attempt to blame their mother.

In a context of limited research and low public recognition of CPV in most European countries, practitioners can struggle to obtain information and training regarding the most effective ways of dealing with this form of abuse. Where there are specialised programmes, these are usually small-scale with low levels of resourcing and they often struggle to survive. Service managers need to acknowledge that CPV is a serious and complex problem and try to find solutions. As discussed earlier, polarising the concepts of 'victim' or 'perpetrator' in CPV work denies 'the complexity inherent to the problem and means that there is no space for the issue to emerge in the public domain' (Hunter *et al.* 2010, p.282). It is a crucial time for policymakers to grasp a new policy construct of working with children as children in the neo-liberal conditions prevalent in the twenty-first century and to build on the interventions and learning of the European action research described here (see also Wilcox and Pooley 2015). As Anderson and Routt have argued, what is needed is 'An integrated approach that combines the efforts of all interested professionals [and] begin to address this hidden form of family violence' (Anderson and Routt 2011, p.15).

Acknowledgment

We would like to acknowledge the European Union's Daphne III programme which funded the RCPV project. The contents of this publication are the sole responsibility of Paula Wilcox and Michelle Pooley and can in no way be taken to reflect the views of the European Union.

References

Agnew, R. and Huguley, S. (1989) 'Adolescent violence towards parents.' *Journal of Marriage and the Family 51*, 699–711.

Aroca, M. C., Bellver, M. M. C. and Alba R. J. L. (2012) 'La teoría del aprendizaje social como modelo explicativo de la violencia filio-parental.' *Revista Complutense de Educación 23*, 2, 487–511.

Baker, H. (2012) 'Problematising the relationship between teenage boys and parent abuse: constructions of masculinity and violence.' *Social Policy and Society 11*, 2, 265–276.

Break4Change (2013) *Toolkit for Professionals Working with Families Where Young People are Violent/Abusive Towards Their Parent or Out of Control.* Unpublished RCPV document.

Browne, K. D. and Hamilton, C. E. (1998) 'Physical violence between young adults and their parents: associations with a history of child maltreatment.' *Journal of Family Violence 13*, 1, 59–79.

Calvete, E., Izaskun, O., Bertino, L., Gonzalez, Z. *et al.* (2014) 'Child-to-parent violence in adolescents: the perspectives of the parents, children and professionals in a sample of Spanish focus group participants.' *Journal of Family Violence 29*, 343–352.

Condry, R. and Miles, C. (2014) 'Adolescent to parent violence: framing and mapping a hidden problem.' *Criminology and Criminal Justice 14*, 3, 257–275.

Coogan, D. (2012) 'Marking the boundaries: when troublesome becomes abusive and children cross a line in family violence.' *Feedback, The Journal of the Family Therapy Association of Ireland,* July, 74–86.

Cornell, C. P. and Gelles, R. J. (1982) 'Adolescent-to-parent violence.' *The Urban Social Change Review 15*, 1, 8–14.

Cottrell, B. (2003) *Parent Abuse: The Abuse of Parents by Their Teenage Children.* Canada: National Clearing House on Family Violence.

Cottrell, B. (2005) *When Teens Abuse Their Parents.* Nova Scotia: Fernwood Publishing.

Cottrell, B. and Monk, P. (2004) 'Adolescent-to-parent abuse: a qualitative overview of common themes.' *Journal of Family Issues 25*, 8, 1072–1095.

Daly, K. and Nancarrow, H. (2009) 'Restorative Justice and Youth Violence towards Parents.' In J. Ptacek (ed.) *Restorative Justice and Violence against Women.* NY: Oxford University Press.

Gallagher, E. (2004) 'Parents victimised by their children.' *Australia New Zealand Journal of Family Therapy (ANZJFT) 25*, 1, 1–12.

Gallagher, E. (2007) *Comparing Child to Parent Violence (CPV) with Intimate Partner Violence (IPV).* Available at www.eddiegallagher.id.au, accessed on 15 December 2014.

Gondolf, E. W. (2002) *Batterer Intervention Systems: Issues, Outcomes, and Recommendations.* Thousand Oaks, CA: Sage Publications.

Harbin, H. and Madden, D. (1979) 'Battered parents: a new syndrome.' *American Journal of Psychiatry 136*, 1288–1291.

Hendrick, H. (1997) *Children and Childhood in English Society 1880–1990.* Cambridge: Cambridge University Press.

Holt, A. (2008) 'Room for Resistance? Parenting Orders, Disciplinary Power, and the Production of "the Bad Parent".' In P. Squires (ed.) *ASBO Nation: The Criminalisation of Nuisance.* Bristol: Policy Press.

Holt, A. (2011) '"The terrorist in my home": teenagers' violence towards parents – constructions of parent experiences in public online message boards.' *Child and Family Social Work 16*, 4, 454–463.

Home Office (2013) *New Government Domestic Violence and Abuse Definition.* Circular 003/2013. London: Home Office.

Honjo, S. and Wakabayashi, S. (1988) 'Family violence in Japan: a compilation of data from the Department of Psychiatry Nagoya University Hospital.' *Japanese Journal of Psychiatry and Neurology 42*, 1, 5–10. Howard, J. (2011) *Adolescent Violence in the Home – The Missing Link in Family Violence Prevention and Response.* Australian Domestic and Family Violence Clearinghouse. Available at www.adfvc.unsw.edu.au/PDF%20files/Stakeholder_Paper_11.pdf, accessed on 15 December 2014.

Hunter, C., Nixon, J. and Parr, S. (2010) 'Mother abuse: a matter of youth justice, child welfare or domestic violence.' *Journal of Law and Society 37*, 2, 264–284.

Kennair, N. and Mellor, D. (2007) 'Parent abuse: a review.' *Child Psychiatry Human Development 38*, 203–219.

Laurent, A. and Derry, A. (1999) 'Violence of French adolescents toward their parents.' *Journal of Adolescent Health 25*, 1, 21–26.

Lewis, C. (2009) 'The day my daughter hit me.' *The Guardian Online*, 27 June. Available at www.theguardian.com/lifeandstyle/2009/jun/27/parental-abuse-domestic-violence, accessed on 15 December 2014.

Matey, P. (2011) 'When children abuse their parents', *El Mundo*, 7 October. Available at http://translate.google.co.uk/translate?hl=en&sl=es&u=http://www.elmundo.es/elmundosalud/2011/10/06/noticias/1317926422.html&prev=search, accessed on 23 December 2014.

Pagelow, M. (1990) 'Effects of domestic violence on children and their consequences for custody and visitation agreements.' *Mediation Quarterly 7*, 4, 347–363.

Parentline Plus (2010) *When Family Life Hurts: Family Experience of Aggression in Children*. Parentline Plus. Available at www.familylives.org.uk/media_manager/public/209/Documents/Reports/When%20family%20life%20hurts%202010.pdf, accessed on 15 December 2014.

Paterson, R., Luntz, H., Perlesz, A. and Cotton, S. (2002) 'Adolescent violence towards parents: maintaining family connections when the going gets tough.' *Australia New Zealand Journal of Family Therapy (ANZJFT) 23*, 90–100.

Paulson, M. J., Coombs, R. H. and Landsverk, J. (1990) 'Youth who physically assault their parents.' *Journal of Family Violence 5*, 2, 121–133.

Peek, C. W., Fischer, J. L. and Kidwell, J. S. (1985) 'Teenage violence toward parents: a neglected dimension of family violence.' *Journal of Marriage and the Family 47*, 4, 1051–1058.

Registrados 200 casos de maltrato familiar por parte de menores (2013) ABC. Available at sevilla.abc.es/cordoba/20130204/sevp-registrados-casos-maltrato-familiar-20130204.html, accessed on 22 June 2015.

Routt, G. and Anderson, L. (2015) *Adolescent Violence in the Home: Restorative Approaches to Building Healthy, Respectful Family Relationships*. Abingdon: Routledge.

Routt, G. and Anderson, L. (2011) 'Adolescent violence towards parents.' *Journal of Aggression, Maltreatment and Trauma 20*, 1–19.

Smith, S., Baker, D., Buchan, A. and Bodiwala, G. (1992) 'Adult domestic violence.' *Health Trends 24*, 3, 97–99.

Triple P Website (n.d.) Available at www.triplep.net/glo-en/home, accessed on 15 December 2014.

Wilcox, P. (2012) 'Is parent abuse a form of domestic violence?' *Social Policy and Society 11*, 2, 277–288.

Wilcox, P. and Pooley, M. (2015) *Responding to child to parent violence and abuse in Europe: Research and data mapping*. Available at www.rcpv.eu/research, accessed on 22 June 2015.

CHAPTER 6

Forced Marriage *Is* a Child Protection Matter

Zahra Alijah and Khatidja Chantler

Introduction

Forced marriage is recognised nationally and internationally as a fundamental breach of human rights. A forced marriage is where one or both parties do not consent to the marriage and where duress (emotional, physical or sexual violence) is used by family members to exert consent. Forced marriage is therefore conceptualised as a violation of the person's bodily integrity, dignity and autonomy. In policy discourses, arranged marriages are positioned as distinct from forced marriage since consent is sought from both parties and family members' role is to introduce potential marriage partners to one another. However, research indicates that this distinction is often not as clear-cut in practice as presented in policy (Gangoli, Razak and McCarry 2006; Hester *et al.* 2007). Such research indicates that a continuum model more accurately reflects the relationship between arranged and forced marriage.

The prevalence of forced marriage in the UK is difficult to establish; however, 5,000–8,000 incidents of forced marriage are thought to occur each year (Kazimirski *et al.* 2009). The Forced Marriage Unit (FMU) (a joint unit of the Foreign and Commonwealth Office and Home Office) is the key UK agency which has developed guidance for social workers, teachers, police and health professionals about how to tackle forced marriage (HM Government 2010); it provides direct assistance to those experiencing forced marriage, supports professionals to support victims and publishes statistics on forced marriage based on cases in which they have been involved. Current figures from the FMU show that 11 per cent of victims were under 16, and 11 per cent were 16–17 years of age

(HM Government 2014). However, it should be noted that ages were not available for all victims. This young age profile highlights the central role that teachers should play in preventing forced marriage. This chapter aims to explore how national policy and guidance are interpreted at a local level, highlighting positive practice as well as gaps in local authorities' and schools' work around forced marriage, focusing specifically on Manchester in north-west England. We will achieve this through an analysis of: (i) school and local authority policies on safeguarding and absences from school from 2007–2014; (ii) interview material from a consultation exercise with two school safeguarding leads in Manchester; and (iii) an intervention involving young people to raise awareness of forced marriage. On the basis of our analysis, we provide some recommendations to enhance policy and practice to better protect school-age young people from forced marriage.

The legal framework – England and Wales

Over recent years, there has been a concerted effort by the UK government to protect victims of forced marriage and here we provide a brief outline of key legal interventions. Three broad areas are considered: immigration rules, civil protection and criminalisation. In relation to immigration rules, the age at which a UK citizen can sponsor a non-EU national for the purposes of marriage or civil partnership was increased from 16 to 18 years in 2003 and similarly the age at entry for a spousal visa was increased to 18 years in 2004. This increase in age was argued to be a means of preventing forced marriage, and in 2008 it was decided to increase the age for sponsorship and spousal visas to 21. However, this decision was overturned by the Supreme Court in 2011 on the basis of the Quila case (*R (Quila and another) v Sec of State for the Home Dept*).

The Civil Protection Act (Forced Marriage) 2007 was operationalised in November 2008. This act enables victims or other relevant third parties (including the police, social workers and local authorities) to make an application to a special court for a Forced Marriage Protection Order (FMPO). The Family Law Act (1996) (Forced Marriage) (Relevant Third Party) enabled local authorities to apply directly to the court for a FMPO. Others can also apply (e.g. concerned friends) if they have the leave of the court to do so. These orders apply to children, young people and adults and specify conditions which must not be breached. Examples of such conditions include requirements to deposit the young person's passport at a specified location (e.g. a school or local authority social services department) and not to remove a young person from the UK. Breaching an order has until very recently been dealt with via civil measures but these are generally accepted as being ineffective.

In March 2014, the breach of a FMPO became a criminal offence (Anti-Social Behaviour, Crime and Policing Act, 2014), and this came into force on 16 June 2014. This act has also created a specific criminal offence of forced marriage despite existing criminal legislation which could be used to protect victims for example, grievous bodily harm, abduction, rape and child protection legislation. There is anecdotal evidence that schools and children's social services departments may be unprepared for the implementation of the Act, should the Act result in an increase in referrals, as is the case in Scotland where criminalisation was introduced earlier. This indicates that it is even more urgent that gaps in the system for child safeguarding are addressed.

Forced marriage, child protection and schools

One of the central challenges in relation to dealing with forced marriage is to recognise forced marriage as a child abuse issue for school-age children. The multi-agency *statutory* guidance on forced marriage makes it very clear that forced marriage is a child protection issue and that the provisions within the Children Act 1989 should be used to protect school-age victims of forced marriage, alongside FMPOs where appropriate. The government also hopes that the criminalisation of forced marriage will send a strong signal, not only to communities in which forced marriage is practised but also to frontline professionals and relevant organisations to intervene in forced marriage. Schools are central to child protection and have a compelling and statutory duty to safeguard and report safeguarding concerns to the local authority (DfE 2014). Information available from reports on the impact of the implementation of FMPOs reveals that frontline staff, including teachers and social workers, are unaware that forced marriage is a child protection issue (MoJ 2009).

In 2008, a link was discovered between absence from school and forced marriage and a lack of appropriate follow-up (Home Affairs Committee 2008), and more recent evidence indicates that the situation has not changed between 2008 and 2011 (Home Affairs Committee 2012).

Schools therefore need to be vigilant about their recording systems for absences and ensure that long-term absences are investigated more fully and passed on to local authorities who hold the key responsibility for safeguarding. Long-term absence from school may be a key risk factor in forced marriage and it is noteworthy that it is not considered necessary by the Secretary of State for Education to improve reporting mechanisms for long-term absences or to make forced marriage awareness training a compulsory element of teacher training. This approach has been criticised by Ofsted inspectors who are concerned that, without a concerted effort at school level and better collaboration between schools and local authorities, opportunities for protecting children will be lost (Home Affairs Committee 2012).

Recognising the signs of forced marriage, eliciting and making referrals and recording of absences by schools and reporting these to the local authority are an important way of triggering the safeguarding process, so this chapter analyses how one local authority (Manchester) has dealt with this issue in its public documents. As noted above, there is often a gap between policy and practice, and we also draw on consultative interviews on forced marriage with two school safeguarding leads to explore the extent to which practice reflects local policy.

The second substantive issue relates to the scope for preventative work within schools on forced marriage. Work in schools on awareness raising with regard to forced marriage is currently very limited and many teachers report feeling uncomfortable about raising the issue (Home Affairs Committee 2012). Again using Manchester as a case study, we analyse an innovative theatre-based intervention, Free2Choose, that aims to raise awareness of forced marriage with young people aged 14–16.

The Manchester context

Manchester is an ethnically diverse city, with just over 33 per cent of the population belonging to a non-white minority ethnic group (Manchester City Council 2014). Tackling forced marriage has been recognised as a priority in Manchester, a city where 17 per cent of the population is estimated to be of South Asian ethnicity. The city also has a rising population of East African and Arab ethnic minorities (Manchester City Council (MCC) 2014). These are all communities in which forced marriage is sometimes practised. Manchester therefore makes for a highly relevant case-study area and it also has one of the 15 specialist courts with jurisdiction to hear FMPO applications. In Manchester, schools along with other statutory, non-statutory and third-sector agencies working with children are explicitly referenced within the city-wide and regional safeguarding and forced marriage strategy, coordinated by two safeguarding boards and the Manchester Domestic Violence Forum (MCC November 2013a, pp.40–42). Forced marriage remains a standing item at the Young People and Children's Scrutiny Committee (MCC November 2013b, p.76), one of a number of committees focused on holding the council executive to account.

Strategy and policy documents relating to domestic violence and child protection explicitly reference forced marriage within the definition of domestic violence and abuse. A Manchester Forced Marriage Safeguarding Standard developed with the Forced Marriage Unit has been in place since 2011 (MCC November 2013a, p.40). This sets out the minimum training and procedural work expected to be undertaken by agencies working with adults and children across the city, including schools. It includes preventative work through awareness-raising among high-risk groups and those engaging with them, early intervention and clear referral pathways.

There is an indication that the number of FMPOs issued in Greater Manchester has increased generally, with a number taken out for young people (MCC December 2012, p.7). It is also known that several of the young people in these cases were taken into the care system (MCC December 2012, p.7). Manchester is the largest city in north-west England which was the fourth highest area in the UK in respect of the percentage of cases handled by the FMU during 2012 and 2013 (HM Government 2013, 2014). However, it should be noted that in 2013, in around 27 per cent of cases, the region was unknown and in 2014 the region was unknown for 19 per cent of cases. It is not possible to say at this stage whether increased awareness has resulted in greater reporting and consultation with the FMU and hence a greater number of FMPOs or whether the incidence of forced marriage is rising or falling. Nationally, there has also been an increase in calls to the National Society for the Prevention of Cruelty to Children (NSPCC) in relation to forced marriage, from 55 calls in 2011 to 141 in 2013 (MCC 2014b).

In 2009, Manchester updated its model safeguarding policy for schools to include a section on forced marriage (Manchester Safeguarding Adults Board 2012, p.42), and a sampling of eight Manchester schools' safeguarding policies for 2013–14 indicates this has had an impact on school policies, with all but one explicitly mentioning forced marriage. One school, part of a national academy chain sponsored by a charitable trust, did not do so. Instead, the policy contained general statements relating to safeguarding and child protection.

The School Model Safeguarding Policy also advises that information on forced marriage should be incorporated within staff safeguarding training, and it directs schools to policy documents on the Manchester Safeguarding Children Board (MSCB) website (MSCB Report 2011, p.42). However, further work needs to be undertaken to learn the extent to which this is translated into practice. Since 2011, Manchester has considered it important to disseminate information on forced marriage in schools (MSCB Report 2011, p.42). A review commissioned in October 2013, looking at forced marriage work across the city, included a study of cases and an audit of training. The findings revealed fragmentation in forced marriage work in Manchester with a recommendation for a more coherent strategy and revised awareness raising within the children's workforce (MSCB 2013, p.5). The strategy is to include a new and revised forced marriage protocol to be known as the 'one chance rule' (MCC Nov 2013b, p.5). School staff, social workers and attendance teams working with schools were recommended to undertake training, not only in prevention and early intervention in forced marriage, but also to enable them to assess the safety of young people who were already abroad (MCC Nov 2013b, p.5). The latter is difficult to implement and contact with the FMU is strongly advised should a young person already be abroad.

The high turnover of social workers, particularly within children's safeguarding teams (MCC 2014a, pp.21–22), and of school staff in disadvantaged urban schools is a national issue (Smithers and Robinson 2005; Allen, Burgess and Mayo 2012) which makes induction training for new staff and refresher training for more established staff critical.

Monitoring school attendance is also a statutory responsibility for schools and local authorities and, in Manchester, this is overseen by an Attendance Board. Manchester local authority and schools also have policies and a protocol in place relating to their statutory responsibilities in respect of monitoring attendance and children missing from education. DfE guidance does not explicitly mention forced marriage, but does have a link to guidance available on the FMU Website (DfE 2013, p.9). Manchester City Council incorporated the guidance along with an explicit reference to forced marriage within the guidelines issued to schools (MCC 2012, p.6). The protocol requires that attendance be investigated by the school in the first instance. If a student does not return to school within a prescribed period, a form relating to removing the student from the school roll must be completed and sent to the local authority. The local authority is then responsible for determining the whereabouts and well-being of the student and to ascertain whether they are receiving appropriate education elsewhere. The local authority also determines whether or not the student can be removed from the school roll.

If a student's parents wish to remove a student from a school, a form requiring the details of the new arrangements for educating the student including the details of the new school and headteacher is required. Again, the local authority is responsible via the attendance office for following this up once it has been passed on by a school. It is here that a potential gap may occur, particularly if the child has been taken overseas (MCC Nov 2013a, p.41). Manchester City Council are addressing this by refreshing policy, procedures and training relating to forced marriage so that frontline professionals are aware of the need to safeguard children who have been removed from the school roll or are being educated abroad, directing them to the Home Office who would then take up the case (MCC Nov 2013a, p.41).

Schools, as well other agencies in Manchester, can access forced marriage training provided by MSCB. However, the review's audit of training indicates frontline staff such as those in schools, social work and attendance may not have been accessing training (MCC 2013a, p.5). Networks for school safeguarding leads and school senior leaders have covered forced marriage periodically, either as an issue in itself or within the context of other safeguarding considerations such as children missing from education and issues associated with particular vulnerable groups, such as children with a disability. This may have brought the issue to the notice of those individual staff members attending. However, our consultation with safeguarding leads indicates that the degree to which this training is cascaded down within schools varies.

One school safeguarding lead, new to the role, who participated in the consultation interviews felt that school safeguarding leads were expected to 'learn as they went along'. She had found a school which was known to be a champion in tackling forced marriage helpful in supporting her in creating a forced marriage strategy for her own school based on the MCC Forced Marriage Protocol. Another school safeguarding lead spoke of competing safeguarding priorities both for staff and within the Personal, Social and Health Education (PSHE) curriculum where forced marriage jostled for space with issues such as e-safety, other forms of domestic abuse, sexual health and grooming.

The school safeguarding leads participating in the consultation interviews reported a lack of confidence in their own knowledge and expressed a 'need to provide staff training for confidence to deliver the session or buy-in someone like [a forced marriage outreach worker] who is an expert to deliver it'.

It was reported by the school safeguarding leads that the more dynamic training methods provided by specialist organisations had the potential for achieving a greater impact on staff and students. This was particularly the case when, as in the Free2Choose intervention, a survivor of forced marriage shared their experience as it was considered that the 'survivor made it more real' and the risk of participants dismissing the training was reduced: 'Before training most teaching staff had a fairly basic level of awareness but now it is the first thing that jumps into their heads.' Undertaking training had led to 'teachers asking a few more questions', one of the school safeguarding leads said. One school safeguarding lead reported that, prior to the training, staff had 'understood the difference between arranged and forced marriage' because many were from backgrounds in which arranged marriages happened, yet they were 'aware that forced marriage happened but not to the extent'; following training, staff were described as 'Now more likely to refer someone who is going on holiday... [there is a] sense that there is a feeling within the school that one passes things out [to someone] who would pass things on'. Another school safeguarding lead said that, although she had undertaken 'a lot of training on forced marriage it is not possible to be an expert in that area... I now need to keep update[d] and to keep staff update[d]... especially as staff turn over.'

At the time of writing, there was no longer funding available to bring in external agencies to deliver training, and one of the child safeguarding leads felt that this, together with curriculum priorities which placed 'PSHE low on the list of education issues' and competing safeguarding priorities, was a constraint in addressing the subject within schools.

Free2Choose – a theatre-based intervention

In March 2013 and 2014, a participatory theatre-based intervention was piloted in Manchester in seven self-selected schools, both mixed and single-sex girls' and boys' schools, all set in ethnically diverse communities. Of the seven schools, two participated in both 2013 and 2014.

The intervention was developed in partnership with the Forced Marriage Unit, Manchester CPS, Women's Aid, other statutory and non-statutory organisations that work on forced marriage and domestic violence and Act on Education, a Manchester-based national theatre company that works in schools. Both authors were on the steering group for the intervention which was devised and delivered as a collaboration between a youth domestic violence and forced marriage specialist, a forced marriage survivor and a forum theatre director. The intervention consisted of three parts. Part one involved awareness-raising on forced marriage with teachers, part two focused on teachers working with their students to create a drama, song, dance or other performance piece dealing with forced marriage; part three was a half-day conference with students who performed their piece on forced marriage and involved a theatre-based drama using professional actors based on Augusto Boal's Theatre of the Oppressed methodology (Boal 1979). The two half-day conferences were attended by 127 pupils in total, with ages ranging from 14 to 17. Here we report on the 2014 half-day conference in terms of its methodology, and the evaluation of the event conducted by Free2Choose (Free2Choose 2014), including the in-service training of staff.

Central to the approach was the philosophy of participation, empowerment and transformation grounded in critical pedagogy (Freire 2003). The active involvement and engagement of students through a problem-solving approach was facilitated in the workshops, theatre production and conference itself, and they were recognised as important social actors who could drive change to address a social injustice, key foundational tenets of critical pedagogy (Adams 2013). It was hoped this would achieve a 'deep' level of learning and consciousness raising, primarily through the co-construction of students' own performance pieces on forced marriage (Freire 2003, p.75).

The public performance of these pieces in front of their peers also worked to raise issues of forced marriage in the public domain in a manner which young people could relate to and which was supposed to awaken their critical consciousness (Freire 2003). Hence, instead of an authoritative approach with teachers or other adults 'instructing' young people, a collaborative social constructivist process was adopted which worked with and through young people's own perceptions and attitudes to forced marriage. In keeping with this central philosophy, a group of actors was briefed on issues of forced marriage and commissioned to perform an interactive drama in the methodology of the Theatre of the Oppressed (Boal 1979). The storyline invited and encouraged audience participation at key points, as well as on an ad hoc basis as the drama unfolded. The basic storyline concerned a Pakistani girl aged 14–15 who lived with her mother and brother. The summer holidays were approaching and her mother was planning a visit to Pakistan for her daughter and herself. The plan was for the mother to marry her daughter off to her nephew, but this motive was kept hidden from the girl. Audience participation was invited at crucial points via a facilitator, a figure equivalent to Boal's Joker (Boal 1979, pp.178–179), who posed questions such as 'what would you like to tell or ask the mum?'; 'what would you say to the brother?'; 'what would you advise the young woman?' Observing the interaction between the actors and young people, it was clear that there was a genuine and sometimes passionate engagement from the young people who interrupted the performance to pose their own questions to the actors. Listening to this dialogic interaction, it was evident that praxis (Freire 2003, p.51) was taking place, with young people reflecting on the problems posed, accessing learning from the piece and from earlier sessions (school training sessions preceded the conference and during the conference itself), articulating their sense of injustice and coming up with potential solutions. This method of participation and active engagement appeared effective in awakening participants' critical consciousness and in generating a dynamic and vibrant atmosphere. Young people were seen to play a full part in developing understandings of and responses to forced marriage, as well as knowledge of sources of help either for themselves or for friends.

The Free2Choose programme conducted its own evaluation with student and teacher participants after the 2014 conference. At the end of conference, students were asked to fill out an evaluation form and write their thoughts on post-it notes. Teachers completed evaluation forms after the separate training they received as part of staff in-service training and at the end of the conference.

The evaluation indicated that students had acquired knowledge and understanding of forced marriage as a form of abuse and were aware of the support available to them. Specifically, they were able to recognise the distinction between forced and arranged marriage, they understood that the former was not acceptable in any religion, could happen regardless of gender, and they could articulate the support available to them. All but two young people indicated they would feel comfortable asking for support if they, a friend or a family member were experiencing any of the issues discussed during the conference (Free2Choose 2014, p.10).

Teachers completed evaluation forms after the separate training they received as part of staff in-service training and at the end of the 2014 conference. The staff training was workshop-based and, as with the conference, included testimony by a forced marriage survivor and input from a solicitor working with forced marriage cases: 'The training placed forced marriage in its wider context of domestic abuse and violence against women so staff recognised it as a human rights abuse, not a cultural issue' (Free2Choose 2014, p.4). The programme evaluation found that, following training, 'Staff feel they have more knowledge of the subject, that this subject needs to be taken more seriously and that in particular they need to be more vigilant, to listen better and to report all concerns they may have' (Free2Choose 2014, p.7). Furthermore, 'staff fed back they would have liked the training over a few sessions' (Free2Choose 2014, p.7). However, there were also challenges identified by the evaluation: 'During the project all the schools found it difficult to fit even one training session into their busy timetable for various reasons such as Ofsted visits and other mandatory training' and it was recognised that 'this would be practically [un]attainable' (Free2Choose 2014, p.13).

Conclusions

Encouragingly, forced marriage legislation is being used in Manchester as evidenced by the increasing number of FMPOs initiated. It is yet to be seen whether the criminalisation of forced marriage will result in further action to combat this form of harm. The review of policy documents indicates that there is recognition of forced marriage as a child protection issue at a policy level, but that practice responses are patchy. In terms of a wider prevention strategy, the evidence suggests that more could be done in terms of raising awareness both for students and teachers. The theatre-based intervention discussed here has two key lessons:

- Theatre-based intervention is valuable in a wider forced marriage prevention strategy which includes staff as well as students. Through a problem-solving approach, students and staff are enabled to become social agents of change, not only raising their awareness of the issues but empowering them to become more inclined to intervene.

- Delivery by an external agency is valued by schools as staff may lack confidence in engaging with the issue. Including the testimony of a forced marriage survivor and placing forced marriage in the context of domestic abuse and safeguarding served to reinforce the importance of active engagement to prevent the potential abuse and breach of human rights.

Manchester has a range of local authority level protocols and training but there is scope for more effective dissemination within schools. Three specific recommendations are made to take this work forward. First, schools that are known to champion tackling forced marriage could support others in developing their own safeguarding strategies which should include a rolling in-service training programme to ensure new staff are trained. This would help to mitigate the current patchy responses to forced marriage in schools and draw on peer mentorship. It is likely that this approach would be welcomed as safeguarding leads will be well aware of the existing pressures on school timetables in respect of PSHE and the time pressures of undertaking extra training on forced marriage. Second, to facilitate training, it will be necessary for resources to be made available as, based on our consultation and the evaluation of Free2Choose, it is clear that external training on forced marriage was valued by teachers. This might also help to ensure that forced marriage is addressed in schools which have competing curriculum and safeguarding priorities. Lastly, more attention should be paid to absences from schools. Collecting absence information, following up absent students and analysing absence and follow-up information at a local authority level may reveal useful knowledge and potential intervention opportunities to protect more young people from forced marriage.

References

Adams Jr, C. N. (2013) 'TIE and Critical Pedagogy.' In J. Anthony and C. Vine (eds) *Learning through Theatre: The Changing Face of Theatre in Education*. Abingdon: Routledge.

Allen, R., Burgess, B. and Mayo, A. (2012) *The Teacher Labour Market, Teacher Turnover and Disadvantaged Schools: New Evidence for England Working Paper*. Bristol: Centre for Market and Public Organisation, University of Bristol. Available at www.bristol.ac.uk/cmpo/publications/papers/2012/wp294.pdf, accessed on 3 March 2014.

Boal, A. (1979) *Theatre of the Oppressed*. London: Pluto Press.

Department for Education (2013) *Children Missing from Education: Statutory Guidance for Local Authorities*. London: DfE. Available at www.gov.uk/government/uploads/system/uploads/attachment_data/file/268987/cme_guidance.pdf, accessed on 30 July 2013.

Department for Education (2014) *Keeping Children Safe in Education: Statutory Guidance for Schools*. London: DfE. Available at www.gov.uk/government/uploads/system/uploads/attachment_data/file/300309/KCSIE_gdnce_FINAL.pdf, accessed on 3 March 2014.

Foreign and Commonwealth Office and HM Government (2012) *Report on the Implementation of the Multi-Statutory Agency Guidance for Dealing with Forced Marriage (2008)*. London: FCO. Available at www.gov.uk/government/uploads/system/uploads/attachment_data/file/136371/Guidance_for_dealing_with_forced_marriage_A4_v1.6_WEB.PDF, accessed on 3 March 2014.

Freire, P. (2000) *Pedagogy of the Oppressed, 30th Anniversary Edition* (trans. Myra Bergman Ramos). New York, NY: Continuum.

Free 2 Choose (2014) *Project Evaluation* (Unpublished).

Gangoli, G., Razak, A. and McCarry, M. (2006) *Forced Marriage and Domestic Violence among South Asian Communities in North East England*. Bristol: University of Bristol and Northern Rock Foundation.

Hester, M., Chantler, K., Gangoli, G., Devgon, J., Sharma, S. and Singleton, A. (2007) *Forced Marriage: The Risk Factors and the Effect of Raising the Minimum Age for a Sponsor, and of Leave to Enter the UK as a Spouse or Fiance(e)*. Bristol and Manchester: School for Policy Studies, University of Bristol, and School of Nursing, Midwifery and Social Work, University of Manchester. Available at www.bristol.ac.uk/sps/research/projects/completed/2007/rk6612/rk6612finalreport.pdf, accessed on 4 August 2009.

HM Government (2010) *Multi-Agency Practice Guidelines: Handling Cases of Forced Marriage*. London: DfE. Available at www.gov.uk/government/uploads/system/uploads/attachment_data/file/35530/forced-marriage-guidelines09.pdf, accessed 8 April 2014.

HM Government (2013) *Statistics January–December 2013*. London: Home Office. Available at www.gov.uk/government/uploads/system/uploads/attachment_data/file/291855/FMU_2013_statistics.pdf, accessed on 8 April 2014.

HM Government (2014) *Statistics January–December 2013*. London: Home Office. Available at www.gov.uk/government/uploads/system/uploads/attachment_data/file/412667/FMU_Stats_2014.pdf, accessed on 8 April 2014.

Home Affairs Committee (2008) *Sixth Report of Session Domestic Violence, Forced Marriage and "Honour" based violence*, HC263. London: Houses of Parliament. Available at www.publications.parliament.uk/pa/cm200708/cmselect/cmhaff/263/263ii.pdf, accessed on 12 January 2015.

Home Affairs Committee (2012) *Eighth Report of Session on Forced Marriage 2010–12*. London: House of Commons Home Affairs Committee. Available at www.publications.parliament.uk/pa/cm201012/cmselect/cmhaff/880/880.pdf, accessed on 8 April 2014.

Kazimirski, A., Keogh, P., Kumari, V., Smith, R. *et al.* (2009) *Forced Marriage: Prevalence and Service Response.* London: Department for Children, Schools and Families.

Manchester City Council (MCC) (2006) *Manchester Children Missing from Education: Guidelines and Practice.* Manchester: MCC. Available at www.mewan.net/behaveattend/getfile.php?src=123/Children+Missing+from+Education.doc, accessed on 3 April 2014.

Manchester City Council (MCC) (2012) *Attendance Strategy: Local Authority Guidelines on Managing Attendance at School.* Manchester: MCC. Available at www.mewan.net/behaveattend/index.php?category_id=72, accessed on 6 August 2013.

Manchester City Council (MCC) (2013a) *Young People and Children Scrutiny Committee Report for Resolution.* Manchester: MCC. Available at www.manchester.gov.uk/meetings/committee/78/young_people_and_children_scrutiny_committee, accessed on 3 April 2014.

Manchester City Council (MCC) (2013b) *Young People and Children Scrutiny Committee: Overview Report.* Manchester: MCC. Available at www.manchester.gov.uk/meetings/committee/78/young_people_and_children_scrutiny_committee, accessed on 3 April 2014.

Manchester City Council (MCC) (2014a) *Young People and Children's Scrutiny Committee Report for Resolution.* Manchester: MCC. Available at www.manchester.gov.uk/meetings/committee/78/young_people_and_children_scrutiny_committee, accessed on 3 April 2014.

Manchester City Council (MCC) (2014b) *AO1 Manchester Factsheet.* Manchester: MCC. Available at www.manchester.gov.uk/downloads/download/4220/public_intelligence_population_publications, accessed on 16 October 2014.

Manchester Safeguarding Adults Board (2012) *Protecting Vulnerable Adults in Manchester: Annual Report 2011/12.* Manchester: MCC. Available at www.manchester.gov.uk/downloads/download/3960/safeguarding_adults_reports, accessed on 8 April 2014.

Manchester Safeguarding Children Board (MSCB) (2013) *Manchester Safeguarding Children Board Annual Report 2012–13.* Manchester: MCC. Avaialble at www.manchesterscb.org.uk/docs/MSCB%20Annual%20Report%20Final%20Full2013.pdf, accessed on 8 April 2014.

Ministry of Justice (MoJ) (2009) *One Year On: The Initial Impact of the Forced Marriage (Civil Protection) Act 2007 In Its First Year of Operation.* London: MoJ. Available at http://webarchive.nationalarchives.gov.uk/20100103073731/http:/www.justice.gov.uk/publications/10508.htm, accessed on 22 May 2015.

R (Quila and another) v Sec of State for the Home Dept [2011] UKSC 45 Office of National Statistics (2011). Available at www.familylawweek.co.uk/site.aspx?i=ed87312, accessed on 16 June 2015.

Smithers, A. and Robinson, P. (2005) *Teacher Turnover, Wastage and Movements between Schools.* London: DfE. Available at http://webarchive.nationalarchives.gov.uk/20130401151715/http:/www.education.gov.uk/publications/eOrderingDownload/RR640.pdf.pdf, accessed on 3 April 2014.

PART THREE

Interventions for Mothers and Children

CHAPTER 7

More Than a Mirage?

Safe Contact for Children and Young People Who Have Been Exposed to Domestic Violence

Lorraine Radford and Marianne Hester

Introduction

Domestic violence does not necessarily stop when couples separate. For one in five women it continues and in some cases it even escalates (Povey *et al.* 2009). Moreover, domestic violence is known to be a common factor in child homicides where the perpetrator is the parent (Brandon *et al.* 2008; Sidebotham *et al.* 2011; Vincent 2009), with child contact and post-separation violence being a particular area of concern (Winter and Gosley 2006). Children's contact arrangements are a flashpoint because they give violent fathers routes to continue their abuse and harassment of ex-partners (Coy *et al.* 2012; Howarth *et al.* 2009; Radford and Hester 2006). Post-separation violence, especially around child contact, was found to be a factor in about half the calls to the police in one recent research study (Stanley *et al.* 2010) and for 30 per cent in another (Hester 2013). Despite growing evidence that children have been killed (Saunders 2004), harmed (Parker *et al.* 2008; Thiara and Gill, 2011) or unwillingly pushed into contact with violent fathers (Fortin, Hunt and Scanlon, 2012; Timms, Bailey and Thoburn 2008) and a number of policy and practice changes aimed at addressing the problem of domestic violence and 'risky parenting', family court system responses have shown a stubborn resistance to change (Hunt and Macleod 2008; Hunter and Barnett 2013). In this chapter we review the challenging environment of contemporary policy and practice; how concerns about domestic violence and children can become marginalised in the family court system and professionals' options for supporting safety for women and children.

Policy context

In recent years there has been a growing awareness of the harm caused to children by domestic violence, and several policy and practice initiatives have been introduced in response in the UK, mirroring changes made in the USA, Canada, Australia, New Zealand and Sweden (Eriksson 2010 and 2011; Jaffe, Lemon and Poisson 2003). In England, policy changes have included putting domestic violence on the child protection agenda. Section 120 of the Adoption and Children Act 2002, introduced in 2005, recognised a child's 'seeing or overhearing' violence as likely to cause significant harm and brought an increase in police and child protection services activity (Stanley *et al.* 2009). Awareness that an individual's experiences and needs for support during and in the aftermath of domestic violence can vary (Kelly and Johnson 2008) has over the past decade led to a move away from treating all domestic violence cases as the same and to the introduction of methods to identify and respond to high-risk cases in particular. Within the criminal justice system especially, this has resulted in a greater emphasis on risk assessment, using assessment tools such as the DASH (domestic abuse, stalking and harassment risk assessment tool), a focus on risk management via mechanisms such as MARACs (multi-agency risk assessment conferences) and coordinated community responses that aim to bring together and improve joint working across a range of agencies and services (Radford *et al.* 2011).

Domestic violence is known to be a common problem in cases concerning post-separation child care arrangements in the family courts. A review for the Ministry of Justice in England found 53 per cent of private family law cases involve allegations of domestic violence or harm to a child (Cassidy and Davey 2011). Most post-separation arrangements for children – where the child will live, how contact with the non-resident parent will take place and other important decisions – are made by agreement by the parents without the need for court involvement. Only about 10 per cent of cases proceed to litigation (Peacey and Hunt 2010), a trend mirrored in North America, Australia and New Zealand and in many countries in Europe. The Canadian psychologist Peter Jaffe has argued that 'differentiated responses' should be established in family courts to allow the majority of cases to continue to be settled by parental agreement, but those involving any allegations of domestic violence or child maltreatment should be treated differently so that safety is the primary concern (Jaffe *et al.* 2003; Jaffe *et al.* 2008). In the family justice system, steps have been taken to improve the identification of domestic violence through good practice guidelines for domestic violence cases and by recommending findings of fact hearings (Children's Act Sub-Committee 2000; Lord Chancellor's Department 2002; Practice Direction 2008; Practice Direction 2009) as well as by the introduction of self-disclosure screening forms (Aris and Harrison 2007). More recently, risk assessment and active support measures have been introduced into the work of CAFCASS, the agency responsible for child well-being in the family courts (Radford 2013). CAFCASS officers' roles under the Children and Adoption Act 2006 shifted from writing reports for the court to assisting and monitoring contact more directly. Courts gained new powers to require parents to undertake a 'contact activity' such as attending a parenting programme or referral to a domestic violence perpetrator programme (DVPP). Conflict on parental separation and divorce is generally agreed to be harmful for children and family courts have responded by stressing parental agreement. Recent changes to the family justice system in England in the form of the Children and Families Act 2014 have been radical in taking the focus on agreement and mediation further than before, making attendance at a mediation and information assessment meeting compulsory for most cases unless there are good reasons for parents to be exempted, such as domestic violence. Court directions now state:

> The Family Court presumes that the involvement of a parent in a child's life will further the child's welfare, so long as the parent can be involved in a way that does not put the child or other parent at risk of suffering harm. (Practice Direction 2014, p.5)

The double disappearing act

We have a longstanding interest in understanding and challenging the 'double disappearing act' that too often takes place in service responses to children and domestic violence. By this we mean how the needs and rights of children affected by domestic violence often disappear from the focus of attention when police, child protection services or family court officials get involved (the first disappearance), and how domestic violence as a problem for women and children fails to emerge or gets swallowed up under other more preoccupying issues (the second disappearance). This double disappearance can occur either way round but most commonly the voice, needs and rights of the child disappear, or fail to emerge, whilst attention focuses on the domestic violence. The domestic violence then ends up being either downgraded as a problem or transformed into the more general problem of 'parenting'. Post-separation contact with violent fathers provides a classic example of the double disappearing act in practice.

Poor working together across agencies partly explains why this happens and why agencies end up failing to protect children and their mothers, despite sometimes having the best intentions. Systemic contradictions exist between those professionals working against domestic violence, professionals working with child protection and professionals working on post-separation arrangements for children in the family courts. The differences in culture, practice and discourse are so great that professionals in these three areas have been described as occupying three different 'planets', illustrated in Figure 7.1.

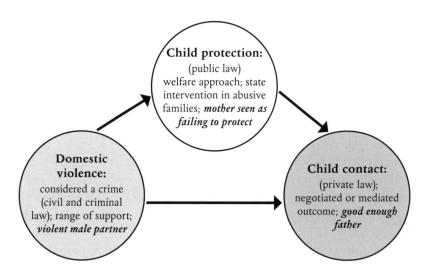

Figure 7.1 The 'three planets model' of agency responses to children and domestic violence (from Hester 2011)

On the domestic violence planet sit refuges and criminal justice agencies that work with victims and perpetrators. The focus is on gender inequality and dealing with violence from men to women. A multi-agency, coordinated community response to high-risk cases is promoted so that victims, mostly women, who are assessed as being at 'high risk' of potentially lethal domestic violence, get support and perpetrators, who are mostly men, face criminal sanctions. Children are generally not a focus or responses to protect adult victims are assumed to deal similarly with the needs of children (Radford *et al.* 2011). Lower-risk cases get fewer services so that the risk assessment can act as a rationing device for stretched police services, resulting in geographically variable and inconsistent policing responses (HMIC 2014).

By contrast, the child protection planet, inhabited by social workers and child protection services, is concerned about children and what is considered by the state to be in children's best interests. The legal framework is provided by laws on child protection, working in partnership with parents to provide this rather than following the route to prosecution. The focus of work on the child protection planet is a gender-neutral focus on 'families'. Work with families invariably involves work with mothers and seldom includes a response to the violent man. Although it is recognised that the violence is from the man to the woman, it is the woman's responsibility, or 'failure' to protect, that gains most attention on the child protection planet. Professionals on the child protection planet ideally expect a woman to leave an abusive partner in order to protect her child, and, if she does not, they can threaten removal of the child (Humphreys and Thiara 2002). Alternatively, they may provide support in the form of a family intervention service, family support or a parenting programme, all of which can be experienced as a form of maternal surveillance. On the child protection planet, domestic violence can disappear as a problem because attention shifts to the abused mother as a struggling parent or as heading a 'family with complex needs' (Radford *et al.* 2011).

The third planet, the child contact planet, is occupied by professionals working in the family court system. Whilst the domestic violence and the child protection planets are concerned with past acts of violence and risks of violence in the future, the child contact planet's main concern is to reduce family conflict and court costs by encouraging parents to put differences behind them and make agreements, preferably outside of the court system. In England, child contact and residence orders have been replaced with the supposedly more neutrally named 'child arrangement orders' but the continued involvement (i.e. contact) of both parents in the life of the child is strongly favoured. To encourage agreement, separating couples are required to attend compulsory mediation information and assessment meetings (MIAMs). As family law researchers have observed, the focus on mediation prioritises process over the justice of the outcome

(Hunter, Barlow and Smithson 2014). Reductions in the availability of legal aid introduced by the Legal Aid, Sentencing and Punishment of Offenders Act 2012 (LASPO) further 'encourage' parents to favour agreement over expensive litigation. Legal aid is available for mediation but not for other family law cases. Technically, cases where there has been domestic violence are exempt if adequate evidence of violence can be provided (Legal Aid Agency 2013). However, the focus on future arrangements, the emphasis on agreement and the belief that contact will happen 'no matter what' mean that domestic violence disappears as not being relevant to the child's parental contact. The view that mediation reduces conflict is by no means unique to the English system and is based more on hope than on evidence. That said, government efforts to increase mediation activity have so far backfired with referrals to mediation declining whereas unrepresented cases, where litigants are mostly fathers, have increased (Bloch, McLoed and Toombs 2014; CAFCASS 2014; Department for Education/Ministry for Justice 2014; Ministry of Justice 2014).

As we have documented over the past couple of decades (Hester and Radford 1996; Hester 2002; Radford and Hester 2006; Hester 2011), the contradictions in policy across the three planets and the different cultures of practice that support them have been difficult to change. As yet there is little evidence that efforts to keep a focus on safety and coordinate approaches across the planets have led to safer contact outcomes for children and their mothers (Radford 2013). Although it is too soon to tell what impact the latest policies may have had, research prior to the changes showed that courts often failed to provide any finding of fact in response to allegations of domestic violence (Hunter and Barnett 2013). Additionally, allegations of violence were not taken up, were downgraded, historicised or disputed in mediation (Trinder, Firth and Jenks 2010); contact was barely ever refused (Cassidy and Davey 2011), even in cases with serious child welfare concerns, and minimal provisions were made for safety or supervision (Hunt and Macleod 2008). Women victims of domestic violence who found their way into mediation, often feeling obliged to attend, were frequently traumatised and felt a lack of control over the process and outcome (Hunter *et al.* 2014). Whilst Chapter 10 in this volume provides some valuable evidence in this field, it is regrettable that there is not more research on children's views and experiences of contact in the context of domestic violence. The limited evidence available from research indicates that whilst some children may want to continue to have contact with a violent father, they only want this if they and the rest of their family can be safe (Radford 2013). Other children do not want contact with abusive fathers and can feel pushed into it by the courts (Thiara and Gill 2011). Whereas applications for contact enforcement orders are rare, there are worrying findings from research showing that concerns over safety and risks are the second most common factor in these cases and only half of those with concerns about domestic violence are dealt with as protection cases (Trinder 2014). Some children just want courts to step in, make a decision to end the contact and put a stop to the ongoing harassment (Radford *et al.* 2011). These findings mirror messages from research on direct contact and children in care which show that relationships between parents and children that start off poorly due to violence and abuse rarely improve with time and are most likely to be harmful and upsetting for a child (Farmer and Lutman 2012; Mackaskill 2002). This is also supported by retrospective research with young adults. Fortin *et al.* (2012) surveyed 398 adults aged 18 to 35 years and telephone-interviewed 50 of them about their experiences of contact in childhood, concluding that the foundations of a successful post-separation relationship between a child and parents are laid down *before* the separation happens. For some of the adults, fearful contact had continued unhappily for a number of years:

> For a few respondents, concerns about violence, excessive drinking or bizarre behaviour meant that they did not feel safe with the non-resident parent. One young woman, whose father, as well as being violent to her mother, had knocked the respondent's front teeth out when she was three, had to steel herself to go and see him for a short visit about once a year. She remained afraid of him throughout the six years she and her sister had contact, even though he was now disabled and they only saw him at their grandmother's house. (Fortin *et al.* 2012, p.240)

As the young woman explained, this father seemed to enjoy frightening his children:

> The common thing was that we would go there, we'd make the effort to go down and see him, but as soon as he opened the door he would for fun try and hit us, because he got...it sounds so awful, but he thought it was really funny to scare us. (Fortin *et al.* 2012, p.240)

Contact centres provide variable levels of safety for families living with domestic violence (Crook and Oehme 2007; Parker *et al.* 2008) and provision in the UK has been patchy. A lack of services to support safe contact continues to be a problem. In 2013, CAFCASS commissioned 32 services to support safe contact and referred 500 domestic violence perpetrators to perpetrator programmes (CAFCASS 2014), but there is nonetheless evidence that orders for contact are made as the default option where access to these services is poor (Hunter and Barnett 2013).

Similar findings on the double disappearing act problem can be seen in countries such as the USA, Canada, Australia and Sweden, where keeping the father involved has taken precedence over safety (Cashmore and Parkinson 2011; Eriksson 2010, 2011; Hester 2011; Hughes and Chau 2012). Efforts made in these countries to address the contradictions between the different planets have included integrated programmes for training, assessment and decision making, as in the USA's 'Greenbook' initiative (Edleson and Malik 2008; Rosewater and Moore 2010), further guidance on risk and child protection, as in Australia (Family Violence Committee 2013) and Sweden (Eriksson 2011), and investing in supported and supervised contact services as in Australia, the UK and the USA. In the next sections we will draw on research from the UK and elsewhere to consider some possibilities for professionals to improve safety for children and mothers after separation. We will describe three strategies in turn: developing a shared understanding of domestic violence and coercive control; repositioning children as 'clients' in domestic violence cases; and putting an end to contact as the default option.

Developing a shared understanding

It is clear that there needs to be a firmer focus on the risks to children of living with domestic violence and how these risks to the safety of children and mothers do not simply disappear on parental separation. CAFCASS has recently adopted various assessment measures including a domestic violence risk assessment measure in the form of the DASH (CAFCASS 2014), which could bring about some shared understanding about risks across the criminal justice and family justice systems. Risk assessment measures such as the DASH are, however, only tools and their utility depends largely on the competence and understanding of the individuals who use them. The focus on high-risk cases using measures such as the DASH emphasises the potential lethality of individual incidents rather than a pattern of behaviour over time. Indicators of risk are largely risks for adults which may not all be as relevant for children and young people. Also, the DASH may not uncover adequately how domestic violence perpetrators may use children as a route to abuse of the mother.

In England and Wales, domestic violence is now officially recognised as covering a range of abusive behaviour – physical, sexual, emotional, financial abuse, coercive and controlling behaviour (Home Office 2013). This definition is now included in the new practice direction on domestic violence for the family courts (Family Court 2014):

> 'Domestic violence' includes any incident or pattern of incidents of controlling, coercive or threatening behaviour, violence or abuse between those aged 16 or over who are or have been intimate partners or family members regardless of gender or sexuality. This can encompass, but is not limited to, psychological, physical, sexual, financial, or emotional abuse.
>
> 'Controlling behaviour' means an act or pattern of acts designed to make a person subordinate and/or dependent by isolating them from sources of support, exploiting their resources and capacities for personal gain, depriving them of the means needed for independence, resistance and escape and regulating their everyday behaviour.
>
> 'Coercive behaviour' means an act or a pattern of acts of assault, threats, humiliation and intimidation or other abuse that is used to harm, punish, or frighten the victim. (Practice Direction 2014, clause 3)

The concept of coercive control is helpful in understanding the nature and impact of domestic violence, why a woman can be 'stuck' or trapped in a violent relationship and how continued harassment at the point of child contact may make separation especially difficult (Stark 2007).

Similar recognition of domestic violence as coercive and controlling behaviour is given in guidance issued for the Australian family courts and the recommended risk assessment includes the assessment of 'potency' (the nature and severity of impact of the violence), the 'primary aggressor' (to distinguish cases where victims may use violence in self-defence and cases where the violence may be from both parties to one another) and the 'pattern' of behaviour and coercive control (Family Violence Committee 2013). Although there have been difficulties in the Australian system over whether contact takes primacy over safety (Cashmore and Parkinson 2011), we consider the guidance on assessing the pattern of abuse and coercive control to be a potentially helpful step towards developing a shared understanding of the risks to children in having contact with a violent parent.

Domestic violence perpetrators may manipulate children during contact visits by:

- pumping them for information about the mother's movements and activities

- using children to give information that will help them to track down mothers who have moved away

- getting the children, sometimes unwittingly, to relay threats to the mother

- influencing the children's beliefs or behaviour in order to undermine the mother's parenting

(Radford and Hester 2006)

We believe that building the understanding of domestic violence as coercive control into methods of identification, assessment and response across the multi-agency context could significantly help to bring about the cultural shift in thinking about risk and safety that is required. It could contribute to improved awareness of the dynamics of domestic violence and shift the focus to include perpetrator behaviour and parenting by violent men. Coercive and controlling behaviour can include a perpetrator's efforts to target the children, to draw them into the abuse and to undermine the mother's relationship with the children and her identity as a mother. Practitioner training and assessment methods need to take this into consideration. Figure 7.2, taken from our book *Mothering through Domestic Violence* (Radford and Hester 2006), illustrates some of these strategies likely to impact on the child's relationship with both parents.

Figure 7.2 Coercive control and mothering

This model can be applied directly to understanding domestic violence in post-separation child contact arrangements. Some of the strategies in Figure 7.2 involve the direct use of violence – for example, where contact with the child is used primarily as a route to abuse of the mother or where abducting or threatening to take the child away is used as a lever to get the mother to return to the abuser. Isolation from family and friends is often a feature of domestic violence and can leave women struggling to cope with contact in the context of domestic violence without informal help and social support. Some of the strategies employed by abusers undermine the mother's authority and status in the family – for example, constantly telling the children that the mother is 'stupid' or 'useless' or responsible for the relationship ending. This can be particularly harmful and emotionally manipulative for children in the context of contact meetings. The 'helping' professions – police, child protection services and family courts – may become inadvertently enlisted in the violent father's efforts to maintain coercive control, particularly through repeated applications for child contact which may financially and emotionally exhaust the victim yet be misunderstood by professionals as the father's devoted persistence.

We are certainly not arguing that women and children are passive recipients of violence, abuse and coercive control from violent men. Women and children of most ages often resist controlling tactics, take steps to avoid and evade the abuse, and to protect and emotionally support one another. The impact of the abuse, and sometimes the coping strategies as well, can nonetheless be such that women who have lived with domestic violence feel vulnerable about their parenting. Decisions about child contact need to be made to support safety as the primary objective and to strengthen the relationship between the primary non-abusive caregiver (generally the mother) and child (Laing and Humphreys 2013).

Children's status

There is worrying evidence that children's views about domestic violence are not always heard and the lack of focus specifically on children is one reason why they 'disappear' in single and multi-agency working. Eriksson (2011) has observed how children living with domestic violence are positioned as 'witnesses', 'victims' and occasionally as 'competent participants' in the decision-making process. Tensions between these positions create problems for everyday practice. Age and the nature of the violence can be seen by professionals as barriers to children's competency to express their views even when a child as young as five may have demonstrated this by calling the police (Radford *et al.* 2011). Methods of identifying and assessing children's specific needs in the context of domestic violence and in relation to contact will require some shift in practice to enable children to be seen, talked to and heard. It is important to recognise the context and positioning of the child's experiences when talking to a child who has lived with domestic violence. Eriksson and Näsman (2008) point out that the child often carries the domestic violence as a family secret and lacks opportunities to talk, be heard, to interpret and make sense of the experiences. The child may consequently feel hopeless, lonely, lacking control and carry feelings of shame and blame. Professionals working with children can, by recognising and affirming the child's experiences, enable them to overcome these negative and harmful understandings. Enabling children to have meaningful participation means giving children information on what will happen, how they will be involved, how their views will be assessed, considered and taken into account. This rarely happens at present and observations, assessments, interviews and meetings may be set up without their purpose being clearly explained and without children having any control over the process.

Taking time to see the child separately is an essential first step for all professionals as it is particularly difficult for a child to express his or her views in the presence of an abusive parent. The time limits to decision making recently introduced into the family courts may create barriers to meaningful participation and may need reconsidering in light of the differing needs of children who have lived with abuse. Methods of working with children of different ages with different capacities already exist (Laing and Humphreys 2013) but they need to be applied more readily.

Children's rights to be safe, to have peace at home and time to recover also need to be taken into consideration and to become a priority. Safety for the child and the primary caregiver has to take precedence over contact. Child protection efforts to date have, we argue, contributed to the double disappearance of children and domestic violence by shifting attention away from the violence and the perpetrator's responsibility on to women's parenting. In Sweden, efforts have been made to recognise domestic violence as a crime intended to create harm to the child as well as the mother (Eriksson 2010). Whereas children may sometimes have ambivalent feelings about a violent parent, their rights to be safe from harassment and exposure to post-separation violence need to be defended more rigorously and legislative change may be necessary to ensure this happens. In England, recognition of domestic violence as a pattern of violent and abusive behaviour and coercive control brings behaviour such as stalking and harassment into consideration within the criminal and family courts. Adult victims of domestic violence can currently seek protection from harassment under criminal law. We would argue that children living with domestic violence, especially after parental separation, should have similar protection from a violent parent who uses the prospect of child contact as a route to pursue and harass the mother and child. Courts and professionals who work with them should help children to say 'no' to unsafe contact and challenge the unhelpful view that a violent man is a 'good enough father'.

Contact as the default option

Little attention has been given to the violent man as a parent and an increased focus on this is strongly recommended if we are to place a greater emphasis on safety. Resources exist that could inform professional practice (e.g. Bancroft and Silverman 2002). In England, CAFCASS has new policies on assessment and referral to family law perpetrator programmes. Services such as Caring Dads in Wales which aim to address violence and fathering are currently undergoing evaluation to gather better information on their impact on the safety and well-being of children and mothers (McConnell *et al.* 2014). However, professionals often lack the skills and confidence to engage with violent men and motivate them to take steps to change their behaviour (Donovan and Griffiths 2013). Professionals working with violent men as parents need to bring expertise and approaches from perpetrator programmes into the everyday practice of child protection and family court work. However, even in cases where domestic violence and potential harm to the child have been recognised, contact has been the default option where there exists a lack of services to support children's safety. No direct contact needs to be considered more frequently as an option if there are insufficient resources to ensure safety.

Conclusion

In this chapter we have shown that despite attempts over the past decade or more to increase recognition of domestic violence as a harmful context for children, men's/fathers' violence to women/mothers continues to be minimised in child contact negotiations and outcomes. Contradictions between domestic violence, child protection and child contact remain problematic. We have argued that there is a 'double disappearance' where the needs and rights of children affected by domestic violence often disappear from the focus of attention when police, child protection services or family court officials get involved, and where domestic violence as a problem for both women and children fails to emerge or gets swallowed up under other seemingly more preoccupying issues. These contradictions and disappearances can be mitigated by the more consistent application of existing policies and approaches, specifically: by professionals, whether police, child safeguarding or family courts, developing a shared understanding of the dynamics of domestic violence; by enabling children's voices to be heard and their views considered in any contact negotiations; and by considering no direct contact as a more frequent option.

References

Aris, R. and Harrison, C. (2007) *Domestic Violence and the Supplemental Information Form C1A.* Ministry of Justice Research Series 17/07 December 2007. London: Ministry of Justice.

Bancroft, L. and Silverman, J. (2002) *Assessing Risk to Children from Batterers.* Thousand Oaks, CA: Sage.

Bloch, A., McLoed, R. and Toombs, B. (2014) *Mediation Information and Assessment Meetings (MIAMs) and Mediation in Private Family Law Disputes: Qualitative Research Findings.* London: Ministry of Justice. Available at www.gov.uk/government/organisations/ministry-of-justice/about/research, accessed on 7 November 2014.

Brandon, M., Belderson, P., Warren, C., Howe, D. *et al.* (2008) *Analysing Child Deaths and Serious Injury through Abuse and Neglect: What Can We Learn? A Biennial Analysis of Serious Case Reviews 2003–2005.* Research Report DCSF RR023. London: DCSF.

CAFCASS (2014) *Annual Report.* London: CAFCASS.

Cashmore, J. and Parkinson, P. (2011) 'Reasons for disputes in high conflict families.' *Journal of Family Studies 17,* 186–203.

Cashmore, J. and Parkinson, P. (2012) 'Parenting arrangements for young children: messages from research.' *Australian Journal of Family Law 25,* 3, 236–257.

Cassidy, D. and Davey, S. (2011) *Family Justice and Children's Proceedings: A Review of Public and Private Law Case Files.* Research Summary 51/1. London: Ministry of Justice. Available at www.justice.gov.uk/downloads/publications/research-and-analysis/moj-research/family-justice-childrens-proceedings.pdf, accessed on 7 November 2014.

Children Act Sub-Committee (2000) *A Report to the Lord Chancellor on the Question of Parental Contact in Cases Where There is Domestic Violence.* London: Lord Chancellor's Department.

Coy, M., Perks, K., Scott, E. and Tweedie, R. (2012) *Picking Up the Pieces: Domestic Violence and Child Contact.* London: Rights of Women.

Crook, W. and Oehme, K. (2007) 'Characteristics of supervised visitation programs serving child maltreatment and other cases.' *Brief Treatment and Crisis Intervention 7,* 4, 291–304.

Department for Education/Ministry for Justice (2014) *A Brighter Future for Family Justice: A Round-Up of What's Happened Since the Family Justice Review.* London: Department for Education/Ministry of Justice.

Donovan, C. and Griffiths, S. (2013) 'Domestic violence and voluntary perpetrator programmes: engaging men in the pre-commencement phase.' *British Journal of Social Work 43,* 1–17.

Edleson, J. and Malik, N. (2008) 'Collaborating for family safety: results from the Greenbook multi-site evaluation.' *Journal of Interpersonal Violence 23,* 27, 871–875.

Eriksson, M. (2010) 'Children who "witness" violence as crime victims and changing family law in Sweden.' *Journal of Child Custody 7,* 93–116.

Eriksson, M. (2011) 'Contact, shared parenting, and violence: children as witnesses of domestic violence in Sweden.' *International Journal of Law, Policy and the Family 25,* 2, 165–183.

Eriksson, M. and Näsman, E. (2008) 'Participation in family law proceedings for children whose father is violent to their mother.' *Childhood 15,* 2, 259–275.

Family Violence Committee (2013) *Family Violence Best Practice Principles Edition 3.1 April 2013.* Australia: Family Court.

Farmer, E. and Lutman, E. (2012) *Effective Working with Neglected Children and Their Families: Linking Interventions to Long-Term Outcomes.* London: Jessica Kingsley Publishers.

Fortin, J., Hunt, J. and Scanlon, S. (2012) *Taking a Longer View of Contact: The Perspectives of Young Adults Who Experienced Parental Separation in Their Youth.* Brighton: Sussex Law School.

HMIC (2014) *Everybody's Business: Improving the Police Response to Domestic Abuse.* London: Her Majesty's Inspectorate of Constabulary. Available at www.justiceinspectorates. gov.uk/hmic/wp-content/uploads/2014/04/improving-the-police-response-to-domestic-abuse.pdf, accessed on 22 May 2015.

Hester, M. and Radford, L. (1996) 'Contradictions and Compromises: The Impact of the Children Act on Women and Children's Safety.' In M. Hester, L. Kelly and J. Radford (eds) *Women, Violence and Male Power: Feminist Activism, Research and Practice.* Bristol: Open University Press.

Hester, M. (2002) 'One step forward and three steps back? Children, abuse and parental contact in Denmark.' *Child and Family Law Quarterly 14,* 3, 267–279.

Hester, M. (2011) 'The three planet model: towards an understanding of contradictions in approaches to women and children's safety in contexts of domestic violence.' *British Journal of Social Work 41,* 837–853.

Hester, M. (2013) 'Who does what to whom? Gender and domestic violence perpetrators in English police records.' *European Journal of Criminology 10,* 5, 623–637.

Home Office (2013) *Information for Local Areas on the Change to the Definition of Domestic Violence and Abuse.* London: Home Office/AVA.

Howarth, E., Stimpson, L., Barran, D. and Robinson, A. (2009) *Safety in Numbers: A Multi-Site Evaluation of Independent Domestic Violence Advisor Services.* London: Henry Smith Charity. Available at www.henrysmithcharity.org.uk/documents/ SafetyinNumbersFullReportNov09.pdf, accessed on 22 May 2015.

Hughes, J. and Chau, S. (2012) 'Children's best interests and intimate partner violence in the Canadian family law and child protection systems.' *Critical Social Policy 32,* 4, 677–695.

Humphreys, C. and Thiara, R. (2002) *Routes to Safety: Protection Issues Facing Abused Women and Children and the Role of Outreach Services.* Bristol: Women's Aid Federation.

Hunt, J. and Macleod, A. (2008) *Outcomes of Applications to Court for Contact Orders after Parental Separation or Divorce.* London: Ministry of Justice.

Hunter, R., Barlow, A. and Smithson, J. (2014) 'Mapping paths to family justice: matching parties, cases and processes.' *Family Law,* 1404.

Hunter, R. and Barnett, A. (2013) *Fact-Finding Hearings and the Implementation of the President's Practice Direction: Residence and Contact Orders: Domestic Violence and Harm.* London: Family Justice Council.

Jaffe, P., Johnston, J., Crooks, C. and Bala, N. (2008) 'Custody disputes involving allegations of domestic violence: toward a differentiated approach to parenting plans.' *Family Court Review 46,* 3, 500–522.

Jaffe, P., Lemon, N. and Poisson, S. (2003) *Child Custody and Domestic Violence: A Call for Safety and Accountability.* Thousand Oaks, CA: Sage.

Kelly, J. and Johnson, M. (2008) 'Differentiation among types of intimate partner violence: research update and implications for interventions.' *Family Court Review 46,* 3, 476–499.

Laing, L. and Humphreys, C. (2013) *Social Work and Domestic Violence: Developing Critical and Reflective Practice.* London: Sage.

Legal Aid Agency (2013) *The Legal Aid, Sentencing and Punishment of Offenders Act (LASPO) 2012 – Evidence Requirements for Private Family Law Matters.* London: Legal Aid Agency. Available at www.gov.uk/government/uploads/system/uploads/attachment_data/ file/345515/legal-aid-evidence-for-private-family-law-matters.pdf, accessed on 7 November 2014.

Lord Chancellor's Department (2002) *Guidelines for Good Practice on Parental Contact Where There is Domestic Violence.* London: Lord Chancellor's Department.

Macaskill, C. (2002) *Safe Contact? Children in Permanent Placement and Contact with Their Birth Relatives.* Lyme Regis: Russell House Publishing.

Ministry of Justice (2014) *Court Statistics Quarterly, January to March 2014.* London: Ministry of Justice.

McConnell, M., Barnard, M., Holdsworth, T. and Taylor, J. (2014) *Caring Dads, Safer Children: Interim Evaluation Report.* London: NSPCC. Available at www.nspcc.org.uk/globalassets/documents/evaluation-of-services/caring-dads-safer-children-interim-report.pdf, accessed on 22 May 2015.

Parker, T., Rogers, K., Collins, M. and Edleson, J. (2008) 'Danger zone: battered mothers and their families in supervised visitation.' *Violence against Women 14,* 11, 1313–1325.

Peacey, V. and Hunt, J. (2009) *I'm not saying it was easy...Contact Problems in Separated Families.* London: GingerbreadPovey, D. (2009) *Homicides, Firearm Offences and Intimate Violence 2007/08.* Available at http://webarchive.nationalarchives.gov.uk/20110220105210/rds.homeoffice.gov.uk/rds/pdfs09/hosb0209.pdf, accessed on 22 May 2015.

Practice Direction (2008) *Residence and Contact Orders: Domestic Violence and Harm.* 9 May 2008, Family Division.

Practice Direction (2009*) Residence and Contact Orders: Domestic Violence and Harm.* 14 January 2009, Sir Mark Potter, President of the Family Division.

Practice Direction (2014) *Child Arrangements and Contact Orders: Domestic Violence and Harm.* London: Family Court.

Radford, L., Aitken, R., Miller, P., Roberts, J., Ellis, J. and Firkic, A. (2011) *Meeting the Needs of Children Living With Domestic Violence in London.* London: NSPCC/Refuge/City Bridge Trust. Available at www.nspcc.org.uk/Inform, accessed on 7 November 2014.

Radford, L. (2013) 'Domestic Violence, Safety and Child Contact in England: Hiding Violent Men in the Shadows of Parenting.' In N. Lombard and N. Macmillan (eds) *Violence Against Women: Research Highlights.* London: Jessica Kingsley Publishers.

Radford, L. and Hester, M. (2006) *Mothering through Domestic Violence.* London: Jessica Kingsley Publishers.

Rosewater, A. and Moore, K. (2010) *Addressing Domestic Violence, Child Safety and Well-Being: Collaborative Strategies for California Families.* California: California Leadership Group on Domestic Violence and Child Well-Being.

Saunders, H. (2004) *Twenty-Nine Child Homicides: Lessons Still to Be Learnt on Domestic Violence and Child Protection.* Bristol: Women's Aid.

Sidebotham, P., Brandon, M., Bailey, S., Belderson, S. and Hawley, C. (2011) *Serious and Fatal Child Maltreatment: Setting Serious Case Review Data in the Context with Other Data on Violent and Maltreatment Deaths in 2009–10.* Research Report DFE-RR167. London: Department for Education. Available at www.education.gov.uk/publications/eOrderingDownload/DFE-RR167.pdf, accessed on 7 November 2014.

Stanley, N. (2011) *Children Experiencing Domestic Violence: A Research Review.* Dartington: Research in Practice. Available at www.rip.org.uk/publications/research-reviews, accessed on 7 November 2014.

Stanley, N., Miller, P., Richardson Foster, H. and Thomson, G. (2010) *Children and Families Experiencing Domestic Violence: Police and Children's Services Responses.* London: NSPCC. Available at www.nspcc.org.uk/Inform, accessed on 7 November 2014.

Stark, E. (2007) *Coercive Control: How Men Entrap Women in Personal Life: Interpersonal Violence.* New York, NY: Oxford University Press.

Thiara, R. and Gill, A. (2011) *Domestic Violence, Child Contact and Post-Separation Violence: Issues for South Asian and African-Caribbean Women and Children.* London: NSPCC. Available at www.nspcc.org.uk/Inform, accessed on 7 November 2014.

Trinder, L., Firth, A. and Jenks, C. (2010) '"So presumably things have moved on since then?" The management of risk allegations in child contact dispute resolution.' *International Journal of Law, Policy and the Family 24*, 1, 29–53.

Trinder, L. (2014) *Enforcing Child Contact Orders: Are the Family Courts Getting It Right?* London: Nuffield Foundation.

Vincent, S. (2009) *Child Death and Serious Case Review Processes in the UK*. Research Brief No. 5, February 2009. Edinburgh: University of Edinburgh/NSPCC Centre for UK-Wide Learning in Child Protection.

Winter, V. and Gosley, J. (2006) *NSW Child Death Review Team: Annual Report 2006*. NSW, Australia: NSW Commission for Children and Young People.

CHAPTER 8

Supporting the Relationship Between Mothers and Children in the Aftermath of Domestic Violence

Cathy Humphreys, Ravi K. Thiara, Cathy Sharp and Jocelyn Jones

The 'siloing' of services for women and services for children has profoundly affected the structure of interventions offered to women and children living with and separating from domestic violence. Even in areas where the co-location of services occurs, such as in refuges, joint work is not necessarily undertaken with women and children together. In this chapter, we will present the case for connecting work with women and work with children recovering from experiences of domestic violence. This is not to argue that women and children do not have their individual support needs; rather our impetus for this approach is located in the emerging evidence that recovery for both women and children is promoted by joint work rather than through individual work alone (Graham-Bergmann *et al.* 2007; Lieberman, Ippen and Van Horn 2006).

Two contrasting examples are presented in this chapter to illustrate the direction that joint work might take. The first promotes strengthening the mother–child relationship through facilitating communication between mothers and their children and is based on the work undertaken in the Talking to My Mum project (Humphreys *et al.* 2006a, 2006b). The second example reports on parallel groups for women and their children and draws on the large-scale Scottish initiative in this area, known as Cedar (Children Experiencing Domestic Abuse Recovery) (Sharp and Jones 2011). Both projects held in common a participatory action learning approach which supported 'changing things in the process of studying them' (Wicks, Reason and Bradbury 2008, pp.15–30), thus simultaneously building the evidence base whilst developing practice and extending the participation of women and children. Most importantly, women and children experiencing the intervention were involved in and fed back into the action research process.

Background

Strengthening the mother–child relationship in the aftermath of domestic violence has been relatively slow in gaining traction as a legitimate intervention in a crisis-driven service system. Certainly, attention to the impact of domestic violence on the mother–child relationship has been growing (Casanueva *et al.* 2008; Radford and Hester 2006) but the translation of this knowledge to policy and practice continues to be limited. A number of issues are relevant here.

The conceptualisation of domestic violence as an attack on the mother–child relationship remains marginalised within the field of domestic violence (Humphreys, Thiara and Skamballis 2011; Laing and Humphreys 2013). Differing approaches to the recognition of individual trauma for women and for children alongside understandings of the impacts on women's mental health and the cognitive, behavioural and emotional well-being of children remain inappropriately siloed. Whilst recognising that the physical health (Rivara *et al.* 2007) and the emotional and behavioural development of children are compromised by domestic violence (Holt, Buckley and Whelan 2008; Kitzmann *et al.* 2013), the extent to which this impact is created by the domestic violence perpetrator undermining, directly or indirectly, the relationship between women and their children has been given less attention. Morris (2009) refers to these tactics of abuse as the Abusive Household Gender Regime (AHGR) to highlight the pervasive and gendered nature of the abuse.

To some extent, the 'failure to protect' discourse which focuses on the survivor's relationship with her children has dominated the practice intervention (Nixon 2011) and provides an example of a parallel 'failure to understand' from the professionals involved. Women are inappropriately held responsible for the protection of children, with little or no emphasis on the 'invisible' perpetrator of violence and the provision of appropriate justice interventions and services for women and their children (Radford and Hester 2006). In this process, the myriad ways in which the relationship between women and their children is undermined by the tactics of power, control and abuse is relegated to the margins of the professional's vision.

Little weight is placed on the ways in which the woman's availability to her children may be undermined by abuse. The woman's physical health may be compromised, sometimes through hospitalisation, but more frequently by painful disabling around her own home with issues such as back problems, painful bruising and a lack of sleep undermining her immune system (Humphreys 2007). Similarly, the attack on her mental and emotional well-being, creating depression, anxiety and trauma symptoms (Jordan, Campbell, Follingstad 2010), also indirectly affects the woman's ability to be with her children.

Whilst emphasising the multiple ways in which domestic violence directly and indirectly impacts on women's relationships with their children, the resilience of that relationship should also not be underestimated. A large-scale US study sampled from a child protection population by Casanueva *et al.* (2008) demonstrated that women took active steps to compensate for the violence of their partners. The parenting scores of women where the domestic violence was past rather than current were significantly higher (i.e. better) and the women were also comparable or more positive in their parenting behaviours than women drawn from a large-scale national study of disadvantaged families (Bradley *et al.* 2001). Interestingly, smacking was less common in the sample of women who had experienced domestic violence.

A further barrier to supporting work to strengthen the mother–child relationship in the aftermath of abuse is created not only by the separation of adult and children's services but also by the training of workers. Training generally focuses upon basic counselling skills with adults or children and sometimes addresses the complexity of relationship-based work. However, those workers with more extensive training in relationship counselling work which builds confidence and skills to work with women and children together (or with other family relationships) are not generally mainstream posts, but rather specialist roles with specialist skills which relatively few workers in the domestic violence sector have (Humphreys *et al.* 2011). A lack of confidence also reduces workers' 'readiness' to carry out joint work with women and children.

In spite of a number of barriers, work focused on strengthening the relationships between women and their children in the aftermath of violence has continued to develop. The randomised control trial by Lieberman *et al.* (2006) which provided mother–child psychotherapy for a year for the intervention group and case management and individual counselling for women and children in the control group showed significant and sustained improvements in behaviour and trauma measures for children and in the women's general distress levels relative to the control group.

Many parallel group programmes for women and children who have experienced domestic violence have developed in England, Canada, the US and Australia. These groups are providing further evidence that recovery for women and children is more effective when interventions are linked. For example, an efficacy trial by Graham-Bermann *et al.* (2007) compared parallel groups for women and their children with individual counselling for children, and a group of children on the waiting list. The results indicated that the recovery of women and children was stronger if both women and children were experiencing parallel group interventions.

This chapter goes on to describe two initiatives which supported interventions to strengthen the relationships between women and children in the aftermath of domestic violence.

Talking to My Mum – supporting mother–child communication

It's not hush, hush anymore (Child, family 3)

In describing the Talking to My Mum project, we briefly explain the action research methodology and then go on to draw out the communication issues this project addressed and the impact reported by women and children who engaged with supported communication activities.

Methodology

Based on repeated cycles of planning, action and reflection, the three-year Talking to My Mum project adopted an action research methodology (Wicks *et al.* 2008) and included three research cycles. Initial focus groups with workers, mothers and children identified issues that needed to be addressed to strengthen communication between mothers and children. Action research cycles then followed with each consisting of the implementation of mother–child activity packs, feedback and reflection from mothers, children and workers, followed by the incorporation of this feedback into the developing materials for the subsequent cycle. The research involved children aged five to 16 years and included research sites in ten refuges, two NSPCC teams, a specialist domestic violence service in London and a rape crisis centre. A total of 45 families and 52 children participated in the research. Of the participating children, 27 were boys and 25 were girls. Twelve of the families were Asian.

Three activity packs were initially developed aimed at two age groups and three stages of the journey after leaving domestic violence. The activities packs were eventually published as resource books which are now widely available: *Talking to My Mum: A Picture Workbook for Workers, Mothers and Children Affected by Domestic Abuse* and *Talking About Domestic Abuse: A Photo Activity Workbook to Develop Communication Between Mothers and Young People* (Humphreys *et al.* 2006a, 2006b).

Mother–child communication in the context of domestic violence

Talking to My Mum (TTMM) provides interesting insights into the process of strengthening communication between mothers and their children – in the aftermath of domestic violence. The crucial role of 'readiness' at multiple levels in this process – organisational, worker, mothers and children has been highlighted elsewhere and is an prerequisite for effective joint work with women and children (Humphreys *et al.* 2011). The factor reported as facilitating womens' readiness to strenghten the communication with their children included: the importance of having a safe place to live away from abuse; a period of stability; a relationship of trust with support workers; the ability to confront and name the effects of domestic violence on children and having the opportunity to receive support for their own needs.

Women and children who participated in TTMM often made reference to the range of tactics used by abusive men to undermine the mother–child relationship. In particular, the constant undermining of the parenting role of the mother *in front of the children* was a consistent theme, alongside the contrasting theme of *exclusion from their children*, an issue that was particularly pronounced for some Asian women:

> They didn't used to leave the baby with me, his sisters used to take him out all the time. I never had much time with him. I was like their servant. (Mother, family 28)

The destructive impact of secrecy and lack of communication about the situation between mothers and children also greatly affected their relationship, and this was something that continued for many after leaving domestic violence:

> I never used to get to talk to my mum…because he had big ears… he was like Dumbo because he could hear everything…I could never like get to talk to Mum unless we were out or anything. (Child, family 40)

Crucially, TTMM provided an opportunity for mothers to raise issues they had not discussed before with their children as well as to simply check in with each other about their well-being after leaving the abusive situation. Whilst those women who enjoyed a good relationship with their child were most open to engaging with the project, those who needed support and motivation to repair poor relationships with their children also reported the positive difference that the intervention made for them. Where there were ongoing contact issues which challenged their relationship, TTMM provided a way of dealing with some of these emotional issues.

Children consistently referred to three themes when talking about the motivation and benefits of engaging with the TTMM activities: spending time with their mothers, helping their mothers and other children, and talking about their worries:

> It felt OK to do it because I wanted to help other children. I wanted to do it because it would help me to understand my mum's feelings and my feelings. And it did help. (Child, family 25)

Those children who were less engaged with the activities were those who found it most difficult to talk about the past and their feelings.

The value of talking

When the issue of speaking with their children about their lives, including their experiences of domestic violence, was raised, most, but not all, women emphasised the value of doing this. For many, TTMM was viewed as a way of speaking to their children about the past in an enjoyable way and to explain their feelings, to enhance their understanding so as to improve their relationship.

> I just thought it would be good for me to talk to the children, just as a help to talk to them... and it did help me – it did make me aware of things that I wasn't aware of with the children which is why I continued. (Mother, family 12)

For some, the evident effect on their children was sufficient motivation to acknowledge that they required support to address the issue. Eight of the 45 families identified that their children were experiencing significant problems with anger and saw the activities as a way of addressing this.

Children commented that their relationship with their mother had improved after the activities as they had been able to understand things from their mother's perspective and had got to know their mothers a 'bit more' and share thoughts:

> It's like because we never got to talk our feelings out and when we was doing the pack we got to tell each other what was going on in our heads... And got to tell her my feelings and what I felt inside... Because I got things out my mind that I was concerned about. (Child, family 20)

Given the close regulation by abusive men of mother–child relationships, most women and children in our research reported that opening up communication between them about the abuse had made their relationship stronger. Thus, spending time together, even where families only did a few activities, was the dominant theme that emerged from the feedback from both mothers and children:

> They [the activities] give you a structure to spend time...because of the structure there it makes it easier to spend that time together otherwise they're off watching telly or off doing something, or you're off doing something. (Worker, family 12)

Women reported that the activities made them acknowledge/listen for the first time to their children's experiences and feelings about abuse and to recognise the actual impact it had on them. Listening to the extent of the effects on their children challenged the mothers' view that simply removing children from the situation of abuse and making them physically safe, although crucial, had not entirely dealt with the impact on children. Even mothers with strong relationships with their children were surprised at how much children had kept to themselves.

Impact of Talking To My Mum – making a positive difference

After completing the activities, the 45 women were asked to rate how well the activities had worked for them on a scale of 1–10 (1 = didn't work at all and 10 = very positive). The majority of mothers were very positive (43%) or positive (33%), with only five mothers scoring at the midway point, and there were no mothers for whom the packs had not worked. An interesting finding from the research was the changing perception of mothers about the extent of their communication with children about domestic violence. For instance, women were asked before (T1) and after completing the activities (T2) about the extent to which they had spoken to their children about the domestic violence. At the outset (T1), *before engagement* with the project, 60 per cent of mothers believed they had spoken a lot, or quite a lot about domestic violence with their children. In contrast, at T2 conducted *after* completing the activities, the majority of mothers reported that they had had little communication with their children before embarking on the TTMM activities. Thus, many women changed their perception of the extent of their previous communication with their children, so that, at T2, 33 per cent reported they had never or rarely spoken to their children about the abuse before they became involved in the research, and 66 per cent put themselves at the mid-point or below.

Women were more likely to have spoken to older children about the abuse and it was also apparent that 'communication about the abuse' often meant different things for different families. Even where women described their relationship as 'very close' and they made time to be with their children, they reported not talking about the abuse: 'We do a lot of activities together…but that's the physical…sitting down talking together…that's something not a lot of people do' (family 16). For a few, the process of opening up communication had taken place over time, and the research was a way of further strengthening relationships they had already spent many months trying to rebuild after the abuse.

Children knew what was happening when they were living with the abuse but they often perceived women's attempts to conceal what was going on as a message that they did not want to talk about it, resulting in secrecy and a 'conspiracy of silence' between mothers and children. The following was a typical comment made by many of the older children: 'I didn't ask her because I knew what was happening' (family 28). Similarly, many mothers also made comments such as: 'I never talked to him about it but he knew what was happening' (family 29).

In summary, although the chronic undermining of the mother–child relationship by abusive men is widely acknowledged, it is also the case that this relationship can recover and strengthen once safety is established and if appropriate support is provided. Many mother–child relationships, even if negatively affected, are strengthened without any intervention as women and children draw on their own resources. However, where the impact is chronic and complex or where the capacity of mothers is impaired by the effects of abuse, the role of supportive interventions aimed at rebuilding the mother's capacity is crucial.

The origins and development of the Cedar groupwork model

Cedar (Children Experiencing Domestic Abuse Recovery) is a psycho-educational, multi-agency initiative for children and young people who had behavioural, emotional and social difficulties as a consequence of their experience of domestic abuse. It was developed in Scotland, based on the Community Groupwork Treatment Programme (CGP) originating in Ontario, Canada (Marshall *et al.* 1995), and also developed in London, UK (Debbonaire 2007; Nolas, Neville and Sanders-McDonagh 2012), and in Australia (Bunston 2006 and see Chapter 9). Cedar provided a therapeutic 12-week group work programme for children and young people in recovery from domestic abuse, alongside a concurrent group work programme for their mothers.

Cedar was piloted between 2008 and 2011 in three local authority areas of Scotland – the city of Edinburgh, Fife and Forth Valley. Delivery of the pilots was led by Scottish Women's Aid working closely in partnership with the three local authorities. The pilot used an action research approach to support ongoing reflective practice, wider dialogue and greater participation of children, young people and mothers. The Cedar evaluation used an inquiry process to bridge the research/practice divide, enhance the use of 'practitioner wisdom' and promote new forms of collaboration, particularly to empower children and young people (Sharp and Jones 2011). Cedar was an ideal programme in which to adopt this approach as the programme values were strongly child- and mother-focused (Loosely *et al.* 2006).

In 2009 and 2010, 52 in-depth qualitative interviews were conducted with children, young people (n=27) and their mothers (n=25). These interviews and other evaluation evidence about the structure of the programme are drawn upon here to continue the exploration of the processes for strengthening the relationships between women and their children in the aftermath of domestic abuse.

Supports for strengthening the mother–child relationship

The Cedar programme provided a number of different strategies aimed at strengthening the relationship between women and their children.

Assessment as a form of engagement with families

The formal Cedar assessment process centred on the needs of the child and the function of the mothers' group was to provide mothers with information about their children's participation in groups. The Cedar coordinators developed a skilful, non-judgemental way to engage with children and mothers; this enabled potential group members to feel comfortable, listened to and able to make choices for themselves. Mothers suggested that the assessment process for Cedar was done 'with' them and not 'to' them and helped overcome their initial reservations:

The whole thing surprised me because I was quite negative at first ... I mean I knew the workers came out for the visit – everything went fine, but I still had it in the back of my head 'it's going to be one of those domestic violence groups' sort of thing. I was really reserved, I really, really was. (Mother)

The high participation and completion rates for mothers in groups alongside their children were testament to the quality of this initial assessment process. Psychological and emotional readiness are key to the success of interventions and these are linked to a woman's sense of self-worth. The extent to which she has begun to acknowledge pre-existing strengths and strategies used to protect her children in the context of the isolating, shaming and self-blaming context of domestic abuse is also relevant. The importance of attention to the 'assessment as engagement' process cannot be underestimated.

Cedar curriculum, structure and strengths-based approach

The structured curriculum and range of activities on offer helped to transform understandings of domestic abuse and reduced self-blame. It taught children strategies to recognise their feelings and deal with their anger and provided a language to talk about feelings and experiences through varied creative and playful activities. It made good use of visual images and memorable metaphors, which aided communication in group and at home. For example, the iceberg exercise was found to be particularly beneficial (Figures 8.1 and 8.2).

Session 3: Through the eyes of a mother

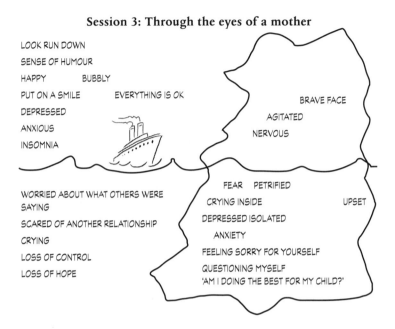

Figure 8.1 The iceberg exercise from a mothers' group: 'Through the eyes of a mother'

Session 3: Through the eyes of a child

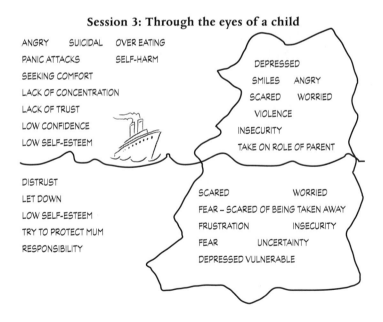

Figure 8.2 The iceberg exercise from a mothers' group: 'Through the eyes of a child'

> [The tip of the iceberg was] bad behaviour…but what was going on beneath the surface was all the hurt, the pain, the confusion but the bit that you saw was basically, 'God, what a horrible child!' (Mother)
>
> We once did this activity like – it was an iceberg…at the top it's quite small, but then under the sea it goes big…so like, if somebody feels quite, quite angry, then they've got a lot more feeling underneath. (Girl, aged 12)

Concurrent groups

Based on experiential rather than didactic learning, the concurrent approach can promote the insight, empathy and reframing that are essential to support more sustainable and transformational learning. Concurrent groups for mothers and children were also a form of motivation and a means of recruiting previously 'hard to reach' families. Involvement in groups gave mothers the opportunity to express their support for their children in a visible, practical and non-stigmatising way. The playfulness of the environment within the mothers' group and the mirroring of the content of the children's group underlined the fact that Cedar was ultimately for the children. In describing how Cedar brought about a transformation in her way of thinking and concrete changes in her parenting, one mother said: 'It's definitely through the eyes of a bairn [child], Cedar, isn't it?' It was important that mothers' groups took place before children's groups so that they could focus on what the children would be doing in their session. Experience suggests that constant attention should be paid to maintaining the balance in the mothers' group between the focus on the children and addressing mothers' personal issues.

Peer learning

The way that groups were run also generated the conditions in which both mothers and children could learn with and from their peers. Witnessing each other's experiences, children and mothers learned that the abuse was not their fault but an abuse of power which had served to isolate and control them: this realisation reduced self-blame and, with it, altered self-perceptions. As children and mothers listened to and took in others' narratives of suffering and resilience, they began tapping into their own agency to respond: hidden capacities to support others, which positively influenced self-perceptions, were revealed. To be able to give and receive peer support enhanced learning and promoted recovery for children and mothers. Such reciprocity is a unique resource for recovery from domestic abuse and a core element of the way that Cedar works.

The influence of Cedar on the mother–child relationship

Cedar helps to end the 'conspiracy of silence' around domestic abuse – 'the hurting and the shouting' – in the family; and for many it opened up new ways of talking about the past and relating to each other which were not charged with negative emotion.

The groups demonstrated a positive impact on children's and mothers' emotional literacy and capacity to form healthier family relationships through a new shared understanding of domestic abuse which made sense of the past:

> I learnt not to blame myself…plus I found a way to communicate with Fiona without screaming and losing my head… The house is a lot calmer. (Mother of 14-year-old daughter)

As the understanding of the effects of domestic abuse increased and communication improved, something like a cloud lifted from the family. This was expressed in terms of increased confidence, mixing more, playing with peers outside in the community, a change in a child's zest for life and handling bullying better.

Once relationships started to heal, there could be many spin-offs, including family members beginning to relax and enjoy being in each other's company. This further reinforced a positive sense of self-worth and well-being: 'I'm getting on better with my daughter and also it makes me feel that I'm worth something, whereas before it was a case of I'm no' [not] worth anything' (mother with teenage daughter).

Mothers tended to describe a greater degree of change in the mother–child relationship following the Cedar programme than their children. Where improvements were reported by younger children, they tended to be about improved communication with their mother in response to something they were distressed about – for example, an issue with another child. Some reported having a good relationship with their mother before they attended Cedar. The best outcome for teenagers and their mothers was acquiring a shared understanding about domestic abuse, which enabled them to communicate better:

> We understand each other a lot more now, so in a sense yes, we get on a lot better than we did...after the group we just understand what each other went through, so it's a lot more like she is my mum again kind of... I really just wanted a relationship with my mum and just to have a calm house and be able to just chill out basically, and that's what I got from the group anyway. (Girl, aged 14)

> He understands what I went through and I understand what he went through. So I think in that case, we can talk to each other more now... We sit down and have a conversation, so I think that helps. (Mother of a 13-year-old boy)

Older children reported being more able to deal with anger at a practical level, giving examples of how they acted or would act now in response to apparent provocation. Enhanced emotional literacy gave children and young people increased insight into their feelings and strategies to manage previously overwhelming feelings, particularly of anger. This learning, shared by their mother (and other siblings in larger families), led to changes in behaviour which introduced a less fraught atmosphere to the home.

However, it is important to acknowledge that mothers especially came to the groups with different starting points. For example, some women were just beginning to understand the nature and extent of abuse in their own childhoods, and they might therefore require more support to sustain improvements in the mother–child relationship and parenting in general. Outcomes for mothers were not secondary to those for the children and self-care for mothers was deemed to be important. A distinct advantage of Cedar is that it offers a non-stigmatising way for mothers to access more individualised support or, where needed, specialist drug and alcohol or mental health services towards the end of the programme when they felt optimistic about the future. It is crucial to capitalise on this to sustain the transformative influence of Cedar to maximise recovery from domestic abuse and childhood adversity.

Customising approaches to women and children in the aftermath of domestic abuse

Many women and children struggle with their relationship following separation from a domestically abusive man. However, the issues they confront may not be amenable to standard parenting programmes. In fact, women may be deterred or indeed insulted by the notion that parenting skills are required to strengthen and reinvigorate relationships undermined by domestic abuse. Reclaiming self-efficacy and confidence, recognising the impact of the past and finding a language to talk about feelings are issues which are consistently identified as critical by women and children. Perhaps more than anything else, finding 'normalcy', playfulness and spending time together without the spectre of fear casting a shadow over the relationship are key ingredients for recovery. The variability of the issues facing women and their children ideally requires a response, customised to the specific circumstances which have undermined the relationship and which can help to address the trauma and fear that have provided the backdrop and the conditions for mothering in circumstances of adversity.

Acknowledgements

With acknowledgement and thanks to Scottish Women's Aid (www.cedarnetwork.org.uk).

References

Bradley, R. H., Corwyn, R. F., McAdoo, H. P. and Coll, C. G. (2001) 'The home environments of children in the United States part I: variations by age, ethnicity, and poverty status.' *Child Development 72*, 6, 1844–1867.

Bunston, W. (2006) 'One Way of Responding to Family Violence: "Putting on a PARKAS".' In W. Bunston and A. Heynatz (eds) *Addressing Family Violence Programs: Groupwork Interventions for Infants, Children and Their Parents*. Melbourne: Royal Children's Hospital Mental Health Services for Children.

Casanueva, C., Martin, S., Runyan, D., Barth, R. and Bradley, R. (2008) 'Quality of maternal parenting among intimate-partner violence victims involved with the child welfare system.' *Journal of Family Violence 23*, 6, 413–427.

Debbonaire, T. (2007) *An Evaluation of the Sutton Stronger Families Group Treatment Programme for Children Exposed to Domestic Violence.* Ontario, Canada: Centre for Research on Violence against Women and Children.

Graham-Bermann, S. A., Lynch, S., Banyard, V., Devoe, E. R. and Halabu, H. (2007) 'Community-based intervention for children exposed to intimate partner violence: an efficacy trial.' *Journal of Consulting and Clinical Psychology 75*, 2, 199–209.

Holt, S., Buckley, H. and Whelan, S. (2008) 'The impact of exposure to domestic violence on children and young people: a review of the literature.' *Child Abuse and Neglect 32*, 797–810.

Humphreys, C. (2013) 'Responding to children living with family violence.' *VCOSS Insight 9*, 40–42.

Humphreys, C., Thiara, R. K. and Skamballis, A. (2011) 'Readiness to change: mother–child relationship and domestic violence intervention.' *British Journal of Social Work 41*, 1, 166–184.

Humphreys, C., Mullender, A., Thiara, R. K. and Skamballis, A. (2006a) *Talking to My Mum: A Picture Workbook for Workers, Mothers and Children Affected by Domestic Abuse.* London: Jessica Kingsley Publishers.

Humphreys, C., Mullender, A., Thiara, R. K. and Skamballis, A. (2006b) *Talking About Domestic Abuse: A Photo Activity Workbook to Develop Communication between Mothers and Young People.* London: Jessica Kingsley Publishers.

Humphreys, C. (2007) 'A health inequalities perspective on violence against women.' *Health and Social Care in the Community 15*, 2, 120–127.

Jordan, C., Campbell, R. and Follingstad, D. (2010) 'Violence and women's mental health: the impact of physical, sexual, and psychological aggression.' *Annual Review of Clinical Psychology 6*, 607–628.

Kitzmann, K., Gaylord, N., Holt, A. and Kenny, E. (2003) 'Child witnesses to domestic violence: a meta-analytic review.' *Journal of Consulting and Clinical Psychology 71*, 2, 339–352.

Laing, L. and Humphreys, C. (2013) *Social Work and Domestic Violence: Critical and Reflective Practice.* London: Sage Publications.

Lieberman, A. F., Ippen, C. G. and Van Horn, P. (2006) 'Child–parent psychotherapy: 6-month follow-up of a randomized controlled trial.' *Journal of the American Academy of Child and Adolescent Psychiatry 45*, 8, 913–918.

Loosley, S., Drouillard, D., Ritchie, D. and Abercromby, S. (2006) *Groupwork with Children Exposed to Woman Abuse: A Concurrent Group Program for Children and Their Mothers, Children's Program Manual.* Ontario, Canada: Children's Aid Society.

Marshall, L., Miller, N., Miller-Hewitt, S., Sudermann, M. and Watson, L. (1995) *Evaluation of Groups for Children Who Have Witnessed Violence.* London, Ontario: Centre for Research on Violence against Women and Children, Fanshawe College, London Coordinating Committee to End Woman Abuse and the University of Western Ontario.

Morris, A. (2009) 'Gendered dynamics of abuse and violence in families: considering the abusive household gender regime.' *Child Abuse Review 18*, 414–427.

Nixon, K. (2011) 'Children's exposure to intimate partner violence in Alberta, Canada: the construction of a policy problem.' *Journal of Policy Practice 10*, 4, 268–287.

Nolas, S. M., Neville, L. and Sanders-McDonagh, E. (2012) *Evaluation of the Community Group Programme for Children and Young People: Final Report.* Brighton: University of Sussex.

Radford, L. and Hester, M. (2006) *Mothering through Domestic Violence.* London: Jessica Kingsley Publishers.

Rivara, P., Anderson, M., Fishman, P., Bonomi, A., Reid, R. and Carrell, D. (2007) 'Intimate partner violence and health care costs and utilization for children living in the home.' *Paediatrics 120*, 6, 1270–1277.

Sharp, C., Jones, J. with Netto, G. and Humphreys, C. (2011) *We Thought They Didn't See: Cedar in Scotland – Children and Mothers Experiencing Domestic Abuse Recovery. Evaluation Report.* Research for Real. Available at www.cedarnetwork.org.uk/wp-content/uploads/2011/03/Evaluation-Report-DOWNLOAD1.pdf, accessed on 22 February 2015.

Wicks, P., Reason, P. and Bradbury, H. (2008) 'Living Inquiry: Personal, Political and Philosophical Groundings for Action Research Practice.' In P. Reason and H. Bradbury (eds) *The SAGE Handbook of Action Research, 2nd Edition.* London: Sage.

CHAPTER 9

Infant-led Practice

Responding to Infants and Their Mothers (and Fathers) in the Aftermath of Domestic Violence

Wendy Bunston

The inclusion of infants in the minds as well as the work places of practitioners engaged in addressing domestic violence is a recent phenomenon. In part, this has resulted from neuroscience demonstrating conclusively what many have always believed: that what happens in childhood lasts a lifetime (Carrion, Wong and Kletter 2013; Schore 2003b; Shonkoff 2010; Siegel 2012; Solomon and Heide 2005; Teicher 2002; Teicher *et al.* 2003). When violence occurs during infancy and early childhood, it is no longer a question of whether it impacts on neurobiological, social and psychological development rather it is how much and in what way (Schechter and Willheim 2009). Just how the infant is included in our work to address the impacts of domestic violence is informed by what is known as 'infant-led' practice (Bunston 2008a, 2008b; Thomson Salo 2007). This approach asks the worker to consider the infant as possessing their own subjectivity and agency and not to be seen simply as an extension of their parent (Thomson-Salo and Paul 2001). The infant is experienced as a new and emerging human being, dependent on as well as shaped by their caregiving environment, and capable of shaping that caregiving environment in return (Stern 2003). Further still, 'infant-led' work sees the infant as an active participant, offering possible entry points for creating therapeutic change in caregiving systems that have become unworkable (Thomson-Salo *et al.* 1999).

This chapter will explore how this important advance in our thinking has enhanced practices of working towards disrupting the impact and transmission of violence within intimate familial relationships. It will describe clearly what 'infant-led practice' involves, how research on infant development informs practice and will offer examples of how this has been undertaken with mothers in individual family work as well as within group work. It will also touch on work that has included fathers. Critical to 'infant-led' work in any area of practice, but particularly so in the area of addressing domestic violence, is ensuring the safety of the infant. Further examples will be included which illustrate the issues involved in keeping infants safe in mind and in practice.

Infant-led practice within a context of family violence

At first glance, the concept of 'infant-led' practice appears straightforward and can be simply interpreted as placing the infant front and centre in the practitioner's thinking and ensuring that their needs are met. For example, in order to work successfully with older children and young adults, we have learnt that we must first engage and then collaborate with them. Our dominant vehicle for negotiating this exchange is verbal. 'Infant-led' practice is more nuanced than this. This work largely remains in the preverbal domain. It is not about filling up the therapeutic space by just talking about the infant with the caregiver, but about truly working towards 'being with the infant' over 'doing things to' the infant (Bunston 2008b; Jordan 2011; Paul and Thomson-Salo 1997). Engaging with an infant involves demonstrating a gentle curiosity about them and inviting their participation. It is respectfully addressing the infant and awaiting reciprocal cues from the infant.

The infant responding to your smile, returning your gaze, a small hand extended: these may all be cues that an infant has registered your interest and is curious about you in return. We can all interpret meanings behind language, the intonation of speech, facial expressions and body language. Infants are highly attuned to their environments and are careful observers of those around them. They can also clearly signal their distress, their comfort or discomfort in the presence of others. Morgan (2007) suggests that infants need the therapeutic space to be safe, reliable and truthful. 'Safety' refers to the infant feeling safe within their internal world, 'reliability' to providing a relationship over time and 'truthfulness' to being available to what the baby thinks and feels. We may know much about infant work and parent work, but as Morgan notes:

We know nothing about this baby, we know nothing about this mother and this father, but we give them our full awareness, our thinking, our knowledge, so that something new can emerge for all of us who are involved in the work, for the baby, the mother, the father and for the therapist. (Morgan 2007, p.13)

The neuro-biology of trauma

Where the infant has been exposed to family violence, additional complexities come into play. Depending on the length, severity, type of and exposure to the violence, and the capacity or incapacity of the caregiving environment to protect or mediate the impacts of the violence, the infant may well have had been forced to rely on their own immature and very limited defences. Immediately post-birth, infants are particularly reactive to stress and within the first two years they are highly dependent on their caregiving system to co-regulate their emotional states as they begin learning to do so for themselves (Rifkin-Graboi, Borelli and Enlow 2009; Schore 2001). The younger the infant and the more frequent the exposure, the more likely the defence will be to shut down and disappear into a frozen, dissociative state (Schore 2003a).

Infancy is a time of immense neuro-biological development and all energy and resources at the infant's disposal are directed towards growth. In circumstances of severe stress, with no available or adequate safe haven, the infant literally needs to hide, to shut down and conserve energy should it be needed to respond to danger. The need to safeguard and to conserve energy leads to an under-stimulation or under-use of important synaptic connections that are rapidly developing to shape the form and function of neural development (Siegel 2001). We are still coming to understand more fully the adverse effects of intimate partner violence on the baby in utero (Quinlivan and Evans 2001; Sarkar 2008). Rifkin-Graboi et al. (2009) suggest that the newborn has limited memories of extreme stress and in novel experiences stress reactivity is 'likely to be driven more by evolutionarily based predispositions and other individual characteristics of the infant' (p.60).

It is when traumatic and frightening experiences are repeated, however, that the infant comes to expect certain responses, behaviours or interactions from their caregiving environment and adapts their responses, behaviours and interactions accordingly:

The generally held belief in neural science is that the patterns of neuronal connections determine the ways in which the brain functions and the mind is created... It is in this manner that interpersonal experiences directly shape the genetically driven unfolding of the human brain. (Siegel 2001, p.72)

Repeated early exposure to trauma and violence influences neural pathways and, ultimately, the hardwiring of the brain. As Perry *et al.* (1995) note, accumulative emotional states brought on by trauma become 'personality traits' over time. As Arvidson *et al.* (2011, p.38) explain:

For young children, traumatic experiences may occur prior to the acquisition of expressive language skills. Young children may lack a specific, identifiable traumatic event and do not have the skills necessary to process trauma through a coherent, sequential, verbal narrative. Trauma processing with young children often occurs in the moment when a child experiences heightened physiological reactions. The restoration of internal safety happens when the child's distress is identified, validated, and modulated by a caregiver.

The caregiving environment is the incubator within which infants grow their capacity to communicate what they are feeling. How well this 'caregiving incubator' functions depends to a considerable extent on the experiences, past and present, that shape the relational world of the caregivers.

Practice implications

It is often not only the infant who is overwhelmed by ongoing violence. Both infant and mother may be traumatised, compromising the ability of both to effectively process their emotions. Further, each may even act as a trigger for the other (Schore 2001). What we might effectively offer is ourselves as something of an intermediary. No matter the support role we offer (i.e. counsellor, group facilitator, family support, refuge worker), we can learn to be more available and present to both mother and infant. We offer our mind, our relationship and our presence to sit with both infant and mother in order to facilitate communication. We, for that moment, become part of the caregiving system and add something new. We can 'be with' (contemplative) their world rather than 'do' something to it (reactive).

Notwithstanding the importance of 'doing', particularly in instances of immediate crisis or danger, making space 'to be' can leave workers feeling unprotected and powerless (Bunston 2011; Bunston and Sketchley 2012). Our ability to recognise and sit with such powerful feelings (to think about our feelings and theirs) may provide real and invaluable insights into what the infants and mothers we work with are feeling. Taken a step further, sometimes our timely ability to sensitively put words to those feelings, not as givens but as gentle questions, may bring out in the open a feeling state that can then be processed (tolerated and thought about) together.

Ironically, a 'doing' developmental activity associated with infancy is the importance of learning routines, such as quickly settling an infant into sleeping and eating patterns. This is something seen as even more critical for an infant exposed to family violence (Arvidson *et al.* 2011). The safety of creating respectful routines is to be encouraged as long as one is cognisant of the fact that exposure to relational violence also creates its own routines. Infants shutting down can replicate the infant 'going to sleep'. Just placing a traumatised infant in a cot and away from their caregiver may be countertherapeutic. They may need instead to be near a soothing presence, rather than left alone to manage such overwhelming and frightening feelings. Within a refuge setting, for example, should the mother herself be highly agitated, it may be the most calm, responsive and comforting person present who can offer immediate relational and physiological relief to that infant, whilst also remaining a calming presence for the caregiver.

Infants can become quickly attuned to the signals of 'what is to come'. We need to endeavour to learn from the infant what their own unique routines have involved, and to pick up on the signals they might give us about what they have come to expect from their world. This involves waiting, watching and wondering about what might be happening for the infant (Cohen 2006). For example, certain smells (alcohol), sounds (slamming doors), sights (broken toys) or relational triggers (mother pulling back as their infant approaches) can all arouse a cascade of sensory and physiological memories. More important than our desire to set up a new routine for them is to first come to know the infant and understand what triggers their stress and what alleviates it. Following a routine should not take precedence over coming to understand their world and exploring what allows them to feel safe and encourages their growth and exploration. Even if we get it wrong, or if their mother misses the mark, growth occurs when we genuinely seek to get it right and together strive to repair relationships (Tronick 2007).

'The principles of regulation theory that apply to the mother–infant relationship also apply to the clinician–patient relationship' (Schore 2005, p.211). They apply to all relationships which are significant to us as we exist and are shaped in relationship to others, and none more so than in infancy (Cozolino 2006). Our being with this infant and this mother therapeutically is not about educating: it is about learning, ours and theirs. We can offer relational capacity building by relating to the infant in the context of their relationship with their mothers, and fathers, leaving an imprint of difference in how to be with each other. This is what we strive for, to enhance and support thinking and relating to support what 'good enough' caregiving can offer (Winnicott 2005).

> Coordinated visual eye-to-eye messages, auditory vocalizations, and tactile and body gestures serve as channels of communicative signals that induce instant emotional effects... Attachment communications, therefore, are 'built into the nervous system', inducing substantial changes in the developing brain. (Schore 2005, p.207)

Importantly, this approach is not intended to exclude the urgent imperatives of what an infant needs physically. If we see that an infant is 'at risk' through lack of adequate care, physically and/or mentally, we also need to be able to act quickly and respond accordingly. The five-week-old infant who is losing weight, or is not regularly bathed and covered in sores, or who is put down to sleep in unsafe bedding or left unattended for hours, needs our minds to recognise that this infant is suffering. As committed as we are to the mothers and fathers, who may themselves present horrific backgrounds of trauma, who may seem little more than youngsters (particularly teenage parents) and who may still be 'at risk', the infant is fully dependent on the care of others. It is sobering to acknowledge that infancy is when we are most vulnerable, with the risk of death greater than at any other time during childhood and adolescence (AIHW 2012; Brandon *et al.* 2008).

Applying what we know to our practice with infants

This section is intended to illustrate how the theory and approaches described above can be used in practice. Space allows for the following case examples to be cursory only, providing a strand of what occurs in the work overall, but each aims to illustrate critical elements of the work undertaken. Building on the ideas of offering an available, reflective mind and calm and attuned presence, these examples will explore how to be with infants and their mothers. This is illustrated both within a group and individual context and is drawn from work undertaken within a child and adolescent mental health programme based at a children's hospital in Melbourne, Australia. A two-tiered group work programme, PARKAS (Parents Accepting Responsibility Kids Are Safe), was originally developed to address the impacts of domestic violence on children and their mothers (Bunston 2001, 2002). It soon became apparent that both the children and the mothers themselves had experienced violence from early childhood and a much earlier intervention response was needed. A community-based infant/mother group work intervention called the Peek-A-Boo Club was soon developed along with a refuge-based programme called BuBs on Board (Bunston 2006, 2008a; Bunston and Glennen 2008).

It is also important to note that infant-led work in the context of domestic violence can often be very time limited, particularly where a mother and her child or children have become homeless as a result of leaving the relationship. Whilst this work should not be rushed, this does not mean that it cannot be respectfully bold and open to offering opportunities to avert and begin to process trauma from the very first contact. How well this is done comes with confidence, practice and, most importantly, by accessing good supervision (Bunston 2013a; Bunston, Pavlidis and Leyden 2003).

Case Study: Darcy

Mary had left an extremely violent relationship some six weeks before I met her. She and her two children Darcy (16 months) and Matilda (30 months) had engaged with a family support worker who was worried about what the children had witnessed and wished to refer the family to an infant/mother group. Mary was very reluctant to attend a group but agreed to an initial one-off session for herself and the children.

The referring worker offered to wait in the reception area but it was very apparent that the whole family wanted her to participate in the session and the worker, subsequently, became a very important player in the work. A total of six sessions were completed with this family as transitional housing was found for them in a different region two months after the work commenced.

Darcy was not yet walking unaided and tended to crawl around the room. Every so often he would suddenly become stiff and, facing head down with his legs together and resting on his toes, he would balance on his elbows in a plank position. He would remain in this position for some 60 to 80 seconds then just as suddenly resume his crawling. On other occasions Darcy would appear to suddenly get cramp and he would curl up and become very agitated and distressed. After these two things occurred, I asked Mary what she thought was happening for Darcy. Mary explained that she had taken him to see a doctor and a specialist who felt his difficulties were bowel-related but that tests had not been able to prove anything conclusively.

When Darcy cramped up, Mary would attempt to comfort him, asking what was wrong, but this had little success and she would then look towards me helplessly as if to say, 'what can I do?' The hypothesis held by his mother and specialist was that Darcy was most likely constipated so they were endeavouring to treat these symptoms by attending to his diet. Whilst it was clearly important to undertake a full medical assessment of Darcy, there did, however, appear to be little capacity to contemplate that there might be a psychological explanation for Darcy's symptoms. Mary had told the two children that they were on holiday, not that they had left their father or why. Matilda would often ask after her daddy and when they would see him. Mary avoided answering this question and would endeavour to distract her or change the topic.

It was very difficult for this family unit to talk about what had happened to them and particularly to talk about the father. This work was conducted on the floor, sitting on cushions and with toys and space for the infants to explore. When Darcy moved into his 'plank position', I lay next to him and wondered aloud if it was hard not to see his dad, and hard for the family to talk about some of the painful and frightening things about their dad. I wondered if perhaps it was so painful for Darcy that it made him feel stuck inside. Words were eventually found to begin to talk about some of the fear, sadness and trauma they had all experienced. Mary remained very reluctant to share too much, particularly in relation to her own past, but she began to talk to the children about why they were no longer living at home and why they were not returning home. Their worker used what occurred in the sessions to continue making space for this family to give words to what they might be feeling outside of the sessions.

This description of the work undertaken intends to give a flavour of what was involved in trying to 'be with' and make meaning out of what Darcy might be communicating, rather than 'doing to' Darcy. Darcy's symptoms did abate and Mary and the children experienced something new – the idea that these two infants had very powerful emotional material and responses (to what had happened at home and to losing their father) that were not being processed. My curiosity about her infants in turn led to Mary being curious about me, what I was doing and why. This resulted in her becoming more contemplative about their internal rather than their external worlds. The family support worker was very effective in bringing this same level of thoughtfulness into her own work with the family, and although this did not 'cure' or resolve their trauma, it perhaps made it a little more bearable.

Case study: Pia

Pia, 14 months old, had been removed from her parents' care and was residing with another family. Child protection services wished to explore partial reunification with her mother, Arna, and referred the two to our infant/mother group. Arna presented herself as a very loud and sometimes frightening figure. We undertook a thorough assessment session with Pia and Arna (and asked the child protection worker to sit out of this session) before accepting Pia into the group. As with all our assessment sessions, we spoke honestly and clearly about our mandate (and commitment) to report if we found an infant was 'at risk' of harm. We made it very clear to Arna and the child protection worker that we would not proceed with Pia in the group if we felt her mother's presence proved too overwhelming for her, given their lengthy separation from one another. We also made it very clear to Arna and the worker that we were not there to assess their relationship for the courts and we would not meet separately with the worker (as child protection had requested) to emphasise that they, Pia and Arna were our clients, not child protection services.

Arna possessed a very engaging sense of humour and was a very big presence in the group. She was very vocal about Pia's father's violence and about how she would not tolerate his 'rubbish', often giving him 'as good back'. Pia was a very self-possessed little girl, and whilst it was evident that she recognised her mother, she did not use her, or any other mother, for social referencing or support and seemed able to cue very quickly into the facilitators as the more reliable caregivers in the room. As the dynamics of the group settled into their own rhythms, we were able to observe how Pia and Arna related to one another, how Arna would rush at Pia and then back off, offended at her approach not being reciprocated. We were also able to pick up Pia's very tiny cues, how she would circle around her mother, occasionally look at her and, when Arna failed to notice, move on to somewhere else.

We offered some reflections out loud when we started to 'catch those moments' and expressed our curiosity about how this little family might begin to 'safely' get to know each other again. A significant moment occurred in the group some three weeks in when Arna began to criticise Pia's father, using very colourful and offensive language. One of the facilitators (who had formed a very positive relationship with Arna) boldly jumped in and very genuinely stated that she found that language too much, that it was not OK to speak like that in front of the infants, the mothers or the facilitators. She also reflected that it put Pia in a really tough place as she had regular supervised access with her father, and by all reports this was positive. This did not discount the violence Arna had experienced nor absolve Arna of the violence she had exposed Pia to herself.

Much discussion was had in supervision later that day about 'that moment' and the facilitator's anxiety that maybe she had said too much and perhaps lost Arna from the group. It would appear that it did the reverse: there was a marked change in Arna from that moment on and we were able actively to help Arna within the group to 'self-regulate' and reflect on what she did that made it easier for Pia to make her tentative approaches towards her, and what pushed her away. Arna was still able to talk about her distress over Pia's father but in such a way that it did not frighten Pia (or anyone else). There was a marked shift in their relationship and the beginning of a 'getting to know' one another within the group, with Pia even taking to sitting in her mother's lap. Placing Pia's needs and safety as central, building a strong rapport with Arna by not partnering with child protection services but by partnering with Arna and Pia as a dyad, and then negotiating an open relationship with child protection services brought in new ways of being with each other.

Case study: Benny

Benny was a little over two when I started to see him and his mother, Jenny, for individual work. He struggled with some developmental delays and had seen his father physically assault his mother on numerous occasions. His father, John, had a diagnosed mental health difficulty and could be erratic in taking his medication. Jenny still loved John but felt she had to leave him in order to create some stability for herself and Benny. I had been seeing Benny and his mother for over 12 months and Jenny was reporting that there had been much improvement in the relationship between Benny and his dad, in part due to her setting firm limits around when he could visit and clear expectations about how he should behave with Benny. It appeared that John loved Benny very much and was keen to comply with Jenny's expectations and form a positive relationship with his son.

Alongside this work, I had been developing and running a group work intervention for fathers (who had been through a men's behaviour change programme) and their infants (Bunston 2013b). I had previously worked jointly with some fathers and children (Bunston 2001, 2008b) and had some positive outcomes, so I was keen to explore how to bring fathers, who were motivated to change, safely into the therapeutic space. I had previously discussed with Jenny the possibility of including John in a session even though John had not attended any counselling for himself. Despite Jenny's scepticism and an initial refusal, John did eventually agree to attend a session. I was introduced to John by Jenny, and Benny very excitedly showed his father around the room, the toys he played with, and tried to engage his father in one of the regular games we played together.

John began to play with one set of toys, then moved on quickly to something else and then another, a pattern Benny had displayed when first beginning counselling, but which had decreased with him showing a much greater attention span and depth of imaginative play over the past six months. The session seemed to proceed a little awkwardly but well enough, until I began to ask more direct questions of John and about his childhood. As I focused on John, I missed seeing Benny's cues and his warnings. I could see John tensing up and not liking my questions, but it was not until Benny came up to me and hit my arms, saying 'don't talk to my daddy', that I realised how anxious Benny had become and that he had been showing me how acutely he was cued into his father's moods and ability to become volatile. I backed off from where I had been taking the session and returned to taking my lead from Benny.

That was the first and last session I had with John (he made it clear that he would not return) and I have spent much time reflecting on the implications of this session. There is much that can be taken from this session, discussed and questioned: was it right or wrong for me to have included his father? I was concerned that I had made unsafe a space which had become very safe for Benny and his mother, and I was much relieved when Benny bounced into the next session and greeted me with his usual enthusiasm. We discussed what had happened and I suggested that I had perhaps put my interest in including John ahead of what Benny and Jenny needed or wanted. On reflection, I think I lost sight of Benny in my mind and in the room. This does not mean that I want to dispel the thought of fathers who have been violent out of the counselling space, as such rigidity is not helpful for the infant, mother or counsellor. Fathers are and remain critical figures who can ideally be integrated in a healthy way into the emotional world of the infant, psychologically if not in person. It does mean that this work needs to be approached cautiously, and with greater consideration than I showed in this instance.

Bringing 'Dads on Board' in our work with infants

A much more positive example of including fathers in the therapeutic space has comprised the development of a groupwork programme for fathers after their involvement in a men's behaviour change programme (Bunston 2013b). This involved two eight-week pilot projects for fathers which involved both the infant and, in all but one case, the mother of the infant. This work saw the fathers better equipped to move into more self-reflective work. These fathers had made a public commitment to address their violent behaviours and had become accustomed to the structure which accompanies participating in a groupwork process. When fathers have not been willing or available or it has clearly not been appropriate to involve them in this work, it has been important to bring the capacity to think and talk about the infant's father into the therapeutic space in order to think about their meaning and significance for the growing infant. This can enable the infant to derive some goodness from that relationship and tolerate that which had been destructive (Jones and Bunston 2012).

Fathers, as with mothers, are a reality in the infant's life, although for some fathers this may be only through their role in the infant's conception. Whether the father lives with or has court-ordered access with their child, or through the growing child's imaginative creation of their father and how this real or imagined relationship is internalised, this shapes the person that the child grows into. Our job is to work with infants, children and their families to find ways to bring honour safely to the significance of these attachments, irrespective of how we may judge them.

Conclusion

'Infant-led' work operates in the realm of discovery. It replicates the conditions applicable to enabling an infant to grow and develop safe relationships with their caregiving environment and with their sense of self. The key, integral ingredients needed include: providing a safe base, ensuring the infant comes to no harm and being available, through relationships, to discover and make meaning. The presence of violence, often predating these ingredients, means that infant-led work in the context of violence requires a greater sensitivity to and thoughtfulness about ensuring that both the external world and internal world are safe to enter and work in. It is about facing the infant's truth, with its often overwhelming complexity, and not running from the complexity. Instead, holding still and offering something of ourselves that is reliable and reflects back something new and nourishing to the infant and in their relationships with their mother and father.

References

AIHW (2012) *A Picture of Australia's Children 2012.* Canberra: Australian Institute of Health and Welfare. Available at www.aihw.gov.au/WorkArea/DownloadAsset. aspx?id=10737423340, accessed on 22 February 2015.

Arvidson, J., Kinniburgh, K., Howard, K., Spinazzola, J. *et al.* (2011) 'Treatment of complex trauma in young children: developmental and cultural considerations in application of the arc intervention model.' *Journal of Child and Adolescent Trauma 4*, 1, 34–51.

Brandon, M., Belderson, P., Warren, C., Howe, D. *et al.* (2008) *Analysing Child Deaths and Serious Injury through Abuse and Neglect: What Can We Learn? A Biennial Analysis of Serious Case Reviews 2003–2005* (DCSF-RR023). UK: Department for Children, Schools and Families. Available at http://dera.ioe.ac.uk/7190/1/dcsf-rr023.pdf, accessed on 22 February 2015.

Bunston, W. (2001) *PARKAS: Parents Accepting Responsibility Kids Are Safe.* Victoria, Australia: MHSKY.

Bunston, W. (2002) 'One way of responding to family violence: "putting on a PARKAS".' *Children Australia 27*, 4, 24–27.

Bunston, W. (2006) 'The Peek a Boo Club: Group work for infants and mothers affected by family violence.' *The Signal 14*, 1, 1–7.

Bunston, W. (2008a) 'Baby lead the way: mental health groupwork for infants, children and mothers affected by family violence.' *Journal of Family Studies 14*, 334–341.

Bunston, W. (2008b) 'Who's Left Holding the Baby: Infant-Led Systems Work in IPV.' In J. Hamel (ed.) *Intimate Partner Violence and Family Abuse.* New York, NY: Springer Publishing Company.

Bunston, W. (2011) 'Let's start at the very beginning: the sound of infants, mental health, homelessness and you.' *Parity 24*, 2, 37–39. Available at http://search.informit. com.au/documentSummary;dn=908022936502962;res=IELFSC, accessed on 22 February 2015.

Bunston, W. (2013a) 'The Group Who Holds the Group: Supervision as a Critical Component in a Group with Infants Affected by Family Violence.' In L. M. Grobman and J. Clements (eds) *Riding the Mutual Aid Bus and Other Adventures in Group Work.* Harrisburg, PA: White Hat Communications.

Bunston, W. (2013b) '"What about the fathers?" Bringing "Dads on Board™" with their infants and toddlers following violence.' *Journal of Family Studies 19*, 1, 70–79.

Bunston, W. and Glennen, K. (2008) '"Bub" on board: family violence and mother/ infant work in women's shelters.' *Parity 21*, 8, 27–31.

Bunston, W., Pavlidis, T. and Leyden, P. (2003) 'Putting the GRO into groupwork.' *Australian Social Work, 56*, 1, 40–49.

Bunston, W. and Sketchley, R. (2012) *Refuge for Babies in Crisis.* Melbourne, Australia: RCH-IMHP. Available at www.bswhn.org.au/attachments/article/629/Refuge%20 for%20Babies%20Manual%20FinalWEB.pdf, accessed on 22 February 2015.

Carrion, V., Wong, S. and Kletter, H. (2013) 'Update on neuroimaging and cognitive functioning in maltreatment-related pediatric PTSD: treatment implications.' *Journal of Family Violence 28*, 1, 53–61.

Cohen, N. J. (2006) 'Watch, wait, and wonder: an infant-led approach to infant–parent psychotherapy.' *The Signal: Newsletter of the World Association for Infant Mental Health 14*, 2.

Cozolino, L. (2006) 'The social brain.' *Psychotherapy in Australia 12*, 2, 12–16.

Jones, S. and Bunston, W. (2012) 'The "original couple": enabling mothers and infants to think about what destroys as well as engenders love, when there has been intimate partner violence.' *Couple and Family Psychoanalysis 2*, 2, 215–232.

Jordan, B. (2011) 'Focusing the lens: the infant's point of view. Discussion of "Brief interventions with parents, infants, and young children: a framework for thinking."' *Infant Mental Health Journal 32*, 6, 687–693.

Morgan, A. (2007) 'What I Am Trying to Do When I See the Infant with His or Her Parents.' In F. Thomson-Salo and C. Paul (eds) *The Baby as Subject, 2nd Edition.* Melbourne: Stonnington Press.

Paul, C. and Thomson-Salo, F. (1997) 'Infant-led innovations in a mother-baby therapy group.' *Journal of Child Psychotherapy 23*, 2, 219–244.

Perry, B., Pollard, R., Blakley, T., Baker, W. and Vigilante, D. (1995) 'Childhood trauma, the neurobiology of adaptation, and "use-dependent" development of the brain: how "states" become "traits".' *Infant Mental Health Journal 16*, 4, 271–291.

Quinlivan, J. A. and Evans, S. F. (2001) 'A prospective cohort study of the impact of domestic violence on young teenage pregnancy outcomes.' *Journal of Pediatric and Adolescent Gynecology 14*, 1, 17–23.

Rifkin-Graboi, A., Borelli, J. L. and Enlow, M. B. (2009) 'Neurobiology of Stress in Infancy.' In C. H. Zeanah Jr (ed.) *Handbook of Infant Mental Health, 3rd Edition.* New York, NY: Guilford Press.

Sarkar, N. N. (2008) 'The impact of intimate partner violence on women's reproductive health and pregnancy outcome.' *Journal of Obstetrics and Gynaecology 28*, 3, 266–271.

Schechter, D. S. and Willheim, E. (2009) 'The Effects of Violent Experiences on Infants and Young Children.' In J. C. H. Zenah (ed.) *Handbook of Infant Mental Health.* New York, NY: Guilford Press.

Schore, A. (2001) 'The effects of early relational trauma on the right brain development, affect regulation, and infant mental health.' *Infant Mental Health Journal 22*, 1–2, 201–269.

Schore, A. N. (2003a) *Affect Dysregulation and Disorders of the Self.* New York, NY: W. W. Norton & Company.

Schore, A. N. (2003b) *Affect Regulation and the Repair of the Self (Vol. 2).* New York, NY: W. W. Norton & Company.

Schore, A. N. (2005) 'Back to basics attachment, affect regulation, and the developing right brain: linking developmental neuroscience to pediatrics.' *Pediatrics in Review 26*, 6, 204–217.

Shonkoff, J. P. (2010) 'Building a new biodevelopmental framework to guide the future of early childhood policy.' *Child Development 81*, 1, 357–367.

Siegel, D. J. (2001) 'Toward an interpersonal neurobiology of the developing mind: attachment relationships, "mindsight", and neural integration.' *Infant Mental Health Journal 22*, 1–2, 67–94.

Siegel, D. J. (2012) *Developing Mind: How Relationships and the Brain Interact to Shape Who We Are.* New York, NY: Guilford Press.

Solomon, E. P. and Heide, K. M. (2005) 'The biology of trauma: implications for treatment.' *Journal of Interpersonal Violence 20*, 1, 51–60.

Stern, D. N. (2003) *The Interpersonal World of the Infant: A View from Psychoanalysis and Developmental Psychology.* London: Karnac Books.

Teicher, M. H. (2002) 'Scars that won't heal.' *Scientific American 286*, 3, 68–75.

Teicher, M. H., Andersen, S. L., Polcari, A., Anderson, C. M., Navalta, C. P. and Kim, D. M. (2003) 'The neurobiological consequences of early stress and childhood maltreatment.' *Neuroscience & Biobehavioral Reviews 27*, 1–2, 33–44.

Thomson-Salo, F. and Paul, C. (2001) 'Some principles of infant–parent psychotherapy: Ann Morgan's contribution.' *The Signal 9*, 1–2, 14–19.

Thomson-Salo, F., Paul, C., Morgan, A., Jones, S. *et al.* (1999) '"Free to be playful": therapeutic work with infants.' *Infant Observation 3*, 1, 47–62.

Thomson-Salo, F. (2007) 'Relating to the Infant as Subject in the Context of Family Violence.' In F. Thomson-Salo and C. Paul (eds) *The Baby as Subject, 2nd Edition.* Victoria, Australia: Stonnington Press.

Tronick, E. Z. (2007) *The Neurobehavioral and Social-Emotional Development of Infants and Children.* New York, NY: W. W. Norton & Company.

Winnicott, D. W. (2005) *Playing and Reality.* New York, NY: Routledge Classics. (Original work published Tavistock Publications, 1971.)

PART FOUR

Working with Abusive Fathers

CHAPTER 10

Focusing on Fathering in the Context of Domestic Abuse

Children's and Fathers' Perspectives

Stephanie Holt

Introduction

The past three decades have witnessed significant developments in domestic abuse research, policy and practice, not least in the expansion of the lens of research and practice interest to include a consideration of the scope and consequences of children's exposure to domestic abuse. This has resulted in a depth of empirical knowledge about its prevalence and the impact this experience has on its youngest victims (Stanley 2011). In tandem with this developing empirical knowledge base there is a growing interest in and awareness of the role of fathers in family life and in child development (Lamb 2004).

The influence of fathers on child development is such that children with highly involved fathers are understood to demonstrate increased cognitive abilities and empathy, less stereotyped beliefs and a greater internal locus of control (Lamb 2004), with the absence of fathers considered harmful for children as it is argued that many aspects of the fathering role subsequently remain unfulfilled (Lamb 1997). Whilst the absence of fathers from children's lives has been mooted as a significant problem for their healthy development (Lamb 2004), other research finds the mere presence of fathers in children's lives not enough to promote children's well-being (Amato and Gilbreth 1999). Amato and Gilbreth (1999) conclude that this arises from the diverse nature of paternal relationships because, for example, we can assume that an abusive or withdrawn and distant paternal relationship will have a significantly different impact on child outcomes than a relationship with a devoted and responsive father. The quality of a father's involvement is therefore the significant factor affecting child well-being and predicting child adjustment, not the extent of such involvement (Amato and Gilbreth 1999). Although there has been a relative lack of attention to the father–child relationship in domestically violent families (Guille 2004), what little information does exist paints a picture concerning negative fathering practices combined with poor outcomes for children (Bancroft and Silverman 2002).

Cognisant of these debates and developments, this chapter focuses on the impact of domestic abuse on fathering and the father–child relationship from the perspectives of the two key players in that dyadic relationship. This chapter draws on doctoral research conducted by the author in the Republic of Ireland. The research highlights the potentially deleterious impact that both the absence of parental contact *and* ongoing and perhaps unwanted contact with an abusive father can have on the developing child. This chapter also reflects a commitment to honouring the principle of 'listening to the voice of the child' as required by Ireland's National Children's Strategy (Department of Health and Children 2000) by recognising and accepting children as active, sentient social actors in the unfolding story of their ongoing development in family life.

The fathering of domestically abusive men

Empirical evidence regarding the father–child relationship in domestically violent families characterises these fathers as individuals with low self-esteem and a poorly developed sense of identity, resulting in neediness, dependency, self-absorption, a lack of trust in others and an inability to see the impact of their violence on their children (Bancroft and Silverman 2002; Rothman, Mandel and Silverman 2008). They are described as physically punitive but not physically affectionate (Holden and Richie 1991), employing more disciplinary and less constructive parenting behaviours than their non-violent equivalents (Fox and Benson 2004). Research also highlights the complex relationships these children have with both of their parents (Levendosky *et al.* 2003). Peled's research (1998) with 14 pre-adolescent children found them implementing strategies to both minimise the negative view of their fathers *and* find ways to see their fathers in a positive light. Both strategies evoked complex emotions when it came to making choices involving their parents.

Post-separation contact is a potentially abusive experience for children who are 'caught in the crossfire' (Kernic *et al.* 2005, p.991) and who are exposed to the physical, sexual and psychological abuse of their mother during contact visits (see Chapter 7 in this book; Radford, Sayer and AMICA 1999; Saunders and Barron 2003). A strong correlation exists between child contact and child physical and/or sexual abuse, with Australian research finding this typically to involve multiple forms of abuse 'at the more severe end of the child abuse continuum' (Brown and Alexander 2007, p.14). Furthermore, there is a growing concern about maternal and child deaths connected to child contact arrangements (Holt 2008; Saunders 2004). Arriving late or not at all for contact, not spending time with their children and rigidity around arrangements that are unresponsive to children's changing needs are commonly cited examples of poor post-separation fathering and contrary to those characteristics of parenting identified as central to the achievement of quality contact (Reece 2006; Smart 2004; Trinder, Beck and Connolly 2002). Jaffe, Crooks and Balo's (2005) review of the literature cautions that contact facilitates children's exposure to poor role modelling whilst Peled (2000) reminds us that the 'instrumental approach' of abusive men's post-parenting behaviour results in a construction of fatherhood in terms of 'rights to' children with little emphasis on nurturing (Smart 2004).

Fox, Sayers and Bruce's (2002) qualitative study with eight perpetrator programme participants found the men expressing complex and diverse feelings concerning their fathering, including guilt, shame, regret and accountability, whilst participants in Perel and Peled's (2008) research reflected on their longing for close relationships with their children. This yearning existed alongside restriction, distance and absence. Indeed, Perel and Peled's (2008) research identified the many ways in which the men constructed their image as a good father through their perceived role as providers, protectors and educators. Both their actual and perceived paternal aspirations were, however, eclipsed by numerous personal limitations and difficulties, including childhoods characterised by absent, distant and emotionally challenged fathers who were simultaneously aggressive, controlling and abusive (Perel and Peled 2008). Krampe (2009, p.882) uses the term 'connection' to refer to a father's involvement in the child's life, indicating that this connection implies more than physical presence, and this concept is perhaps best encompassed in what Krampe (2009, p.875) refers to as 'psychological presence', signifying psychological nearness and accessibility to the child.

These somewhat conflicting descriptions of fathering demand that we consider abusive men as fathers through a dual lens of harm and vulnerability (Perel and Peled 2008). Whilst fathers are identified as craving a deep and meaningful relationship with their children (Harne 2004), generally reflective of more contemporary fathering practices (Lamb 1997), they are also found to be influenced by more traditional (less emotionally involved) approaches to fathering (Perel and Peled 2008). This contradiction was found to be particularly heightened for violent fathers (Perel and Peled 2008). Concerns regarding the capacity of abusive men to change and take responsibility for their behaviour (Buchbinder and Eisikovits 2008) need to be acknowledged, as does the limited insight abusive men have demonstrated into the impact of their behaviour on their children (Harne 2004).

However, there is a marked absence of consideration of the fathering of abusive men in perpetrator programmes and as yet limited evidence about the effectiveness of programmes for abusive men who are fathers (Peled 2000). The proposals made for a new approach to measuring outcomes on such programmes in the chapter by Alderson, Kelly and Westmarland included in this volume are relevant here. Perel and Peled (2008) argue that interventions for perpetrators may facilitate change but that this change can occur only when they both acknowledge and take responsibility for their behaviour and are actively attempting to stop it. With the research evidence establishing that abusive men are rarely able to prioritise their children's needs over their own (Sturge and Glaser 2000), Perel and Peled (2008) conclude that abusive men should be viewed simultaneously as dangerous and needy, and that this requires denunciation of their abusive behaviour whilst responding to their vulnerability.

Participation or protection? Constructing children within the contact debate

The debate concerning children's participation in decision making regarding contact has been heavily focused on the issue of competence (Pryor and Rodgers 2001). However, research participants as young as five have clearly demonstrated that they can articulate, through a variety of means employed to elicit their views, age-appropriate understandings of what has been happening in their family. Furthermore, they can provide coherent and rational reasoning to support their position on contact with their father (Holt 2011; Kilkelly and Savage 2012). Research also finds that even when children expressed unhappiness with their current arrangements for contact – this did not necessarily mean they wanted an end to contact – in fact very few did so. Rather they expressed a deep yearning for a different kind of relationship with their father – a meaningful relationship that could exist independently of their parents' relationship (Holt 2011).

Despite clear rhetorical commitment to the concept of children's rights (Roche 1999), as evidenced by the international and domestic embracing of the UNCRC, the research on post-separation contact highlights a rather conservative approach to protecting rather than empowering children and they continue to be viewed through a protectionist lens (Mantle *et al.* 2007). Kaganas and Day Sclater's (2004) observation, that how children are understood or constructed in terms of their capacity or their vulnerability determines how they are responded to, resonates loudly from a review of the research. A clear commitment to a protectionist or welfare agenda (Mantle *et al.* 2007) is grounded in the belief that such involvement makes 'unreasonable demands on their maturity' (Pryor and Rodgers 2001, p.112), manifesting itself in considerable ambivalence and concern expressed about the appropriateness of children's involvement in this domain. Neale (2002) condemns this orientation for critically limiting children's participation, whilst Laing (2006) asserts that claims to proceed in the child's best interests cannot be valid where the child's view is not sought, heard or considered.

Research methods

Both quantitative and qualitative data collection methods were employed for the research which was conducted over two phases. Phase one collected survey data from separated mothers accessed through a national network of Irish services providing refuge and outreach services to women and children experiencing domestic abuse. The survey involved the completion of two questionnaires: one by 147 mothers of 317 children who were or had been engaged in post-separation contact with their fathers over the previous year. The other was completed by 72 mothers whose 132 children had not been engaged in contact over the same period. Data were systematically collected in respect of a 'number of variables' broadly concerned with the prevalence of post-separation contact. These variables captured socio-demographic familial details and contact arrangements; the child's involvement in the decision-making process; the use of domestic violence orders; mothers' satisfaction with contact arrangements; the extent and nature of professional supports and child and women protection and welfare concerns.

Phase two of the study sought in-depth understanding of the phenomenon of contact as it was directly experienced by all those concerned. Focus group interviews were chosen as the primary method for interviewing the children, mothers and professionals, with individual interviews the chosen method for interviewing fathers. The phase two sample was sourced through professional gate-keepers. Participants included 16 children and young people, nine mothers, six fathers and 30 legal, health and social care professionals. Whilst some of the mothers and children were from the same family, none of the fathers were related to any of the mothers and children. Cognisant of the emotional well-being of participants, the sampling criteria were restricted to families where the parents had been separated for at least one year prior to participation in the research interview.

Whilst initial access to the children and young people was facilitated through the participating organisations and with parental consent, the researcher also secured the informed consent of the children and young people themselves. Relevant ethical approvals were also obtained. Sixteen children and young people (five male and 11 female) aged between seven and 24 participated in focus groups, individual or sibling group interviews which utilised age-appropriate vignettes to stimulate discussion.

Discussion of findings

Overview of contact experience

The findings of this research paint a largely negative picture of contact for the majority of participating mothers, fathers and children, confirming concerns for the continued abuse of women and children through contact (Buckley, Holt and Whelan 2007). Echoing Radford and Sayer's (1999) research with a similar (though smaller) sample of domestic abuse survivors, analysis of phase one data found child protection and welfare concerns expressed by mothers for 68.7 per cent of the 147 families or for 62.5 per cent of the 317 children engaged in contact. The predominant concern emerging across both phases of the research was for the emotional welfare of children engaged in contact, representing 74 per cent of all child protection and welfare concerns noted in the survey sample. Participants across both phases of the research described children's continuing exposure to the verbal abuse and derogation of the mother, when contact was being arranged, at hand-over points and during contact. Children clearly articulated their distress at hearing this abuse, their efforts to stop it and their sense of powerlessness when they were unable to, as this child explained:

> I feel torn between Mum and Dad, because I always want to see him but when I do see him, he's talking about Mum and it makes me feel a bit awkward really. (Robert, 8)

Post-separation fathering – the child's perspective

In common with the children in Smart's (2004) research, children described contact arrangements that they felt reflected their father's need for control, with a marked absence of reciprocity in the parent–child relationships and an absence of nurturing as highlighted by Peled (2000). For example, one participant described an arrangement where she and her sisters telephoned their father at set times each week. Outside of those calls she noted:

> He never ever rings us, never ever. Sometimes when he is in a mood he won't even be bothered talking to us. (Rachel, 11)

In a similar vein, Ciara (9) and Todd (7) reported that they were allowed only one telephone contact with their mother when staying overnight with their father, something Ciara described as particularly distressing because she was struggling with mental health issues that she needed her mother's support with:

> Sometimes even when I am really upset and need to talk to her, Dad won't let me. (Ciara, 9)

This may be an indication of their father's difficulty in accepting his role as the non-resident parent and giving permission to their mother to be the primary carer, a task Trinder *et al.* (2002) identified as integral to functional post-separation parenting. It may also be a reflection of the low self-esteem of abusive men (Bancroft and Silverman 2002) when a child's expressed need for their primary parent is experienced by the contact parent as rejection (Smart 2004).

Participating children and young people expressed a level of both apathy and frustration with contact, with their father's lack of interest in them and unwillingness to spend time with them fuelling their indifference and irritation. Unreliability and unpredictability were also something that children began to anticipate, as this young participant explains:

> Sometimes he makes up an excuse and then he doesn't see us…so we're just hanging around for ages waiting. (Cathy, 9)

The quality of the father–child relationship was a determining dynamic affecting the contact experience for most, if not all, of the young participants. For example, Eva (16) and her sister Leah (12) introduced the idea of a 'proper' dad, and were very clear about what this entailed, as this extract from their interview illustrates:

> To be a 'proper' dad, he doesn't have to bring us anywhere, he doesn't have to spend anything, we just wouldn't have to feel awkward around him, we could actually talk to him, just being in the same room as him and not being all tense and awkward. (Eva, 16)
>
> … And feel like you have to talk to fill in the gaps. (Leah, 12)

'Being there' in the above quote implies more than physical presence, and is conveyed by Krampe's terms 'psychological presence' (2009, p.875) or 'connection' (p.882), a concept that arose frequently in this research. One father, Steve, considered that his children were 'always on my mind. I need to connect with them all the time.' Reflecting on her experiences of being fathered, Eva (16) conversely stated that her father 'doesn't know me; he knows nothing about me or my life', whilst her sister, Leah (12), asserted that 'he might be my father but it takes a lot more to be my dad and he is not in my life'.

Reflecting existing research (Peled 2000), the conflicting feelings of love and hate, of yearning for and rejection of a fathering relationship also emerged with clarity from the children's narratives:

> Lots of the time I really, really, hate him, but at the end of the day, he is still my dad. (Rachel, 11)

Fathering and being fathered – the fathers' perspectives

The six participating fathers in this research identified fathering as one of the most significant facets of their lives. However, previously established concerns about the capacity of men to change their abusive behaviour and their limited insight into that behaviour also emerged (Buchbinder and Eisikovits 2008). Whilst four of the six participating fathers acknowledged their abusive relationship with their child's mother, some did so more openly and extensively than others. Their responses ranged from guilt and shame at what they had exposed their children to, to a sense of injustice and indefensible marginalisation from their children's lives. Resonating with Rothman *et al.*'s (2008) research, there were clear indications that whilst some of the men could demonstrate insight into how their behaviour had impacted on their children, this insight was not always accompanied by a willingness or perceived need to alter that behaviour. For example, Brian stated that he was only attending the perpetrator programme so that this might positively influence his application for increased contact, whilst Luke, who was incarcerated at the time of interview for holding his ex-partner hostage at knifepoint in front of their children, asserted that she needed help with her parenting and that he was the 'good' parent.

All the fathers' narratives were tainted with a deep sense of loss, but for some this was more heavily flavoured with deep-seated resentment and bitterness at what they saw as their ex-partner's vindictiveness in preventing them seeing their child, without acknowledging that their behaviour towards their ex-partner had resulted in the decision for contact to be supervised.

The arrangements for contact were regulated by a court order for three of the six fathers interviewed, but two of those fathers could neither understand nor accept the restrictions imposed. They experienced restricted contact as revengeful behaviour by their ex-partner and co-parenting as obstructing their fathering. The role of provider was highlighted by all participating fathers as an important facet of their fathering role, and by mothers and children as a mechanism by which fathers could continue to exercise control over the family finances. The 'provider' role was somewhat resentfully engaged in by one father who equated the provision of maintenance with a 'charge' for seeing his child:

> A tenner an hour to see my kid, that's what it feels like. How can I be a father in four hours a week? She wants me to have nothing to do with him, but she'll take the money. (Brian, father)

The above quote reflects Brian's construction of his partner as 'malicious' for restricting his time with his child, but without the recognition that his violence might render him 'dangerous'. Furthermore, Holden and Richie's (1991) assessment of abusive men as physically punitive but not physically affectionate, employing more disciplinary but less constructive parenting behaviours than their non-violent equivalents, resonated in this research. Two children said they could not recall their father ever hugging them or telling them he loved them. Nine-year-old Ciara concluded that her father 'just doesn't care at all', whilst thirteen-year-old Kate stated: 'he can hardly take care of himself – how can he take care of us too?' Implicit in this is a question of capacity, specifically the capacity of abusive men to rise to the challenges inherent in fathering.

For all participating fathers, 'hope' was cited as a coping mechanism, couched in their aspirations for their future or potential fathering. The inherent contradiction between their expressed yearning for closeness and the concerns raised by the participating women and children allow us to question whether their parenting ambitions were a means to continue contact with a partner they had previously abused.

The men's descriptions of their parenting poignantly mirrored their recollections of their own experiences of being parented, an experience grounded in traditional fathering discourses (Perel and Peled 2008). Their accounts of their childhoods were characterised by absent, distant and emotionally challenged fathers who were also intermittently aggressive and abusive. For example, Steve spoke about a childhood where his father was 'never there', whilst Tom also reflected on parental absence for the first 13 years of his life, when he was brought up by his grandmother as his mother 'couldn't cope', later returning to a family he had no relationship with when his grandmother died.

Children's participation in decision making about contact

In respect of a child's competence, the question is often raised as to whether children can articulate an understanding of what is happening in their family, why their parents are separated and what their wishes are in relation to contact with their father. The young participants in this research clearly demonstrated that they could articulate, through a variety of means, age-appropriate understandings of what was happening in their family and could provide coherent and rational reasoning to support their position on contact with their father, as this nine-year-old explains:

> Visits should be about the kids, not the adults. (Sara, 9)

They could also lucidly explain why they didn't enjoy spending time with their father, as another nine-year-old commented:

> Parents aren't supposed to say mean horrible things and make you feel bad. My dad makes me feel bad and stupid but my mum doesn't. Mum says me and Todd are the most important things in her life… I know that's true 'cos she doesn't make me feel bad and stupid. (Ciara, 9)

And they were able to describe the type of relationship they wanted with their father:

> All we ever wanted was a proper dad, and that's not rocket science… he just has to spend time with us. (Eva, 16)

They also expressed a need to be informed in an inclusive manner about what was happening to their family and varying levels of desire to have a choice in their participation in that debate.

Overwhelmingly, the articulate, insightful data drawn from the children's interviews in this research concur with Butler *et al.*'s (2002, p.99) view that 'they are also the most reliable witness of their own experience' and this also confirms their competency to understand and manage their post-separation lives. Where they were consulted, the overwhelming experience of those children was that their views were neither listened to nor taken seriously, as Todd explains:

> We didn't want to spend time with him [father] at all. The guy
> [psychological assessor] did [listen] but the judge didn't [listen].
> (Todd, 7)

It was clear from the interview process and from analysis of their narrative
that where children had either been given a choice, or been allowed to
exercise their will not to have contact, and this wish was respected by the
court, their sense of empowerment and self-esteem was palpably evident,
as Eva explains:

> When we wrote that letter to him saying we didn't want to see him
> anymore because he just kept hurting mam and that hurt us too and
> we just couldn't take any more…it's hard to explain but it's always
> been his move, like in chess, we were always waiting for his move…
> it feels now that we have check-mated him and he doesn't know
> what to do 'cos that never happened before. (Eva, 16)

Finally, there were also some children and young people who had become
so disillusioned with their relationship with their father, or lack of it, that
they had either ended contact or wished it to end. This quote from Eva
poignantly illustrates this position:

> I don't really believe in fathers, I think they're a bit useless but
> that's just because of our experience but maybe some of them could
> be OK, and they should be investigated properly, and have proper
> detailed statements from children whether or not they want to
> see them, instead of assuming it was good for you and you'd miss
> out otherwise. They thought we were missing out…but how can
> you miss something if you never rightly had it? I've never had it
> [relationship with father] so I can't miss it. (Eva, 16)

The findings concur with those of Laing (2006) who observes that
claims to proceed in the child's best interests cannot be valid if the child's
view is not sought, heard or considered. Given the lack of professional
attempts to engage with children, the findings of this research therefore
question how children's competency to participate can be adjudicated on
in the absence of any attempt to engage them meaningfully in the debate.
This research found a potent blanket exclusion of children of any age
participating in the decision-making process and a subsequent denial of
real participatory rights.

Conclusion

This chapter concludes by confirming previously expressed concerns about the quality of parenting of abusive fathers, their compromised insight into their children's needs and their capacity to put those needs before their own (Sturge and Glaser 2000). Whilst many of the children and young people had 'father presence' in their lives, their narratives concurred with Pyror and Rodgers' (2001) assertion that 'the mere presence of fathers is not enough', with participants describing regular yet rigid visits with fathers who were angry or simply lacked the fundamental skills to interact with their children. There was no evidence of commitment to post-separation fathering and fathering capacity; moreover, the absence of 'father presence' from the epicentre of the children's lives rendered the father'child relationship meaningless for many of the young participants. In common with the testaments of the children in Mullender et al.'s study (2002), children participating in this research clearly articulated their distress, their sense of powerlessness and their constant watchfulness and fear of what could or might happen. This research questions whose needs contact was meeting and whose rights were being acknowledged in situations where a focus on equal parenting and the contact period provided abusive men with legitimate opportunities for continued abuse of their ex-partner, whilst simultaneously denying the child their right to adequate and appropriate parenting during contact.

As in other studies (Fox et al. 2002), the fathers participating in this research expressed a deep yearning for a better quality of relationship with their children. Whilst their capacity to achieve that was not possible to establish within the remit of this study, what was clear was that the potential for abusive men to become better fathers cannot be accommodated or responded to within a system that only recognises vulnerability arising from their absence and not the vulnerability and risk that accompany their presence. A lack of attention to abusive men as fathers, or alternatively viewing them as either abusive men or fathers, not only undermines the support and protection needs of mothers and children, but also fails to challenge the potential of 'good enough' fathering through the provision of an infrastructure of interventions for all of the key players involved. This chapter challenges those charged with supporting, protecting or regulating the lives of the key players involved in contact to focus on the reality of abusive men's behaviour rather than an ideology of involved fatherhood. This requires a significant paradigm shift to prioritise the construction of fathers as 'risk' in the context of post-separation father–child contact. Doing so does not mean prioritising means of excluding fathers from children's lives; rather, what is critical is to find ways to ensure that abusive men can be 'good enough' fathers. This involves acknowledging and addressing the continued presence of domestic abuse and holding abusive men accountable for their abusive partnering and parenting whilst simultaneously viewing them through a dual lens of risk and vulnerability.

The findings from this research also identify a particular construction of children as vulnerable and in need of protection. When they were given a voice through the medium of this research, children and young people clearly indicated that they did not want protection from the debate and the decision-making process. Instead, they spoke of their wish and need for meaningful and active involvement in decisions that affected their lives and they reflected on how their life experiences had been compromised as a result of their exclusion from the decision-making process that had determined contact arrangements with their fathers. What came across clearly in the accounts of participants who engaged either with the survey or interview process is that children felt their voices were seldom heard, and, if they were heard, usually discounted (Mantle *et al.* 2007).

This chapter argues that promoting children's welfare by protecting them from involvement in the process is somewhat akin to closing the stable door after the horse has bolted and adds further insult to the injury of their invisibility within the domestic abuse domain. Concurring with other observers (Butler 2002), it is palpably apparent that children *are* already involved in the process of their parents' separation or divorce and that, furthermore, the reality of their exposure to domestic abuse has been emphatically established and remains unquestioned. This experience therefore needs to be acknowledged and respected. Roche (1999) asserts that this respect is reflected in their right to participate in a debate which, after all, is about them. This, however, requires a repositioning of children as central to this debate so they do not continue to be silenced victims in an ideological battle fought on their behalf but in the absence of their voice.

References

Amato, P. R. and Gilbreth, J. G. (1999) 'Nonresident fathers and children's well-being: a meta analysis.' *Journal of Marriage and the Family 61*, 3, 557–573.

Bancroft, L. and Silverman, J. G. (2002) *The Batterer as Parent: Addressing the Impact of Domestic Violence on Family Dynamics.* New York, NY: Sage.

Brown, T. and Alexander, R. (2007) *Child Abuse and Family Law: Understanding the Issues Facing Human Service and Legal Professionals.* Crows Nest, NSW: Allen & Unwin.

Buchbinder, E. and Eisikovits, Z. (2008) 'Doing treatment: batterers' experience of intervention.' *Children and Youth Services Review 30*, 6, 616–630.

Buckley, H., Holt, S. and Whelan, S. (2007) 'Listen to me! Children's experiences of domestic violence.' *Child Abuse Review 16*, 5, 296–310.

Butler, I., Scanlan, L., Douglas, G. and Murch, M. (2002) 'Children's involvement in their parents' divorce: implications for practice.' *Children & Society 16*, 2, 89–102.

Department of Health and Children (2000) *National Children's Strategy: Our Children, Their Lives.* Dublin: The Stationery Office.

Fox, G. L., Sayers, J. and Bruce, C. (2002) 'Beyond bravado: redemption and rehabilitation in the fathering accounts of men who batter.' *Marriage and Family Review 32*, 3, 137–163.

Fox, G. L. and Benson, M. L. (2004) 'Violent Men, Bad Dads? Fathering Profiles of Men Involved in Intimate Partner Violence.' In R. D. Day and M. E. Lamb (eds) *Conceptualizing and Measuring Father Involvement.* Mahwah, NJ: Lawrence Erlbaum.

Guille, L. (2004) 'Men who batter and their children: an integrated review.' *Aggression and Violent Behaviour 9*, 2, 129–163.

Harne, L. (2004) 'Childcare, Violence and Fathering: Are Violent Fathers Who Look after Their Children Likely to Be Less Abusive?' In R. Klein and B. Wallner (eds) *Gender, Conflict and Violence.* Vienna: Studien Verlag.

Holden, G. W. and Richie, K. L. (1991) 'Linking extreme marital discord, child rearing, and child behaviour problems: evidence from battered women.' *Child Development 62*, 2, 311–327.

Holt, S. (2011) 'Domestic abuse and child contact: positioning children in the decision-making process.' *Journal of Child Care in Practice 17*, 4, 327–346.

Holt, S. (2008) 'Domestic Violence and Child Contact: Issues and Dilemmas for Child Protection and Welfare Practice.' In K. Burns and D. Lynch (eds) *Child Protection and Welfare Social Work: Contemporary Themes and Practice Perspectives.* Dublin: A & A. Farmer.

Jaffe, P. G., Crooks, C. V. and Bala, N. (2005) *Making Appropriate Parenting Arrangements in Family Violence Cases: Applying the Literature to Identify Promising Practices.* Canada: Department of Justice.

Kaganas, F. and Day Sclater, S. (2004) 'Contact disputes: Narrative constructions of "good" parents.' *Feminist Legal Studies 12*, 1, 1–27.

Kernic, M. A., Monary-Ernsdorff, D. J., Koepsell, J. K. and Holt, V. L. (2005) 'Children in the crossfire: child custody determinations among couples with a history of intimate partner violence.' *Violence against Women 11*, 8, 991–1021.

Kilkelly, U. and Savage, E. (2012) 'Legal and Ethical Dimensions of Communicating with Children and Their Families.' In V. Lambert, T. Long and D. Kelleher (eds) *Communication Skills for Children's Nurses.* London: Open University Press, Magreaw Hill House.

Krampe, E. M. (2009) 'When is the father really there? A conceptual reformulation of father presence.' *Journal of Family Issues 30*, 7, 875–897.

Laing, K. (2006) 'Doing the right thing: cohabiting parents, separation and child contact.' *International Journal of Law, Policy and the Family 20*, 2, 169–180.

Lamb, M. E. (ed.) (1997) *The Role of the Father in Child Development, 2nd Edition.* Toronto: John Wiley & Sons.

Lamb, M. E. (ed.) (2004) *The Role of the Father in Child Development, 4th Edition.* New York, NY: Wiley.

Levendosky, A. A., Huth-Bocks, A. C., Shapiro, D. L. and Semel, M. A. (2003) 'The impact of domestic violence on the maternal–child relationship and preschool-age children's functioning.' *Journal of Family Psychology 17,* 3, 275–287.

Mantle, G., Moules, T., Johnson, K., Leslie, J., Parsons, S. and Shaffer, R. (2007) 'Whose wishes and feelings? Children's autonomy and parental influence in family court enquiries.' *British Journal of Social Work 37,* 5, 785–805.

Mullender, A., Hague, G., Iman, U., Kelly, L., Malos, E. and Regan, L. (2002) *Children's Perspectives on Domestic Violence.* London: Sage.

Neale, B. (2002) 'Dialogues with children: children, divorce and citizenship.' *Childhood 9,* 4, 455–475.

Peled, E. (2000) 'Parenting of men who abuse women: issues and dilemmas.' *British Journal of Social Work 30,* 1, 25–36.

Peled, E. (1998) 'The experience of living with violence for pre-adolescent children of battered women.' *Youth and Society 29,* 4, 395–430.

Perel, G. and Peled, E. (2008) 'The fathering of violent men: constriction and yearning.' *Violence against Women 14,* 4, 457–482.

Pryor, J. and Rodgers, B. (2001) *Children in Changing Families: Life after Parental Separation.* Oxford: Blackwell Press.

Radford, L., Sayer, S. and AMICA (1999) *Unreasonable Fears? Child Contact in the Context of Domestic Violence: A Survey of Mothers' Perceptions of Harm.* Bristol: Women's Aid Federation of England.

Reece, H. (2006) 'UK women's groups' child contact campaign: "So Long as it is Safe".' *Child and Family Law Quarterly 18,* 4, 538–561.

Roche, J. (1999) 'Children and Divorce: A Private Affair?' In S. Slater and C. Piper (eds) *Undercurrents of Divorce.* Aldershot: Dartmouth.

Rothman, E. F., Mandel, D. G. and Silverman, J. G. (2008) 'Abusers' perceptions of the effect of their intimate partner violence on children.' *Violence against Women 13,* 11, 1179–1191.

Saunders, H. (2004) *Twenty-Nine Child Homicides: Lessons Still To Be Learnt on Domestic Violence and Child Protection.* Bristol: Women's Aid Federation of England.

Saunders, H. and Barron, J. (2003) *Failure to Protect? Domestic Violence and the Experiences of Abused Women and Children in the Family Courts.* Bristol: WAFE.

Smart, C. (2004) 'Equal shares: rights for fathers or recognition for children?' *Critical Social Policy 24,* 4, 484–503.

Stanley, N. (2011) *Children Experiencing Domestic Violence: A Research Review.* Dartington: Research in Practice.

Sturge, C. and Glaser, D. (2000) 'Contact and domestic violence – the experts' Court Report.' *Family Law 30,* 615–629.

Trinder, L., Beek, M. and Connolly, J. (2002) *Making Contact: How Parents and Children Negotiate and Experience Contact after Divorce.* York: Joseph Rowntree Foundation.

CHAPTER 11

Expanding Understandings of Success

Domestic Violence Perpetrator Programmes, Children and Fathering

Sue Alderson, Liz Kelly and Nicole Westmarland

> *Dear Dad,*
>
> *I think that our family is happier now that you have stopped being angry with Mum. Can you be sorry to her and us? Can we do things together like play football and computer games.*
>
> *I love you lots, From P (age 7)*
>
> *Dear Dad,*
>
> *Please don't argue with Mum anymore. Every time you get angry can you please go and calm down in your room on your own. When you are nice and calm all our family is happy and we can go for a nice sunny walk and have a picnic.*
>
> *Lots of love G (age 7)*
>
> *To Dad,*
>
> *I love you so much but when you have finished [the course] would you be sorry and would you argue with Mum again?*
>
> *Lots of love from R (age 8)*

These are letters that three of the 13 children we spoke to wrote to their fathers as part of Project Mirabal – our multi-site longitudinal research on British Domestic Violence Perpetrator Programmes (DVPPs – known as Batterer Intervention Programs (BIPs) in the US or Men's Behaviour

Change Programs (MBCs) in Australia). This chapter describes how and why we integrated fathering and children into the core of the research and how the children we talked to felt about their father attending the DVPP. The aim of the chapter is to widen how outcomes for children in relation to DVPPs are understood.

On invisible fathers

Talking about men who are violent and abusive is a good place to start when thinking about domestic violence and children. This is because we have spent many decades talking about increasing safety for women and children, yet we have hardly any research into what, if anything, makes men stop using violence against their partners and children. As we have argued elsewhere (Westmarland and Kelly 2012), too little attention has been given to domestic violence perpetrators in discussions of women and children's safety.

Many have pointed to the problem of 'invisible fathers' – Brown *et al.* (2009) talk about 'ghost fathers' and Edleson (1998) of 'responsible mothers and invisible men'. As a consequence, whilst practitioners may work with the woman to try to support her to keep the children safe, children's services might threaten to remove the child or children from their mother and police might give advice about keeping safe and installing monitoring equipment and alarms, the direct naming of men's violence against women happens infrequently and interventions with men of any type (DVPPs, police arrest, prison, etc.) remain rare. Stanley *et al.* (2011) found that when children's services receive a referral from the police for domestic violence, the woman, as a mother, becomes the focus of the intervention or assessment by social workers in the vast majority of cases (44 out of 46 of the cases they examined). The Fathers Matters 3 review (Roskill *et al.* 2011) found two key themes relevant to this chapter: first, that social workers failed to assess fathers and other male figures in the child's life and, second, that fathers were marginal to planning, to professional involvement and were rarely explicitly challenged about their behaviour.

The British government's Troubled Families programme (covering England only) takes the invisible father narrative even further and deeper – hiding men's violence against women and children under the rubric of a 'troubled family'. They define 'troubled families' as 'those that have problems and cause problems to the community around them, putting high costs on the public sector' (Department for Communities and Local Government 2014). Throughout the programme, domestic violence has been simultaneously 'there' and 'not there' – a 'deafening silence' as Romito (2008) would call it. For example, the goals of the programme are to: (1) get children back into school; (2) reduce youth crime and anti-social behaviour; (3) put adults on a path back to work; and (4) reduce the high costs these families place on the public sector each year. However, the majority of 'case studies' used in the official reports talk about domestic violence as a central problem and the Troubled Families programme director, Louise Casey, has herself said:

> Violence appears in many cases to be endemic – not just domestic violence between parents but violence between siblings, between parent and child, outside the house and inside the house. Violence, verbal and physical abuse was described in an almost matter-of-fact way. (Casey 2012, p.2)

Crossley (2014) highlights that despite the above statement, domestic violence was excluded from the initial criteria and the programme's official documents tend to marginalise the issue. He also problematises both the payments-by-results approach when working with domestic violence and the suitability of the whole family approach which lies at the heart of the Troubled Families programme.

Failing to name and make visible violent men reinforces the idea that it is possible to be a 'bad partner' (who uses violence and abuse) yet still be a 'good father'. This came through clearly in the interviews we did with men on DVPPs at the beginning of their time on a programme:

> I'm a good parent, I'd spend every second I had with my son. Play, read, that wasn't a problem. I was good at that. (Matthew, interviewed in Project Mirabal)

> I could have been better as a husband, but as a father, as a dad, I can't be faulted for that one. (Max, interviewed in Project Mirabal)

Project Mirabal – widening understandings of 'success'

Project Mirabal is a large programme of research into British non-criminal justice DVPPs funded by the Economic and Social Research Council, Northern Rock Foundation and Lankelly Chase Foundation. It compares over time a group of women whose partners or ex-partners have attended a DVPP with a second group of women whose partners or ex-partners had not attended a DVPP (and where one was not available in their locality). We also conducted in-depth interviews with men on programmes and partners or ex-partners of men on programmes near the start and the end of their attendance.[1] The overall aim of the research was to explore what DVPPs add to coordinated community responses to domestic violence.

In Project Mirabal, we move away from the notion of 'no more violence' or 'programme completion' as the core outcome measure of 'success':

> Success…means far more than just 'ending the violence'. It would be quite possible for the physical violence to stop but at the same time for women and children to continue to live in unhealthy atmospheres which are laden with tension and threat. (Westmarland, Kelly and Chalder-Mills 2010, p.16)

In a pilot study we conducted 73 interviews with women partners/ex-partners, men attending DVPPS, practitioners (men's workers, women's workers and children's workers) and DVPP funders and commissioners. From these interviews, we developed six measures of success which we operationalise as a set of indicators within the main body of the research.

Of significance for this chapter is that four of the measures (3, 4, 5 and 6) directly relate to children. As such, children have been integral rather than an 'add on' to Project Mirabal – something we have been very committed to as a research team from the beginning. We have discussed these measures and why we need to start thinking more broadly about what 'success' means in relation to DVPPs elsewhere (Westmarland *et al.* 2010; Westmarland and Kelly 2012). Here, we will summarise the four that directly reference children.

---

1   For more information about Project Mirabal see www.dur.ac.uk/criva/projectmirabal.

PROJECT MIRABAL MEASURES OF SUCCESS

1. An improved relationship between men on programmes and their partners/ex-partners which is underpinned by respect and effective communication.

2. For partners/ex-partners to have an expanded 'space for action' which empowers them through restoring their voice and ability to make choices whilst improving their well-being.

3. Safety and freedom from violence and abuse for women and children.

4. Safe, positive and shared parenting.

5. Enhanced awareness of self and others for men on programmes, including an understanding of the impact that domestic violence has had on their partner and children.

6. For children, safer, healthier childhoods in which they feel heard and cared about.

Measure 3 – safety and freedom from violence and abuse for women and children

This is perhaps the most obvious of the measures, given that for women and children being and feeling safer is one of the official objectives of most DVPPs. Following Stark's (2009) work in the US about the importance of freedom, and the way that women participating in our pilot study talked about wanting to be able to have 'normal arguments' and for them and their children to no longer live in fear of violence, we include 'freedom from' the threat of violence as well as actual safety within this measure.

Measure 4 – safe, positive and shared parenting

This measure refers to parenting being safe – for example, for unsupervised contact to be able to take place and for mothers to be able to trust fathers to take children out or take care of them alone. It also entails having more frequent family activities and men being generally more attentive to and interested in the lives of their children. The majority of the women we interviewed desperately wanted their partner or ex-partner to be a better parent for the sake of their child or children, regardless of the relationship they had with them.

For example, one woman described how she managed her time to ensure she was home before the children got in from school in order to prevent friction between them and their father. She explained that whilst he didn't use physical violence against them, he just 'didn't show any interest' in them and do the things that are part and parcel of being a parent: 'when you're a parent you end up doing an awful lot of stuff you would rather not be doing, don't you?... He'd sort of say "oh, no no no!" and I'd say [name of man] that's not very nice, she wants you to take her.' Hence, it was not just safe parenting that was important, but positive and shared parenting.

Measure 5 – enhanced awareness of self and others for men on programmes, including an understanding of the impact that domestic violence has had on their partner and children

The idea of violent men saying 'sorry' for their behaviour towards women and children can seem glib to some. However, the man's ability to listen, empathise and understand what life had been like for those living under his regime of control was important to many of the women and children. This is reflected in the opening letter at the beginning of this chapter where R expresses a wish for his father to be 'sorry'.

Measure 6 – for children, safer, healthier childhoods in which they feel heard and cared about

Although this measure has obvious overlaps with the other measures – particularly 3 and 4 – we felt that it was important to have one measure that related directly and solely to children. Whilst children's safety has in recent years become more central to the work of DVPPs, since men are increasingly referred by children's social services and from the family court, safety goes deeper than physical safety and encompassed physical and emotional health and well-being, happiness, freedom from fear and/or having to protect their mother or siblings.

At the time of writing, we cannot report the quantitative results showing to what extent women reported that men did change in relation to these measures, but that is not the intent of this chapter. Rather we want to explore what focusing on children in work with perpetrators might accomplish.

Impacts in group work

For many men, the sessions on the impact of domestic violence on children and fathering were linked to their motivation to change. It has long been practice-based knowledge that there are two modules in DVPP group work which evoke the strongest responses from men: one on sexual respect, and one on the impact of living with domestic violence on children. It is in these modules that men sometimes walk out, and the material can produce strong denials and a lack of willingness to even consider that they could have acted in these ways. Added to this, some of the men have themselves lived through childhoods involving domestic violence. Having been adamant that they would not act in a way that would harm their children, and adopting a protective masculinity, the realisation that they have harmed their children can be a shock. Most DVPPs have specific exercises using role play or videos which place men in the position of a child observing or overhearing abuse. A common variant is to get the men to sit on the floor, close their eyes and think back to when they were a child. The facilitators then act out a loud, violent argument in the background. The discussion explores how the men felt overhearing it, and from here how their own children might feel:

> I think they get an awakening when they do the [children's] module on the programme. When they can see themselves as they were as children, then that is a wakeup call... It does reduce some of the men to tears. It gets them to think 'that was me as a child'. (DVPP men's worker)

Such emotional responses also enable men to begin to understand children's behavioural changes that did not initially seem to be connected to the way they acted towards their partner or ex-partner. For example, Brendan explained in his second interview that his partner had been struggling with poor behaviour from their four-year-old son. He had at first situated himself as the 'good parent' as the child tended to be well behaved for him but naughty for his mum. However, later he reflected that the child had seen him showing disrespect to his partner:

> I think through the programme I learnt the fact that [my son] didn't have to be in the same room. He didn't probably have to be in the same house. He would pick up on tension just like dogs do, animals do and other people do. He will have...probably seen disrespect between me and his mum.

A common response – reported by men themselves and by their female partners – was that their children were too young to be affected. Here, one programme participant is adamant in the first interview, completed when he was just starting the programme, that his behaviour had not had any impact on his baby:

> *Interviewer: Do you think the abuse between you and your partner affected your daughter?*
>
> Desmond: No, because if we were loud enough to wake her up she would start crying, but we would stop at that point and sort her out. Like, we wouldn't continue arguing when she was awake.

This position meant that this man was unable later in the same interview to provide an example of how his abuse might have affected his daughter. In his second interview, however, a shift of perspective was evident:

> *Interviewer: What do you understand now about the effects to children of being part of an abusive relationship?*
>
> Desmond: That it doesn't matter how old the bairn [child] is really... when there's arguing it doesn't matter whether they're asleep or not, they are still going to hear it and its still going to – it's definitely going to affect them.
>
> *Interviewer: Before the programme did you think this?*

Desmond: I wouldn't have realised that…'cause obviously when I was with [name of partner], [baby] was only six months old – so like during the programme I realised how much it can affect them things like that, even at that age.

What the data on men's engagement with DVPPs show is that some men are strongly and profoundly affected by content which challenges them to recognise what it is like for children to live with abuse. This echoes research by Stanley, Graham-Kevan and Borthwick (2012), which found that children could function as a form of intrinsic motivation – whereby men saw their attendance on a programme and their improved understanding of the impact of abusive behaviour on children as a way of becoming a 'better father'. Similarly, Stanley *et al.* (2012) found that men in the community asked to inform a social marketing campaign targeting men's violence towards women rated 'effects on children' as the most highly effective message they thought would motivate men to change.

Listening to the voices of children

As well as asking questions about children, Project Mirabal also included the voices of a small number of children. Thirteen interviews were undertaken with six boys and seven girls aged between seven and 16 years old whose fathers had recently completed or were close to completing a DVPP. All the children were receiving support from a children's workers linked to the DVPP at the time they were interviewed, and this is how invitations to participate were issued (using a child-focused participant information sheet). Rather than a formal interview, children were invited to complete a 'research book' with the support of a researcher. The research book was bright and colourful and presented in a cartoon format with lots of pictures and space for children to draw their own pictures. If the children were slightly older, the research book was adapted so the same questions were asked but the child was not required to do the pictures if they did not want to. The workbook took the children through questions such as what life was like before their father/father figure attended the DVPP how they were told about his attendance on the DVPP, how they felt before compared with after the DVPP, and how safe they felt.

Life before the DVPP and finding out about it

The children were asked to draw a face and write a word that indicated how they felt about their father before he attended the DVPP. By far, the most common response to this question was that children felt 'sad' (see also Mullender *et al.* 2002). One said she was annoyed, another wrote 'grrrr' and one child drew a face and wrote 'confused, didn't know what was happening' – as shown in Figure 11.1. The children were generally aware of the domestic violence.

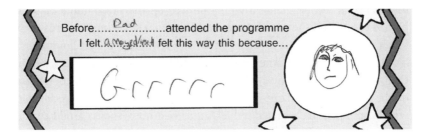

Figure 11.1 Example of feelings from research book

As we have discussed elsewhere, there was no consistent process by which the children were informed, or when they were informed, about their father's participation on a DVPP (Alderson, Westmarland and Kelly 2012). This significantly reduced the potential number of children we could talk to as part of our research, since we were only able to approach children who were aware that their father was attending a DVPP (however, even here, a variety of terms was used to describe it, e.g. 'working with Dad', 'helping Dad get better'). The children were asked how they felt when they became aware of their father's attendance at the DVPP. Almost all the children said they had high hopes that their father's behaviour would change.

The children were also asked to draw a face and indicate a word that described how they felt once they became aware that their father was attending the DVPP. Responses included, 'happy', 'happier', 'it would help him', 'hopeful'. Whether it was their mother or father who told them, the act of being told about their father's participation on the DVPP was extremely important to the children and perceived as commensurate to a promise that the violence would stop.

Feelings towards and activities with their father

The children were asked to circle a list of feelings relating to how they felt about their father prior to attending DVPP and how they felt at the time of interview (which took place near or at the end of the programme). Seventeen different feelings were listed under the column headings before and after. Before the programme the children tended to feel sad, worried and upset before their father attended the programme. Four children felt disappointed, three children felt angry, scared and hurt, and two children felt confused, guilty, bored and 'nothing'. In contrast, children's feelings towards their father changed whilst he was on the programme or once he had completed the programme. Six children felt 'loving' towards their father, five felt 'happy' and 'okay'. Four children said they felt 'joyful' and 'excited' towards their father and three said they felt 'warm' towards him. One child said he felt 'nothing' towards his father after his participation on the programme and one circled 'worried'. This last feeling was clarified with a note next to 'worried' which explained how he was afraid that 'a big argument might happen'.

Nearly all of the children reported that their relationship with their father had improved whilst or since he had been attending the programme. These improvements were mostly seen in the light of spending more time together and engaging in activities the children enjoyed.

> Kevin: We watch TV together sometimes and we play guitar and listen to music... We've made an area in the garage where I can plug in my amp and we can play there.
>
> *Interviewer: Would you say your relationship is better [with your father] than it was before [DVPP]?*
>
> Kevin: Yeah it's better now. Because before, every so often, he would get angry.

For many of the children, spending quality time with their father and other members of the family was defined as engaging in activities together. In some cases, children were really excited about the newfound relationship they had formed with their father and the family bonding that had taken place. Two sisters interviewed together who lived with their father and who had two younger siblings spoke animatedly about the new activities they were discussing as a family.

Sally: We do more stuff now.

Sam: Yeah, like we go to the pictures now.

Sally: And we go out with Dad's girlfriend.

Interviewer: So you're spending more time together doing stuff with your dad and his girlfriend?

Sally: Yes, he wants to try and get us all involved in free swimming as well.

Sam: And sometimes on a night we all watch collections of DVDs.

The completed research books demonstrated how time spent with fathers and other members of their families had improved since men's participation on a DVPP. Whilst many children were doing some of the same activities with their father before and after he attended the DVPP, they spent more time on these and additional activities were reported post-participation in the DVPP. For example, three of the children had started to play football or had been on a camping trip with their father; two of the children were now going to the cinema, having picnics, cooking, doing homework and reading with their father; and one child said he had been for ice-cream with his father on a day out. Other activities that fathers were involved in with their children included swimming, playing the piano and board games. Many of the activities children highlighted cost little or nothing, which confirms that it was the amount and quality of time spent with their father that they valued.

Feelings of safety

One of the tasks for the children completing the research books was to indicate on a ladder scale their perception of how safe they felt before their father participated in the DVPP and the level of safety they felt now. Rung 1 on the ladder indicated feeling unsafe, and rung 10 indicated feeling very safe. Before their father attended the programme, all the children indicated that they thought their level of safety was at or around level 1 and 2 (very unsafe). When asked how safe they felt at the time of interview, one child circled rung 5 (unsafe/fairly safe), two circled rung 9 (very safe) and four children circled rung 10 (extremely safe). This means that the children in this study whose fathers had completed a DVPP group *and* who were themselves receiving support reported a major shift in how safe they felt with him. Whilst a small sample, these data offer some of first evidence that it is possible to explore the meanings and impacts of attending a DVPP for children.

Conclusions

In this chapter we have argued that violent men are still far too often invisible in interventions on domestic violence and are thus rarely held to account. DVPPs are an important exception, since holding men to account and inviting them to change is their raison d'être. In Project Mirabal we have developed a set of more complex indicators of success, four of which are connected to the experiences of children and safe fatherhood. Data from interviews with men attending DVPPs reveal that explicit and emotive content on the impacts on children holds the potential not only to shift men's perspectives but also to reinforce motivations to change. Data from a small group of children whose fathers were attending DVPPs, and who themselves were receiving support, showed that they had noticed and welcomed changes in their fathers' behaviour. This was not just that they felt safer, but they were spending more time with their fathers doing things that children enjoyed. Both sets of data support our contention that measures of success for DVPPs should include changes in both parenting and in children's everyday lives.

References

Alderson, S., Westmarland, N. and Kelly, L. (2012) 'The need for accountability to, and support for, children of men on domestic violence perpetrator programmes.' *Child Abuse Review 22*, 3, 182–193.

Brown, L., Callahan, M., Strega, S., Walmsley, C. and Dominelli, L. (2009) 'Manufacturing ghost fathers: the paradox of father presence and absence in child welfare.' *Child and Family Social Work 14*, 1, 25–34.

Casey, L. (2012) *Listening to Troubled Families.* London: Department for Communities and Local Government.

Crossley, S. (2014) *Domestic Violence and the Troubled Families Programme.* Online blog, 6 February 2014. Available at www.akindoftrouble.wordpress.com accessed on 1 September 2014.

Department for Communities and Local Government (2014) *Helping Troubled Families Turn Their Lives Around.* London: Department for Communities and Local Government. Available at www.gov.uk/government/policies/helping-troubled-families-turn-their-lives-around, accessed on 1 September 2014.

Edleson J. L. (1998) 'Responsible mothers and invisible men: child protection in the case of adult domestic violence.' *Journal of Interpersonal Violence 13*, 2, 294–298.

Mullender, A., Hague, G., Imam, U., Kelly, L., Malos, E. and Regan, L. (2002) *Children's Perspectives on Domestic Violence.* London: Sage.

Romito, P. (2008) *A Deafening Silence: Hidden Violence against Women and Children.* Bristol: Policy Press.

Roskill, C., Fraser, C., Featherstone, B., Haresnape, S. and Lindley, B. (2011) *Working with Risky Fathers. Fathers Matter Volume 3.* London: Family Rights Group.

Stanley, N., Fall, B., Miller, P., Thomson, G. and Watson, J. (2012) 'Men's talk: men's understandings of violence against women and motivations for change.' *Violence against Women 18*, 11, 1300–1318.

Stanley, N., Graham-Kevan, N. and Borthwich, R. (2012) 'Fathers and domestic violence: building motivation for change through perpetrator programmes.' *Child Abuse Review 21*, 4, 264–274.

Stanley, N., Miller, P., Richardson Foster, H. and Thomson, G. (2011) 'A stop-start response: social services intervention with children and families notified following domestic violence incidents.' *British Journal of Social Work 41*, 2, 296–313.

Stark, E. (2009) *Coercive Control: How Men Entrap Women in Personal Life.* New York, NY: Oxford University Press.

Westmarland, N. and Kelly, L. (2012) 'Why extending measurements of "success" in domestic violence perpetrator programmes matters for social work.' *British Journal of Social Work 42*, 3, 1–19.

Westmarland, N., Kelly, L. and Chalder-Mills, J. (2010) *Domestic Violence Perpetrator Programmes – What Counts as Success?* Project Mirabal Briefing Note 1. Durham and London: Durham University and London Metropolitan University.

CHAPTER 12

Reshaping the Child Protection Response to Domestic Violence Through Collaborative Working

Neil Blacklock and Ruth Phillips

Exposure to parental domestic violence can have a negative impact on children's health, development and well-being (Stanley 2011) with outcomes similar to those of children experiencing direct physical abuse (Kitzmann *et al.* 2003). Over the past 20 years there have been repeated calls for improved responses to children and young people living in homes where domestic violence is taking place (Humphreys 2000; Humphreys and Stanley 2006; Mullender 2002; Mullins 1997). The call is often for better support for parents, particularly mothers, support for children exposed to domestic violence and interventions with fathers to increase safety. The need to provide a safe environment for children is, of course, important. However, when a child is removed from their parent(s), either wholly or in part because of the mother's victimisation, it is hard to look on such an outcome as anything but a heart-breaking failure, even when it appears to be the best of a very poor set of options.

As social work has become increasingly aware that children exposed to domestic violence are at risk of harm, the need for an effective social work response to domestic violence becomes more pressing. Finding social work interventions that can eliminate or significantly reduce a child's exposure to parental domestic violence is critical to improving the outcomes for these children. This chapter focuses on some of the attempts to provide such interventions and specifically the collaboration projects that exist between Domestic Violence Perpetrator Programmes

(DVPPs) and local authority children's social services. DVPPs offer structured programmes to assist those who have used violence or abuse towards an intimate partner to end this behaviour and construct positive relationships. In the UK, DVPPs also provide support to the partners and ex-partners of men attending the service. In North America, DVPPs are known as Batterer Intervention Programs and, in Australia, as Men's Behaviour Change Programs.

Without well-constructed and effective ways to respond to domestic violence, professionals can be left with a sense of powerlessness. This can make them susceptible to explanations that, at best, blame the victim for making 'poor choices' in their relationships or, at worst, construct her as co-author in her own abuse. Paradigms underpinned by a sense of powerlessness and blame will, of course, be self-fulfilling.

Improving responses to violence against women has centred on moving the accountability for the abuse, and the responsibility for stopping it, from the victim to the perpetrator and using the state and its institutions to drive that process (Pence and Shepard 1999). Coordinated community responses that frequently focus on the criminal justice system are prime examples of this approach. Here, responsibility for holding the perpetrator accountable has moved away from the victim to the professionals via positive arrest policies, specialist prosecutors, specialist courts, victim advocates, perpetrator rehabilitation programmes, perpetrator risk management and multi-agency structures. There is still a tendency towards victim blaming in the criminal justice system and policy commitments are not always evident on the ground (HMIC 2014). Nevertheless, the changes in the criminal justice response to domestic violence over the past 20 years have been significant. This chapter suggests that a similar paradigm shift in social work could produce a degree of change in response resembling that achieved in the criminal justice system.

Increased focus on domestic violence

The Adoption and Children Act 2002, which came into force in 2005, made exposure to domestic violence a form of harm, following increased awareness of its impact on children's well-being. The statutory recognition of this harm, alongside better identification, impacted on the work of children's social services in terms of the volume of referrals and notifications. Exposure to domestic violence in itself is not one of the five distinct categories of abuse (physical, emotional, sexual, neglect and multiple) under which a child may be subject to a child protection plan but it is frequently classified under neglect or emotional abuse. As Figure 12.1 shows, since 2005 the numbers of child protection plans completed for children in these two categories have shown a steady increase which is not seen for other categories of harm or abuse.

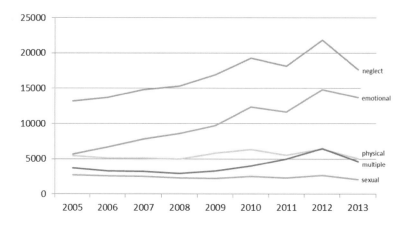

Figure 12.1 Children subject to child protection plans by category of abuse
Based on an analysis of data at www.gov.uk/government/collections/statistics-child-protection and http://webarchive.nationalarchives.gov.uk.

Whilst it is not possible to attribute all of this increase to the identification of domestic violence, it is likely to have contributed to this rise. The result is that many social services departments are struggling to respond to the sheer volume of notifications they are receiving (Stanley *et al.* 2010).

Figures from the advice and advocacy service run by the Family Rights Group for families involved with local authority children's social services (Ashley and Kanow 2014) show that the percentage of families making contact with the service regarding domestic violence has climbed consistently since 2007:

The experience of many mothers, who are domestic violence victims, is that their children become subject to child protection processes, in an environment in which they have few, if any options, given the combined impact of welfare and legal aid reforms, and diminishing support services for victims and indeed reduced perpetrator programmes. (Ashley and Kanow 2014, p.11)

Where's Dad?

Studies have pointed out that engagement with fathers by children's social services is poor (Ashley 2011; Osborn 2014). This lack of engagement with fathers is in part the product of a longstanding, deep-seated cultural view of families:

The family is the building block of society. It's a nursery, a school, a hospital, a leisure place, a place of refuge and a place of rest. It encompasses the whole of society. It fashions beliefs. It's the preparation for the rest of our life and women run it. (Thatcher 1988)

An example of this is the way in which public concerns about anti-social behaviour by young people in the early 2000s led to the introduction of anti-social behaviour orders and parenting orders. Based on the view that parents are accountable for their children's behaviour, the courts were enabled to order parents to attend parenting classes. However, in reality, the majority of 'parents' subject to parenting orders have been mothers (Ghate and Ramella 2002).

Recent years have seen a growth in the number and variety of interventions that focus on parenting as a means of improving outcomes for children, but the majority of such initiatives have very low engagement with fathers so that 'most evaluated interventions to promote child well-being, development and violence-prevention focus exclusively on mothers' (McAllister and Burgess 2012, p.5). Parenting programmes can, by and large, be said to be mothering programmes with a few exceptions such as Caring Dads discussed below.

The Social Exclusion Taskforce's *Think Families* (2007) report identified 'that around 2 per cent of families – or 140,000 families across

Britain – experience complex and multiple problems' (p.4). Echoes of the 'Think Family' approach can be found in the current Troubled Families agenda launched by the British prime minister in 2011. Louise Casey, the lead for the Troubled Families initiative, in her speech to the Women's Aid conference in 2014, stated that domestic violence featured in between 40 per cent and 75 per cent of the lives of these families. Research on Family Intervention Projects (an earlier approach aimed at reducing the number of Troubled Families) found that 67 per cent of those receiving the intervention were lone parents (Lloyd *et al.* 2011), but it is unclear if or in what ways biological fathers, or other father figures, featured in the lives of these families.

It seems that a significant number of fathers who pose a risk to their families are not being engaged with via parenting programmes, Family Intervention (or similar) Projects or statutory children's social services. The reasons for this gap can been seen across 'many ecological levels' (Scourfield 2014, p.975) from the individual to the institutional and social dimensions of engagement. Barriers at every level need to be addressed – from the reluctance of both fathers and mothers (for different reasons) to engage with social care professionals, to the failures of institutions to respond effectively, and cultural ideas about women as primary caregivers. Each level interacts with others to create an environment in which domestic violence victims can be held responsible for the abuse they are suffering whilst perpetrators remain invisible.

Dads as resource

This focus on mothers adds to the impunity experienced by many perpetrators of domestic violence and has led some to see increased engagement with fathers as a route to a more effective social work response (Fatherhood Institute 2015).

Most of the improvements in engaging fathers have 'focused on fathers as a resource for children, rather than seeing them as risks' (Featherstone and Fraser 2012, p.257). A failure to engage with fathers directly means that not only is assessment of risk not as strong as it could be (Baynes and Holland 2012), but the resource that fathers may represent for their children, or that of their extended paternal family, may not be recognised.

'Fathers as resources' initiatives are important as they can challenge the polarised view of fathers as either violent men or good fathers, either risk or resource (Burgess and Osborn 2013). It is suggested that 'label[ling] men as violent without recognition of their role as fathers... negates any chance of changing the negative aspects of these fathers' behaviours to children' (Maxwell *et al.* 2012, p.161). The Fatherhood Institute has done much to promote more father-inclusive approaches (Fatherhood Institute 2015).

Caring Dads, another 'fathers as resource' intervention, provides fathering programmes for men who have used violence towards the mother of their children (see also Chapter 14 of this book). Caring Dads has shown positive outcomes in improving fathering but one study, although with small sample size, found less of an impact in addressing attitudes that support violence:

> The men's positive responses to the child-centred focus of the programme suggest the parenting of their children became safer and more nurturing and this included a greater awareness of the need to avoid abusive behaviour towards the children's mother. A similar shift in the men's attitudes towards women, which would suggest the programme improves women's safety, was not as evident. (McCracken and Deave 2012, p.79)

Whilst this shift from 'parenting...as synonymous with mothering' (Ferguson 2012, p.231) is to be welcomed, the focus on engaging fathers as resources can obscure the gendered inequalities still evident in contemporary families and, crucially, can fail to address directly risks posed by violent fathers (Featherstone 2009). Addressing the ecological factors that have created our low level of engagement with fathers is important as low engagement feeds into low expectations of fathers. A focus on getting more men attending services and higher expectations of what it is to be father are of benefit, but on their own they will not address the underlying issues that support this gendered inequality in the parents' accountability for the safety and well-being of their children that informs much child protection work.

If children's social work is poor at engaging with fathers as a resource, the reluctance to engage is often increased when he is known to be violent or abusive: social workers may fear for their own safety and have reported a lack of skills and/or confidence in how to engage violent fathers (Hester 2011; Phillips 2013). As Ferguson (2012) states, 'a sea change in attitude, culture and approach' (p.231) will be required on the part of children's social care if violent fathers are to be fully engaged and addressed. This would require: an engagement with fathers as both resource and risk; an understanding of the dynamics of coercive control operating within these families and its impact on the children; and where possible, work with him to address his violence.

The arrival of domestic violence prevention programmes (DVPPs)

At the beginning of the 1990s, a handful of organisations started to provide programmes for men who perpetrate domestic violence (Burton, Regan and Kelly 1998; Phillips, Kelly and Westmarland 2013). Since then, there has been a slow but steady growth in the number of these services. In 2004, with the formation of the National Offender Management Service (NOMS), there was a separation of the probation service's offending-focused provision and community programmes.

After 2004, community-based DVPPs were being accessed by men who were either self-referring (with the encouragement of partners and others) or were reaching DVPPs through a myriad of statutory and voluntary sector services. Over the last ten years, referrals from statutory children services to DVPPs have risen dramatically in a pattern that matches the trends shown in Figure 12.1.

Many community DVPPs are influenced by the coordinated community response model which shifts the burden for holding the perpetrators accountable for their behaviour from the victim to the community and its institutions (Pence and Shepard 1999). Children's social services agencies are ideal partners in this project and community DVPPs have actively pursued working relationships with statutory children services. Alongside this development, social work has begun to recognise that a child protection response that was overly focused on separation was inadequate (Stanley *et al.* 2011). As stated in the Munro Review (2011): 'social workers should not believe that the problem [domestic violence] is necessarily solved by separation' (p.92).

The availability of a DVPP for social workers to refer into has a number of benefits:

- The process of being referred tests the motivation and possibility of change for the father.

- The DVPP can help unpick the often confusing narratives from parents about who is doing what, to whom and with what effect.

- The partner safety service, which is a requirement of UK accredited DVPPs, provides support and advice to mothers and others at risk.

- DVPPs have the potential to provide domestic violence expertise in case planning.

Staff at Respect, the UK organisation that sets the accreditation standard for perpetrator services, have noticed that the referral process between children's social services and DVPPs can be slow, as the family move through the referral and assessment processes of two agencies. A significant number of fathers do not make the transition from referral by the social worker to attendance at a DVPP and information sharing between the professionals is frequently poor.

Thus, whilst too many local authority children's social services do not have any access to an accredited DVPP, those that have been working with DVPPs for some time are now making dramatic structural changes to bring these services closer together.

Co-location and collaborative working

The father-focused parenting programmes, improved father engagement and referral to DVPPs are all positive steps but they fail to address the central challenge of how to build domestic violence expertise into the day-to-day work of children's social services and specifically child protection. Co-locating domestic violence services and social work seems to offer a means of meeting this challenge.

To be transformative, however, co-location models must step beyond physical proximity into a new collaborative process. Terminology in this area is problematic – partnership, joined-up, integrated, coordinated, co-located – are all terms used to describe multi-agency working. We use the term collaborative (Atkinson, Jones and Lamont 2007, p.100) to denote the shared goals of both agencies and their independence, rather than integration which assumes a new organisational structure incorporating both agencies.

Co-locating can speed up the processes of referral and information sharing but the co-location is merely the starting point for the collaborative model which entails:

- evolution of practice through the exchange of ideas, skills and information

- partners having independence and equal status

- shared purpose

- shared decision-making processes (with different areas of responsibility).

Collaborative DVPP social work projects bring together partners that have different working cultures and who are independent from each other. A number of local authorities have sought to appoint a social worker with a domestic violence specialism which, whilst acknowledging the problems in current social work responses to domestic violence, often results in a practitioner in a relatively junior role with little independence and who is fundamentally still a social worker. In the DVPP social work projects, the DVPP staff spend part of their working life in a domestic violence specialist setting and consequently their identity and expertise are constantly renewed. With a collaborative approach, the development of shared purpose and understandings between partners has the potential to improve responses on the ecological level, from engaging individuals and improving practice through to effecting institutional and cultural change.

Co-located DVPPs

Co-location in itself is not new. A recent Home Office Report (2014) on Multi-Agency Safeguarding Hubs (MASHs) highlighted the multiple benefits of co-location but, in practical terms, this is frequently geared towards the co-location of statutory agencies. However, it is not unknown for independent domestic violence agencies to co-locate with statutory agencies and there are examples in the provision of Independent Domestic Violence Advisors (IDVAs) and in specialist domestic violence courts (Cook *et al.* 2004; Coy and Kelly 2011).

Co-location projects can be subject to differences in power and authority, both perceived and real, between voluntary and statutory sectors and these require commitment to address. Evaluations of voluntary–statutory co-location offer some insights into the particular dynamics of such arrangements. Kelly *et al.*'s (1999) early evaluation of Domestic Violence Matters (DVM), a project which based civilian crisis counsellors in an Islington police station to support women when police responded to domestic violence incidents, showed initial wariness and hostility from police officers. Similarly, a more recent evaluation of four IDVA schemes (Coy and Kelly 2011) co-located in different organisations, including a police station and a hospital accident and emergency department, reported that 'some schemes continued to be intimidated and/or marginalised by more powerful statutory agencies' (p.2). Overall, however, both DVM and the IDVA schemes were successful in forging better working relationships through co-location, resulting in significant shifts in practice and improved responses to those at risk.

More recently, the Safer Families Project (previously Working with Men) in Edinburgh has co-located with one of the city's children's social services teams to collaboratively provide a response to families of children exposed to domestic violence. Like other UK approaches, this collaborative model situates some of the DVPP intervention work within the social work team.

Another recent co-location project, set up in 2012, places DVPP practitioners from London's Domestic Violence Intervention Project (DVIP) within Hackney children's social services; this collaboration has been the subject of a process evaluation (Phillips 2013) and a forthcoming case study by the second author. Data from this evaluation are used below to illustrate the account of this collaboration. As well as providing an on-site violence prevention programme and partner support service, the DVIP co-location project also offers domestic violence expertise on risk and case management. Both agencies also undertake training focused on improving joint working and shared purpose.

The project has been both welcomed and resisted. On the one hand, the act of commissioning such a project signifies a desire within children's social services to find new ways to address domestic violence and work more effectively with abusive fathers. Yet the sheer volume of domestic violence among social work caseloads is experienced as overwhelming, particularly in the light of statutory obligations and systemic restrictions. These fears are not unfounded: not only have referrals related to domestic violence proliferated generally since 2005 but, as the Home Office (2014) report on multi-agency work highlights, the creation of a multi-agency and/or co-located response has been seen to increase caseloads due to more information leading to a greater awareness of risk. However, the more accurate assessments of risk and need made possible through joined-up work may lead to a reduction in repeat referrals over time (Home Office 2014).

In Hackney, social workers consistently reported the value of regular feedback from DVIP workers and, likewise, DVIP staff benefit from an increased familiarity and understanding of children's social services processes. The ongoing communication, made possible by collaborative co-location, is vital to robust risk assessment and safety planning, and generally enhances understanding about the roles and restrictions of both parties. The following quotes from both DVIP workers and social workers provide evidence of shifts in understanding, information sharing and the willingness to use another service's expertise:

> I think I have a lot better understanding of the pressures that social workers are under, so that I still get frustrated with some of their responses but at the same time I can see why and how. I have a better understanding of the institution, if you like, of social services. (DVIP women's support worker)

> My work with social workers has been very different in the past but this is a lot deeper, it's a lot more rounded, and I think the social workers understand what the service is about better. I think the information sharing is a lot better as well. So before, massive things could happen, like someone getting arrested or social services closing the case, and we wouldn't get told. We're more in the loop now. (DVIP men's worker)

> What I see now, if you take that I started in April and we're now November, nearly December, I see more people going up to [DVIP workers] going 'oh, we've got this here, can you come and listen to this conversation?' and 'what do you think, do we think this is really bad?' or 'how can we keep her safe, but deal with him?' All of that I see going on as the norm, whereas when I first started no one was referring, no one was asking. (Social work team leader)

Safe and Together Model™

The Safe and Together Model™ developed by David Mandel and Associates (see www.endingviolence.com) operates with a similar focus on the perpetrator's behaviour, survivor strengths and the child's well-being. In the model, collaborative working between domestic violence specialists and children's social services provides a mechanism to promote changes in response and longer-term cultural change.

In the US, the model has been used to support collaborative assessment and case management with trained advocates co-located with trained children's social workers. One of the strengths of the model is the training which precedes implementation to develop a shared framework, tools and language for working together. In contrast, in the UK, this shared framework has emerged through the process of collaboration, rather than providing the structure in which the collaboration occurs. It seems likely that this more structured approach to the collaboration will be needed if this approach is to be widely adopted. The Safe and Together Model™ has produced some very promising evidence for its effectiveness in improving outcomes for families.

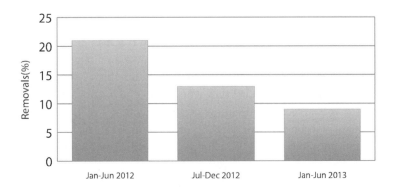

Figure 12.2 Reductions in domestic violence related child removals as a proportion of all removals after implementation of the Safe and Together Model™ in Florida, US

As Figure 12.2 shows, from January 2012 through to June 2012, domestic violence related removals represented 20.6 per cent of children removed from their families in the Bay and Gulf Counties of Florida. These figures cover the first six months of the project when co-located advocates were being recruited and staff were receiving Safe and Together Model™ training. During the next six months, from June 2012 to December 2012, the removal rate dropped to 13.6 per cent. For the most recent six-month period, January 2013 to June 2013, the removal rate dropped even further to 9.1 per cent (Safe and Together 2013).

Challenges for DVPPs

For the domestic violence agency, the collaboration project is linked to the changing profile of their service users which has become increasingly composed of parents of children who are subject to a child protection plan. Ten years ago, DVPP service users who self-referred were the majority of the service's users. However, the funding for this work has become more difficult to secure and one of the challenges for DVPPs is how to maintain broad access to their services when funding can dictate who gains access.

For DVPPs in collaboration projects, there is a recognition that part of their domestic violence work needs to be situated alongside statutory children's social services so that it informs and shapes that response. However, experienced DVPP staff who are able to understand and value both the requirements and culture of social work are required for these partnerships to be effective. Finding or being able to develop these staff in significant numbers will be a struggle for many small DVPPs:

> When we started the process, what we knew was there was going to be all those cultural challenges. We've learnt far more about what is required of our staff in those settings, so that you need staff with real experience and confidence in their practice so that they are able, robustly, to have a sense of 'where can I make a shift here, where might I be able to do something slightly differently than I would ordinarily because we're in a different environment here, or where do I have to say no we can't do it like that?' You need staff who have got the skills to have that dialogue. (DVIP manager)

The long-term value of co-location lies in its ability to influence cultural and structural practices. This involves addressing the low level of accountability and responsibility expected of fathers for the safety and well-being of their children and the correspondingly high level of responsibility placed on mothers. Ideally, this shift will contribute to the development of practices that focus on the father's behaviour, its impact on the child and on the mother's ability to provide care in difficult circumstances. A willingness to deliver their work in different ways, without losing their identity, will be required from DVPP staff. The value of this flexibility was acknowledged by a social work manager:

> DVIP have been really good at looking at and thinking about the needs of the service and whenever I've said to them 'look we need to do this' they've come back and we've been able to shift things in a way that we've wanted them to … For example, we need people to go out and do home visits and be involved much earlier on in the assessment process and that's something that DVIP haven't traditionally done, doing co-located assessments in the home, but we need to look at the needs of how we're going to get the best out of assessments and the strongest assessments, so that's important to think about as well. (Social work manager)

Challenges for statutory children's social services

Up-front investment is needed to make the DVPP social work collaborative model work, both in terms of financial input and staff time. At a time of reduced public spending, there's a risk that the short-term need to make urgent budget reductions may outweigh potential savings further down the line:

> That's the struggle and will be the battle moving forward for DVIP when they're looking to commission in other boroughs, everyone's got scarce resources and everyone's target driven, they want outcomes quickly that aren't necessarily going to happen and DV services across the board we know are being massively cut so it's going to become more of a problem, not go away. (Social work manager)

Time is needed for staff to train together at the beginning of the project and develop an understanding of each other's work, and integration of external staff into the team requires a degree of patience. The anxiety of frontline staff about the impact of a greater focus on domestic violence on already stretched workloads is consistently reported and this needs to be managed and supported. However, all the indicators concerning the volume of domestic violence referrals coming into statutory children's social services have been moving in one direction – upwards – for some years, and to date our attempts to remodel our social work response to address this have been slow.

Forward together

Often the initial attraction of such collaborations for social work is that the joint service delivery provides a transfer of skills on working with fathers and mothers, and whilst this is of value in itself, the longer-term benefit is that this is a mechanism to develop a shared model and purpose. As this collaborative working develops organically in these UK pioneer services, it is important that it is captured and translated into something that can be replicated and evidenced.

Co-location projects can increase the visibility of abusive fathers within social work practice and at the same time equip social workers with the skills and confidence to work directly with male perpetrators of domestic violence. This does not merely reproduce the work of the DVPP but acts to build a greater understanding of how the abusive behaviour impacts on children. This can in turn lead to a different approach with women and more informed decision making. Female partners also have access to the DVPP integrated women's support service, where advocates are available to support them within the child protection process and increase their understanding of the dynamics of domestic violence within their own relationships.

Domestic violence is the most common issue in child protection caseloads. The majority of fathers attending DVPPs have children who are subject to a social work intervention. There is a need to reshape the social work response so that it can address the volume of domestic violence in social work caseloads. These facts alone should make the case for increased attention to the DVPP social work collaborative projects.

References

Ashley, C. (ed.) (2011) *Working with Risky Fathers: Fathers Matter Volume 3: Research Findings on Working with Domestically Abusive Fathers and Their Involvement with Children's Social Care Services.* London: Family Rights Group.

Ashley, C. and Kanow, C. (2014) *Desperate for Help: Report Analysing Calls to Family Rights Group's Advice Service from Families of Children in Need or at Risk.* London: Family Rights Group. Available at www.frg.org.uk/images/Policy_Papers/report-about-advice-service-2007-2013.pdf, accessed on 7 January 2015.

Atkinson, M., Jones, M. and Lamont, E. (2007) *Multi-Agency Working and its Implications for Practice: A Review of the Literature.* Reading: CFBT Education Trust. Available at www.nfer.ac.uk/publications/MAD01/MAD01_home.cfm, accessed on 14 January 2015.

Baynes, P. and Holland, S. (2012) 'Social work with violent men: a child protection file study in an English local authority.' *Child Abuse Review 21*, 1, 53–65.

Burgess, A. and Osborn, M. (2013) *Engaging with Men in Social Care: A Good Practice Guide.* Wiltshire: Fatherhood Institute.

Burton, S., Regan, L. and Kelly, L. (1998) *Supporting Women and Challenging Men: Lessons from the Domestic Violence Intervention Project.* Bristol: Policy Press.

Cook, D., Burton, M., Robinson, A. and Vallely, C. (2004) *Evaluation of Specialist Domestic Violence Courts/Fast Track Systems.* London: Crown Prosecution Service and Department of Constitutional Affairs. Available at www.cps.gov.uk/publications/docs/specialistdvcourts.pdf, accessed on 7 January 2015.

Coy, M. and Kelly, L. (2011) *Islands in the Stream: An Evaluation of Four London Independent Domestic Violence Advocacy Schemes.* London: London Metropolitan University.

Fatherhood Institute (2015) *Engaging with Fathers in Safeguarding.* Available at www.fatherhoodinstitute.org/training-and-consultancy/engaging-with-fathers-in-safeguarding, accessed on 14 January 2015.

Featherstone, B. (2009) *Contemporary Fathering: Theory, Policy and Practice.* Bristol: Policy Press.

Featherstone, B. and Fraser, C. (2012) 'Working with fathers around domestic violence: contemporary debates.' *Child Abuse Review 21*, 4, 255–263.

Ferguson, H. (2012) 'Editorial: Fathers, child abuse and child protection.' *Child Abuse Review 21*, 4, 231–236.

Ghate, D. and Ramella, M. (2002) *Positive Parenting: The National Evaluation of the Youth Justice Board's Parenting Programme.* London: Youth Justice Board for England and Wales.

Hester, M. (2011) 'The three planet model: towards an understanding of contradictions in approaches to women and children's safety in contexts of domestic violence.' *British Journal of Social Work 41*, 5, 837–853.

Home Office (2014) *Multi-Agency Working and Information Sharing Project: Final Report.* London: Home Office. Available at www.gov.uk/government/publications/multi-agency-working-and-information-sharing-project, accessed on 7 January 2015.

Humphreys, C. (2000) *Social Work, Domestic Violence and Child Protection: Challenging Practice.* Bristol: Policy Press.

Humphreys, C. and Stanley, N. (eds) (2006) *Domestic Violence and Child Protection: Directions for Good Practice.* London: Jessica Kingsley Publishers.

Kelly, L., Bindel, J., Burton, S., Butterworth, D., Cook, K. and Regan, L. (1999) *Domestic Violence Matters: An Evaluation of a Development Project.* Home Office Research Study 193. London: Home Office.

Kitzmann, K., Gaylord, N., Holt, A. and Kenny, E. (2003) 'Child witnesses to domestic violence: a meta-analytic review.' *Journal of Consulting and Clinical Psychology 71*, 2, 339–352.

Lloyd, C., Wollny, I., White, C., Gowland, S. and Purdon, S. (2011) *Monitoring and Evaluation of Family Intervention Services and Projects Between February 2007 and March 2011. Research Report DFE-RR174.* London: Department of Education. Available at www.gov.uk/government/publications/monitoring-and-evaluation-of-family-intervention-services-and-projects-between-february-2007-and-march-2011, accessed on 7 January 2015.

Maxwell, N., Scourfield, J., Featherstone, B., Holland, S. and Tolman, R. (2012) 'Engaging fathers in child welfare services: a narrative review of recent research evidence.' *Child and Family Social Work 17,* 2, 160–169.

McAllister, F. and Burgess, A. (2012) *Parenting Programmes and Policy: A Critical Review of Best Practice.* London: Fatherhood Institute. Available at www.men-care.org/data/Parenting-Programmes-and-Policy-Critical-Review-Full-Report.pdf, accessed on 22 May 2015.

McCracken, K. and Deave, T. (2012) *Evaluation of the Caring Dads Cymru Programme.* Wales: Welsh Assembly Government.

Mullender, A. (2002) *Rethinking Domestic Violence: The Social Work and Probation Response.* London: Routledge.

Mullins, A. (1997) *Making a Difference: Practice Guidelines for Professionals Working with Women and Children Experiencing Domestic Violence.* London: NCH, Action for Children.

Munro, E. (2011) *The Munro Review of Child Protection: Final Report.* London: Secretary of State for Education.

Osborn, M. (2014) 'Working with fathers to safeguard children.' *Child Abuse & Neglect 38,* 6, 973–1138.

Pence, E. and Shepard, M. (1999) *Coordinating Community Responses to Domestic Violence: Lessons from Duluth and Beyond.* London: Sage.

Phillips, R. (2013) *DVIP'S Co-Location in Hackney Children's Services: A Process Evaluation.* London: DVIP. Available at www.dvip.org/assets/files/downloads/DVIP%20Co-Location%20In%20Hackney%20Children%20Services%20-%20A%20Process%20Evaluation.pdf, accessed on 7 January 2015.

Phillips, R., Kelly, L. and Westmarland, N. (2013) *Domestic Violence Perpetrator Programmes: An Historical Overview.* London and Durham: London Metropolitan University and Durham University.

Safe and Together (2013) *Florida Co-located Advocates, Florida DCF and Safe and Together Model Combine To Reduce Removal of Children from Domestic Violence Survivors in Half, October 8th, 2013.* Available at http://safe-and-together.endingviolence.com/blog/?p=533, accessed on 14 January 2015.

SETF (2007) *Reaching Out: Think Family.* London: Social Exclusion Task Force. Available at www.cesi.org.uk/publications/reaching-out-think-family, accessed on 7 January 2015.

Scourfield, J. (2014) 'Improving work with fathers to prevent child maltreatment.' *Child Abuse & Neglect 38,* 6, 974–981.

Stanley, N. (2011) *Children Experiencing Domestic Violence: A Research Review.* Dartington: Research in Practice.

Stanley, N., Miller, P., Richardson Foster, H. and Thomson, G. (2010) *Children and Families Experiencing Domestic Violence: Police and Children's Social Services' Responses.* London: NSPCC. Available at www.nspcc.org.uk/preventing-abuse/research-and-resources/children-families-experiencing-domestic-violence, accessed on 7 January 2015.

Stanley, N., Miller, P., Richardson Foster, H. and Thomson, G. (2011) 'A stop-start response: Social services' interventions with children and families notified following domestic violence incidents.' *British Journal of Social Work 41,* 2, 296–313.

Thatcher, M. (1988) Speech to Conservative Women's Conference, Barbican Centre, London, 25 May 1988. Available at www.margaretthatcher.org/document/107248, accessed on 17 April 2015.

PART FIVE

Interagency Work

CHAPTER 13

Working Together, Working Apart

General Practice Professionals' Perspectives
on Interagency Collaboration in Relation to
Children Experiencing Domestic Violence

*Eszter Szilassy, Jessica Drinkwater, Marianne Hester, Cath
Larkins, Nicky Stanley, William Turner and Gene Feder*

General practice, domestic violence and children

Victims and perpetrators of domestic violence are likely to seek
support from a range of health service providers including general
practice (family doctors) (Britton 2012). General practice responses to
domestic violence when both adults (whether victims or perpetrators)
and their children are involved are complex and emerge in the context
of joint working. Multi-agency solutions are required to coordinate
care and interventions for all family members and to assess the risks
for both adults and children. This chapter illuminates general practice
perspectives on interagency collaboration and communication with key
professional groups in this process. The narratives of general practice
professionals describing their interactions with domestic violence
services, children's social services, health visitors and non-primary care
professionals presented here provide us with a unique understanding
of the current institutional and practical barriers as well as facilitators
of effective interagency partnerships in relation to the management of
domestic violence when children are affected.

A focus on general practice or family doctors is relevant because the
prevalence of domestic violence among women attending general practice
is higher than in the wider population, and it is a potential setting for
domestic violence interventions (Hegarty 2006). It is a first point of access

to care, and victims (who are often isolated from other service providers as a result of their partner's controlling behaviour) are more likely to be in contact with general practice than with other agencies. They usually expect that their GP (general practitioner) can offer them safe and practical support and can be fully trusted with disclosures of domestic violence (Feder *et al.* 2006). GPs have a complex duty to coordinate care, facilitate early intervention and provide ongoing support through repeated contacts with the victim and family members over sustained periods. They are potentially in a position to identify early signs of child maltreatment as they may have contact with children well before their referral to specialist services. National (Department for Education 2013) and professional (Royal College of General Practitioners 2009) guidance requires GPs to refer children who are at risk of significant harm due to child abuse and neglect, including their exposure to domestic violence, to children's social services. They can refer patients to other agencies and have a potentially key role in providing information to inform decisions about access to services. It is also part of the general practice remit to receive and store information from other agencies. General practice teams therefore play an important role in responding to domestic violence and are also at the frontline of multi-agency work.

A child-centred and coordinated multi-agency approach is often advocated as the solution to safeguarding and promoting the welfare of children. There is compelling evidence that effective interagency work is vital at all stages of the child protection system (e.g. Ward and Davies 2011). In the UK, high-profile failures in interagency child protection work in recent years (Jay 2014; Laming 2009) have resulted in government guidance emphasising the central role of general practitioners in multi-agency child protection work (Department for Education 2008, 2013; Department of Health 2010). Various measures have been introduced to enhance the role of GPs in this process, including mandatory training, guidance on referral and assessment systems, and improved information exchange procedures between agencies.

Although we have some research evidence about the expectations of other professionals in respect of interagency collaboration (e.g. Birchall and Hallett 1995; Lupton, North and Khan 2000; Lupton, North and Khan 2001), there is still only have a handful of studies about the views and experiences of GPs themselves in respect of child safeguarding (e.g. Miller and Jaye 2007; Tompsett *et al.* 2010; Woodman *et al.* 2013). What constitutes an effective coordinated approach for children experiencing domestic violence is not yet fully understood from the general practice perspective. The RESPONDS study aims to close that gap by providing qualitative evidence on the general practice response to domestic violence in families with children and the barriers to engagement in interagency work from the perspectives of GPs, practice nurses and practice managers.

Study methods

We conducted qualitative semi-structured telephone interviews with 69 general practice professionals across six sites in England between May and December 2013.

Table 13.1 Research participants		GPs (42)	Practice nurses (12)	Practice managers (15)
Sex	Male	17	0	4
	Female	25	12	11
Age range (years)	21–34	8	2	0
	35–44	11	0	2
	45–54	15	8	7
	55–64	5	1	4
	Not known	3	1	2
Experience managing domestic violence (number of cases)	More than five	5	0	
	A few	13	1	
	One	0	2	
	None	18	8	
	None, but aware of case at surgery	6	1	

NB. To see how these figures compare to current national statistics on GP workforce in England, see Health and Social Care Information Centre (2014).

The six sites were chosen to represent different levels of domestic violence service provision and included metropolitan, urban and semi-rural locations across the north and south of England and the Midlands.

The interviews typically lasted between 25 and 60 minutes. Vignettes were employed to elicit practitioners' accounts of their work with parents and children experiencing domestic violence, and a series of questions was asked about practitioners' communication with other organisations including specialist domestic violence services and children's social services and with other health professionals. All interviews were audio-recorded with consent, transcribed verbatim, then loaded on to qualitative data analysis software (NVivo) and analysed thematically using Framework (Ritchie and Spencer 1994). The multidisciplinary research team developed the initial coding frame based on the literature which guided our initial interview schedule and on other concepts which emerged in the course of data collection. It was tested using three pilot interviews and subsequently revised. Each researcher then took a lead on identifying themes within elements of the analysis framework and these were revised and interpreted through research team discussions. The study was guided by two panels of professional and service user experts who contributed to developing the interview schedule and analysis.

Relationships with specialist domestic violence services

When domestic violence is disclosed or suspected, GPs are advised to 'provide all those currently (or recently) affected by domestic violence and abuse with advocacy and advice services tailored to their level of risk and specific needs' which includes providing 'specialist domestic violence and abuse services for children and young people' (NICE 2014, p.17). The service context is relevant here: domestic violence service development is still relatively uneven across the UK. In some areas, few specialist agencies exist to which children experiencing domestic violence could be referred (see Radford *et al.* 2011). Many domestic violence organisations are underfunded and recent austerity measures are undermining specialist provision further (Women's Aid 2014).

Participants' responses illustrated a general unfamiliarity with these specialist organisations and with the services they provide; however, they also reflected the varying levels of service provision in the six research sites. Across the sample, there was general ignorance of existing domestic violence services and general practice professionals expressed reservations about the relevance of such services for their patients. Although the National Institute for Health and Care Excellence (2014) recommends that 'staff know about the services, policies and procedures of all relevant local agencies for children and young people in relation to domestic violence and abuse' (p.16), the majority of our respondents – 22 clinicians (14 GPs and eight practice nurses) and nearly all practice managers were unaware of local or national domestic violence services and did not know if the practice had any links with them. 'No idea, I've never had to access it [the local domestic violence service],' said one GP (GP 19); 'I don't know is the answer…I'd have to go and find out,' replied another GP (GP 13). This lack of awareness was particularly surprising given that about half of the practices included in the study displayed information (posters or leaflets) about domestic violence services in the waiting room or in the women's toilets.

Five respondents, whilst unable to recall any information about these services, thought they would be able to locate the telephone number if required:

> I have never had any contact from them or, do know actually any, about what they really do other than sort of what I've googled and interneted with the patient in the room. (GP 03)

Another four GPs and a practice manager described having some distant relationship with these agencies:

> Very distant, as I say, we've got, we've got the helpline number… it's very rare that you hear from someone with a particular domestic abuse hat on. (GP 39)

Close relationships were reported by six GPs; five of these were in one area where domestic violence training for GPs had been delivered. Practice teams participating in the IRIS programme (Feder *et al.* 2011) had received in-house training and ongoing support with identification, assessment, data handling and safety planning in relation to domestic violence. The only practice manager who reported familiarity with local domestic violence organisations also came from this area:

> I do feel, you know, quite passionate about it [domestic violence]...
> we are more aware of those families that do need that or have that
> vulnerability. (PM 13)

Relationships with children's social services
Making links between child protection and domestic violence in theory and in practice

Child protection concerns appeared to be a relatively infrequent occurrence
in the workloads of general practice professionals participating in the
study. Although 12 GPs said that they had a contact phone number
they could use to communicate with children's social services, only one
described using it. Moreover, of the 42 GPs, only three reported having
made a child protection referral in respect of concerns about a child's
exposure to domestic violence.

Our results are consistent with previous research findings (Tompsett
et al. 2010; Woodman *et al.* 2013) showing that whilst GPs have no
difficulty prioritising the interests of children and are familiar with the
child protection procedures in an emergency or when risks are high, they
are largely uncertain about the course of action when concerns are less
immediate. 'It's the ones in the middle that I struggle with,' noted one GP
(GP 24), referring to low- and medium-risk situations. Where domestic
violence related risks to a child were evident and child protection concerns
were clearly identified, formal protocols for contacting children's social
services could be enlisted. However, in most domestic violence cases that
involved children, the non-abusive parent was seen as the primary patient
by most participants and children experiencing domestic violence were
rarely conceptualised as patients in their own right:

> I think that [talking to the mother is] how you kind of assess the
> kind of impact on the kids. (GP 19)

The RESPONDS study also found that GPs were generally very much
more ready to engage with victims and perpetrators than they were to
talk to children; these findings are reported in full elsewhere (Larkins *et al.*
under review).

Although the majority of those interviewed had no difficulty
establishing a link in theory between domestic violence and the potential
harm it represented for children, about one-third of practitioners only

made this link when prompted by the interviewer. Moreover, more than half of GPs and nearly all practice nurses interviewed said they would not necessarily make a link between child protection concerns and the possibility that domestic violence might be an issue in a family. Some of the reasons given for not exploring the possibility of domestic violence when there were known child protection concerns included domestic violence not being 'first on your radar or list of things to ask about' (GP 31), the problem of 'finding the time to do [it] all' (GP 28), concern that it was a 'difficult conversation to have' (GP 26) and the assumption that children's social services would already be in contact with the family.

General practice professionals' accounts of the quality of their relationships with children's social services were mixed. Their narratives not only reflected the variety of social work practices in England, but also shed light on the respondents' lack of confidence and familiarity in liaising with social workers.

Many respondents described handing the task of communication with children's social services over to the child protection lead in the practice. Most practice nurses would not talk to a social worker themselves (this was understood to be beyond their remit or competence):

> No, no, I don't talk to them [social workers], I mean I would if I had to, I wouldn't have a problem but at the moment I've never had to. (PN 10)

Fourteen clinicians (most of them GPs) described their relationships with children's social services as good or unproblematic. Twelve clinicians (nine were from the same site) described the relationship as 'distant' (GP 16), 'not vast' (GP 22) 'neutral' (GP 17) or 'non-existent' (GP 03). Furthermore, 11 respondents including four practice nurses from different sites described fundamental problems in their relationship with social workers. Many of these accounts voiced frustrations with deficiencies in coordinated work and highlighted systemic problems manifested in gaps – 'a sort of real them and us' (GP 29) – between their own and social workers' practices and assumptions. 'I feel that social services sometimes are this other group, this body somewhere,' said a practice nurse (PN 08) and, according to another practice nurse, 'we [general practice and social care] don't seem to be very linked up' (PN 04).

Interviewees gave numerous examples of difficulties in communication with children's social services. 'One of the most difficult things is knowing who to refer to and contact,' noted a GP (GP 15). A practice nurse from another area expressed that 'it would be useful to know if you'd contacted the right person or, you know, if I, if I rang somebody they would obviously ring me back and speak to me and get, you know, the story from me' (PN 03).

Familiarity with social work processes and procedures

About a third of respondents said they would like to improve their understanding of the structures and context within which social care professionals operated. They also emphasised the absence of face-to-face meetings with social workers – 'you've no idea what they look like' (GP 09) – the lack of named people to confer with and the challenge of 'finding the right person to pin down' (PM 07). They would have welcomed opportunities for joint teaching and or 'more team working' (GP 29) in order to 'know who the social workers are and what makes them tick' (GP 21).

Improved knowledge of other professionals' work could increase appreciation of the boundaries and context of different roles which, in turn, might improve interagency communication. This phenomenon is described by Banks, Dutch and Wang (2008) as 'institutional empathy' and the quest for it was clearly conveyed by one of our respondents:

> I think I'd probably like, like some more clarity on, you know, what, what the police response would be…maybe even talk to people like solicitors and people involved further along the chain, to say well what actually happens to these women, what are the outcomes?… I think just further down the chain I'd like to know what happens rather than just my end of it. (GP 01)

Low levels of engagement in child protection work were acknowledged as a concern by many GPs. One GP (GP 24) noted: 'We just get sent letters about what's going on…but I don't necessarily think that we're involved per se.' Another GP (GP 03) argued that the lack of institutional empathy was a two-way process and that social services 'seem to lack understanding in what a general practitioner's job involves'. In other words, they do 'not really involve us in a way that we'd like to be involved'. A consequence of this was that this GP and her colleagues could feel left out or excluded from child protection processes and from key decisions:

> ...we get these notifications that case conferences have happened and you think well actually I would have liked to have known about that if I'd had a bit more information, a bit more time and you'd made it at a time that we could go to. (GP 03)

GPs' low attendance at and contributions to child protection case conferences has been identified by many commentators (e.g. Devaney 2008; Tompsett *et al.* 2010). Twelve GPs and three practice nurses in our study were aware of this and noted that the timing of meetings together with short notice mitigated against their attendance. Referring to GPs' poor reputations in relation to their attendance at interagency child protection meetings, this GP remarked:

> I went to a case conference of a child recently and the social worker was quite amazed. (GP 38)

However, other GPs did not consider that their role extended beyond the referral process:

> ...so we don't necessarily need to attend, particularly if they haven't got much to contribute. (GP 21)

Child protection referrals and feedback

The high threshold for child protection referrals and children's social services' lack of responsiveness were identified as other sources of frustration for general practice professionals. Most of the accounts emerged in the context of a struggle to understand the remit and responsibilities of child protection social work:

> Social services who were delivering the training said 'there is no point phoning us as we will not take a referral we have too much to do'. This makes you think there is no point even making the phone call. (GP 26)

Some GPs found it challenging that children's social services were increasingly using administrative staff or duty social workers to receive and respond to all incoming referrals. It was described as difficult to communicate complex and sensitive information in the absence of an established ongoing relationship with the person receiving the information:

> I have felt slightly frustrated sometimes ringing the duty social worker…the person on the end of the phone I've never spoken to and never met the family and I give them the scenario and within a few minutes they've told me that they're not worried about it, that it's fine. (GP 10)

In contrast, a safeguarding lead GP who had many years of experience managing domestic violence related cases and was heavily involved in child protection work outside the GP practice, described 'a very close working relationship with a lot of them [social workers]' (GP 36). She felt able to contact social workers 'to just discuss a concern that may not reach their threshold but just to sort of check things out'. Familiarity with those she was communicating with appeared to enhance her readiness to share confidential information:

> I know I'm discussing matters for an appropriate reason…and I'm speaking to another agency who, you know, handle confidential information in a confidential way. (GP 36)

Four GPs suggested that where they were uncertain about whether to refer a family, they would be able to have an informal discussion with a social worker in order to establish the appropriateness of a referral: 'you can talk it through with social services without actually having to formally refer to social services' (GP 11). This process seemed more established in some of the research sites than in others. A practice nurse and two GPs (from different areas) described themselves as more confident in initiating these preliminary discussions since having received training.

Although the Laming Report (Laming 2009) highlighted the importance of social workers providing other professionals with feedback, this remains an infrequent practice (Ward and Davies 2011). The lack of feedback following a child protection referral was described as 'upsetting' and this represented another barrier to effective joint work.

This practice nurse commented rather wistfully on the lack of feedback following a referral:

> I haven't had any feedback from the social worker that I spoke to but I didn't, neither did I expect it…but it would be nice to know what's happening…has somebody acted on that? (PN 11)

However, expectations regarding feedback differed: two GPs and four practice nurses were content to just pass on the necessary information and did not expect feedback.

For some practitioners (11 GPs and three practice nurses), the one-way flow of information and the perceived insensitivity of social workers to the GP's position represented an obstacle to effective decision-making. Five GPs said they would have liked to be involved in the child protection process beyond the early identification stage. 'They [social services] wouldn't speak to us, and I found it hugely frustrating. I still felt the child was at risk,' noted one GP who concluded that: 'It's all about communication and factor sharing, and if we could do that better. I think doctors are always, always very happy to do that too but it seems like the system can be a bit clunky sometimes' (GP 10).

Insufficient understanding of the processes and contexts of other professionals' roles constituted a major source of frustration for the practitioners participating in this study. A lack of 'institutional empathy' restricted general practice professionals' ability to gauge thresholds for child protection referral and their understanding of the consequences of referral. It also explained deficiencies in communication and negatively impacted on efficacy in relation to risk assessment when concerns arose for a child experiencing domestic violence.

One practice nurse clearly articulated these differing approaches to risk assessment and risk thresholds between general practice professionals and social care professionals and her lack of understanding of these differences:

> You feel oh gosh I thought that was fairly urgent and two weeks on, three weeks they've not been seen and why? …that's where I sometimes find they have a different remit to us and how do they [children's social services] assess a priority compared to how we would assess a priority? (PN 08)

Relationships with other health care professionals

Participants gave relatively few details about how partnerships with other health professionals affected their practice with children experiencing domestic violence. In a small number of accounts, hospital paediatric consultants or community paediatricians were involved in the assessment process; these were all cases involving high levels of physical violence ('more of a physical nature rather than a child protection' (GP 12)). Risk of serious physical harm appeared to be the factor that triggered the involvement of these senior specialist practitioners:

> You might feel it isn't, got quite to that level and you perhaps don't want to bother the consultant. (GP 35)

Two GPs (from different areas) mentioned consulting with the geographically based designated safeguarding nurse when they encountered complex, high-risk domestic violence cases:

> I know who the named nurse is as well, designated nurse, and I've got good relationships with those already, so again I could ask them for advice. (GP 39)

Most communication with other health professionals involved health visitors. Nearly all GPs and practice nurses mentioned involving or wanting to involve them in relation to child protection cases. 'We'd go through the health visitors,' asserted a GP (GP 40). However, the strength of general practice staff's relationships with health visitors varied with reorganisation of health visiting services described as exerting significant changes in a number of sites. Most interviewees explained that these relationships had been undermined by the geographical relocation and loss of named practice health visitors from general practice, which 'made things far more difficult. I haven't personally seen our health visitors in probably eighteen months,' complained a GP (GP 39). A practice nurse from another area missed regular practice meetings with health visitors: 'it used to be a good forum, you know, to keep, to keep families who were struggling a bit on the radar for everybody' (PN 09). Her manager articulated similar concerns:

> We don't have a named health visitor for the practice, we don't have a named midwife, and that, that is a problem, we don't know who to contact if we're concerned about somebody. (PM 14)

Although about half of the practitioners reported that reorganisation of health visitor services had reduced their contact, others continued to use health visitors as their conduit to children's social services and consequently had little direct communication with social workers:

> The only contact I have with social services is by keeping up to speed with our Health Visitor. (GP 22)

Despite major shifts in the relationship, in most practices health visitors still attended practice meetings. Health visitors' access to information and knowledge about families was seen as crucial. One GP identified two key elements of an effective response to children experiencing domestic violence: relevant experience of such cases and 'good communication with health visitors because they're aware of all this' (GP 12).

School nurses were referred to by clinicians in just three instances. These accounts described problems in the relationship and portrayed some major deficiencies in joint work and communication. 'Often you play a bit of telephone tennis,' mentioned a GP (GP 16), whilst another GP said that speaking to a school nurse was practically unfeasible, consequently he had never spoken to one: 'In theory, good idea, it's how to track them down' (GP 17). One GP explained that whilst there was now a trend towards school nurses becoming 'more integrated in primary care and that can only be a good thing', school nurses 'still tend to work in isolation' (GP 21).

Strengths and weaknesses of general practice

One of the strengths of general practice is that it can offer direct responses to multiple family members, including victims and perpetrators of domestic violence and their children. It is also well placed to make a key contribution to a multi-agency whole system response to the interface of domestic violence and child protection. There is, however, a continuing discrepancy between the reality and a vision that accords GPs 'both within government guidance and by fellow professionals, a much more pivotal role in all stages of the child protection process than they typically assume themselves' (Lupton et al. 2001, p.177).

Other studies describing the external perceptions of the GP role in child protection (e.g. Carter 2007; Richardson and Asthana 2006) indicated the GP's limited involvement in and isolation from the interagency child protection network. According to Hallett (1995, p.333), whose viewpoint is still acknowledged as relevant by many professionals:

> It seems clear the mandate to work together is not widely accepted by GPs, who may have the status and independence to ignore it. It may be that…they have, in fact little to contribute and the system can and does function in the main without their active participation.

Since this observation, there have been significant policy developments in this field. Doctors have become better trained to detect child abuse and they have clear child protection responsibilities. The National Institute for Health and Care Excellence guidance (2014) on domestic violence now urges all service providers, including general practice, to be informed about the procedures and services of all relevant local agencies for children and young people. However, whilst the roles of general practice professionals may be more clearly defined, they lack relevant training on child protection and domestic violence as well as space and time to interact and reflect on this area of work.

Despite important recent improvements in procedures, training and guidance, our study shows that professionals still operate on different 'planets' (Hester 2011) and connections between planets are limited by a lack of institutional knowledge, interagency trust and self-confidence which limit effective communication and team working.

We also found a varying but generally low level of general practice engagement in child protection work in relation to domestic violence beyond the point of referral. Our research indicates that most general practice professionals do recognise domestic violence as a risk factor for children and are also fully aware of their child protection responsibilities. Yet most failed to establish a link between child maltreatment and the possibility of children's exposure to domestic violence. When domestic violence in the family is identified, GPs tend to focus on the needs of parents rather than those of children.

What hinders the fuller engagement of general practice professionals in this area of work and what are the barriers to more effective interagency partnerships between general practice, social work and the domestic violence sector? This study was an attempt to answer these questions from the perspective of GPs themselves.

Participants in this study felt that general practice still operated on the periphery of the child protection system. Their limited participation in the process restricted their role to referral and information exchange rather than joint work.

Respondents also recognised the importance of informal communication between professionals in relation to domestic violence and children and regretted its absence. Communication at an individual level reinforced by formal methods of interagency interaction were identified as key to effective interagency work. Limited knowledge of the other agency's sphere of operations, poor engagement in joint decision making, low awareness of domestic violence services, a perceived lack of feedback and isolation from other professional groups can all have an adverse impact on practitioners' decision making. They can also have a negative effect on their self-confidence in responding to domestic violence in families.

The diversity of perspectives identified by this research indicates substantial variation between general practice professionals in their perceptions of the nature and strength of connections between domestic violence and child protection. Our findings also point to some salient differences in their expectations regarding interagency collaboration. These differences may raise concerns for the safety of children experiencing domestic violence but they also provide examples of positive practice among general practice professionals. However, mounting pressures on the health system, the increased fragmentation of child protection services, as identified by the recent Jay Review on child sexual exploitation in Northern England (Jay 2014), and the lack of a cohesive and coordinated approach to the complex problem of domestic violence can seriously undermine the overall effectiveness of these individual responses.

Conclusion

In light of these findings, attempts to shift responses to child maltreatment into general practice without at the same time providing the necessary support and resources (training, reflection time, supervision, etc.) and without focusing on improving systems for interagency collaboration cannot be feasible. GPs' work in the field of domestic violence and child protection will be safe and effective only as long as it is understood and managed within a context of interagency work.

Specialised interagency training is not a panacea, but it constitutes an important part of the answer to bridging the gap between child protection and domestic violence (Szilassy *et al.* 2013). We know from previous research that general practice professionals are poorly represented on the advanced interprofessional child protection courses, including training on domestic abuse (Carpenter *et al.* 2010). This research evidence and the findings reported above have informed the design and content of a new interagency training intervention that aims to increase general practice professionals' confidence and skills in managing the complexity of domestic violence when children are affected as well as improving interagency collaboration. This training is currently being piloted; it is hoped that it can be used to inform professional education more widely.

Acknowledgement

This chapter is based on independent research commissioned and funded by the Department of Health Policy Research Programme (Bridging the Knowledge and Practice Gap between Domestic Violence and Child Safeguarding: Developing Policy and Training for General Practice, 115/0003). The views expressed in this publication are those of the authors and not necessarily those of the Department of Health.

References

Banks, D., Dutch, N. and Wang, K. (2008) 'Collaborative efforts to improve system response to families who are experiencing child maltreatment and domestic violence.' *Journal of Interpersonal Violence 23*, 7, 876–902.

Birchall, E. and Hallett, C. (1995) *Working Together in Child Protection. Report Phase Two: A Survey of the Experience and Perceptions of the Six Key Professions.* London: HMSO.

Britton, A. (2012) 'Intimate Violence: 2010/11 BCS.' In K. Smith (ed.) *Home Office Statistical Bulletin 02/12: Homicides, Firearm Offences and Intimate Violence 2009/10. Supplementary Volume 2 to Crime in England and Wales 2010/11.* London: Home Office.

Carpenter, J., Hackett, S., Patsios, D. and Szilassy, E. (2010) *Outcomes of Interagency Training to Safeguard Children: Final Report.* London: Department for Children, Schools and Families/Department of Health.

Carter, Y. (2007) 'Lessons from the past, learning for the future: safeguarding children in primary care.' *British Journal of General Practice 57*, 536, 238–242.

Devaney, J. (2008) 'Inter-professional working in child protection with families with long-term and complex needs.' *Child Abuse Review 17*, 4, 242–261.

Feder, G., Hutson, M., Ramsay, J. and Taket, A. (2006) 'Women exposed to intimate partner violence: expectations and experiences when they encounter health care professionals: a meta-analysis of qualitative studies.' *Archives of Internal Medicine 166,* 1, 22–37.

Feder, G., Davies, R. A., Baird, K., Dunne, D. *et al.* (2011) 'Identification and Referral to Improve Safety (IRIS) of women experiencing domestic violence with a primary care training and support programme: a cluster randomised controlled trial.' *Lancet 378,* 9805, 1788–1795.

Hallett, C. (1995) *Interagency Coordination in Child Protection.* London: HMSO.

Health and Social Care Information Centre (2014) *General and Personal Medical Services: England 2003–2013.* Leeds: HSCIC. Available at www.hscic.gov.uk/catalogue/PUB13849/nhs-staf-2003-2013-gene-prac-rep.pdf, accessed on 12 September 2014.

Hegarty, K. (2006) 'What Is Intimate Partner Abuse and How Common Is It?' In G. Roberts, K. Hegarty and G. Feder (eds) *Intimate Partner Abuse and Health Professionals: New Approaches to Domestic Violence.* Edinburgh: Churchill Livingstone.

Hester, M. (2011) 'The three planet model: towards an understanding of contradictions in approaches to women and children's safety in contexts of domestic violence.' *British Journal of Social Work 41,* 5, 837–853.

Department for Education (2008) *Information Sharing for Practitioners and Managers.* London: HM Government.

Department for Education (2013) *Working Together to Safeguard Children: Statutory Guidance on Inter-Agency Working to Safeguard and Promote the Welfare of Children.* London: HM Government.

Department of Health (2010) *Achieving Equity and Excellence for Children: How Liberating the NHS Will Help Us Meet the Needs of Children and Young People.* London: DoH.

Jay, A. (2014) *Independent Inquiry into Child Sexual Exploitation in Rotherham.* Rotherham: Metropolitan Borough Council.

Laming, H. B. (2009) *The Protection of Children in England: A Progress Report.* London: The Stationery Office.

Larkins, C., Drinkwater, J., Hester, M., Stanley, N., Szilassy, E. and Feder, G. (under review) 'Engaging with abusive fathers but not with children? General practice clinicians' perspectives on involving and supporting children and perpetrators in families experiencing domestic violence and abuse.'

Lupton, C., North, N. and Khan, P. (2000) 'What role for the general practitioner in child protection?' *British Journal of General Practice 50,* 461, 977–981.

Lupton, C., North, N. and Khan, P. (2001) *Working Together or Pulling Apart? The NHS and Child Protection Networks.* Bristol: Policy Press.

Miller, D. and Jaye, C. (2007) 'GPs' perception of their role in the identification and management of family violence.' *Family Practice 24,* 2, 95–101.

National Institute for Health and Care Excellence (NICE) (2014) *Domestic Violence and Abuse: How Health Service, Social Care, and the Organisations They Work with Can Respond Effectively.* London: NICE.

Radford, L., Aitken, R., Miller, P., Ellis, J., Roberts, J. and Firkic, A. (2011) *Meeting the Needs of Children Living with Domestic Violence in London.* Research report. London: Refuge/NSPCC.

Royal College of General Practitioners (2009) *Safeguarding Children and Young People: A Toolkit for General Practice.* London: RCGP.

Richardson, S. and Asthana, S. (2006) 'Inter-agency information sharing in health and social care services: the role of professional culture.' *British Journal of Social Work 36,* 4, 657–669.

Ritchie, J. and Spencer, L. (1994) 'Qualitative Data Analysis for Applied Policy Research.' In A. Bryman and R. G. Burgess (eds) *Analyzing Qualitative Data.* Abingdon: Routledge.

Szilassy, E., Carpenter, J., Patsios, D. and Hackett, S. (2013) 'Outcomes of short course interprofessional training in domestic violence and child protection.' *Violence against Women 19*, 11, 1370–1383.

Tompsett, H., Ashworth, M., Atkins, C., Bell, L. *et al.* (2010) *The Child, the Family and the GP: Tensions and Conflicts of Interest for GPs in Safeguarding Children.* London: Kingston University.

Ward, H. and Davies, C. (2011) *Safeguarding Children across Services: Messages from Research.* London: Jessica Kingsley Publishers.

Women's Aid (2014) *Why We Need to Save Our Services: Women's Aid Data Report on Specialist Domestic Violence Services in England.* Bristol: Women's Aid.

Woodman, J., Gilbert, R., Allister, J., Glaser, D. and Brandon, M. (2013) 'Responses to concerns about child maltreatment: a qualitative study of GPs in England.' *BMJ Open 3*, 12, e003894.

CHAPTER 14

Moving Towards Integrated Domestic Violence Services for Children and Families

Nicky Stanley

This chapter considers multi-agency work in relation to children and families experiencing domestic violence. Numerous studies have testified to the absence of a joined-up approach to the issue of domestic violence (Hester 2011; Stanley *et al.* 2011) and inquiries and reviews into child deaths provide some of the most pressing evidence of the continuing need for organisations to develop more effective mechanisms for communicating information about the risks to children experiencing domestic violence (see, for example, Bradford Safeguarding Children Board 2013; Coventry Safeguarding Children Board 2013). Despite this, progress towards developing more coordinated or integrated systems has been slow. However, new 'whole system' and integrated models of collaboration are emerging and this chapter will trace the movement towards these new forms of multi-agency work.

Difficulties in collaboration and communication can be attributed to a number of factors: varying understandings and conceptions of domestic violence; the tendency of services to focus on either the victim, perpetrator or the child; and those differences in the knowledge base, service thresholds and agency remits and structures which impede multi-agency work on many issues. The lack of a joined-up approach has particular consequences for child protection work in the context of domestic violence. Some agencies or professionals still struggle to acknowledge children's involvement in domestic violence and fail to recognise their needs for support or protection. Mothers are saddled with responsibility for managing violent partners when child protection services fail to engage with those partners or because there are few resources or services for engaging with perpetrators. The threat of punitive social services involvement becomes a disincentive for victims and children to disclose abuse and for other agencies to make referrals. Young people who are experiencing abuse in their own intimate relationships, often after growing up against a background of domestic violence, slip out of the picture for many professionals. Hester (2011) argues that the unspoken but deeply embedded assumptions and orientations of professional groups operating in the field of domestic violence make it difficult for them to acknowledge the different perspectives of other organisations or professions. A lack of shared understanding regarding agencies' roles and remits as well as different services' varying assessment and eligibility criteria make for failures to share information and inappropriate referrals. Children and families are left without support or experience repeated and frustrating attempts to obtain the support they need.

However, domestic violence affects all family members, though in different ways. Not only does it involve all family members but the consequences have implications for many different aspects of experience and identity. The impact of domestic violence encompasses children's health and safety as well as their education, their development and their social relationships (Holt, Buckley and Whelan 2008; Stanley 2011). Moreover, domestic violence often occurs in tandem with other forms of child harm and with family and community problems such as mental health needs, substance misuse, crime, poverty and poor housing which undermine children's health and well-being (Cleaver, Unell and Aldgate 2010; Hamby and Grych 2013). Increasing awareness that children and families experience these problems as overlapping has contributed to new ventures aimed at creating joined-up or integrated services. Before discussing a selection of these new approaches, this chapter will draw on research evidence to explore some of the key challenges to multi-agency collaboration and integration.

Barriers to coordination and communication
Secrecy
As part of their overall mission to protect victims and children from violent perpetrators, domestic violence organisations have traditionally delivered their services in ways that seek to maintain women's and

staff's safety and confidentiality. Services are advertised using secure telephone numbers or protected websites and such information that is available in the public arena is likely to be non-specific and lack detail about the services available. Refuges themselves place a high premium on information about their location and contact details remaining restricted. Inadvertently, this approach may have contributed to the secrecy and stigma that surround domestic violence. Children who stay in refuges often complain about the closed nature of refuge life which restricts communication with friends and family (Överlien 2011; Stafford, Stead and Grimes 2007). Similarly, this lack of visibility may have contributed to poor communication between domestic violence services and other agencies.

Research undertaken with women in Wales in order to inform the national strategy for services addressing violence against women (Berry *et al.* 2014) found that victims themselves would like domestic violence services to be more widely publicised. Women participating in focus groups felt that services for those experiencing abuse and violence were not sufficiently promoted – 'why is it not advertised – it is not getting to the right places!' – and some felt that available information needed to be broadcast more widely: 'there is information but you have to know where to go for it' (Berry *et al.* 2014, p.59). However, as awareness and understanding of domestic violence penetrates public consciousness, largely as a result of the campaigning undertaken by domestic violence organisations, domestic violence services may have increased opportunities to move to a more visible position where both potential users and other professionals have fuller knowledge of what services they offer and how to access them. The example of the Oranje Huis discussed below provides an illustration of a more 'open' approach to delivering domestic violence services.

Lack of institutional empathy

A UK study of police notifications of domestic violence incidents to children's social services (Stanley *et al.* 2010) provides a clear illustration of the ways in which the divergent perspectives and remits of police and children's social workers acted as a barrier to effective communication and collaboration. Social workers receiving notifications from the police described the information transmitted as insufficiently child-focused. This was a direct consequence of police officers' reluctance to engage with children at the site of a domestic violence incident. From the police perspective, children were considered to be on the periphery of the incident and most police officers confined themselves to communicating with the adults present:

> ...when you communicate with the family you communicate with the adults generally speaking and you don't communicate with the children, the only time that you communicate with the children generally is when they are suspects...or they're witnesses. (Specialist supervising officer 1, Richardson-Foster *et al.* 2010, p.231)

Insufficiently detailed information on children's experiences of and responses to incidents was combined with limited understanding of how the information they passed to social workers would be used. Police officers lacked the 'institutional empathy' which would confer understanding of the role and remit of children's social services. Institutional empathy is defined by Banks, Dutch and Wang (2008) as an appreciation of the context shaping the work of another agency (see also Chapter 13 in this book) and, without it, one group of professionals will struggle to comprehend what information another group of professionals requires from them. In the absence of this understanding, the information communicated in police notifications was often incomplete or contained basic errors which made it difficult for social workers to identify the children and families involved in incidents. In some cases, the extent of a child's involvement in an incident was not conveyed. Police officers interviewed suggested that joint training and opportunities to 'shadow' one another might assist in increasing understanding of social workers' tasks and responsibilities:

> ...we need to be having joint training and things like that...to know each other's parts, what we do, because I still don't know what other agencies do properly, I know they do something but I don't know what. (DV specialist police officer, Stanley *et al.* 2011, p.2383)

Gaps in knowledge and partnerships

In the UK context, there are knowledge gaps concerning both child and adolescent mental health services (CAMHS) and schools in respect of their work with children who have experienced domestic violence (Stanley 2011). Although professionals in both these sectors regularly encounter and work with children and families affected by domestic violence, there is little research evidence available that describes or evaluates the work they do and their contribution to multi-agency collaboration in this field is also difficult to discern.

Social workers and other professionals commonly refer children seriously affected by their experience of domestic violence to CAMHS (Stanley *et al.* 2010); however, there is little published material available on CAMHS interventions with children experiencing domestic violence. Radford *et al.* (2011) found that parents and professionals participating in their mapping study of services in London for children experiencing domestic violence reported barriers to accessing CAMHS in the form of long waiting lists and rigid criteria for accessing the service. The government's response (Department for Children, Schools and Families and Department of Health 2010) to the independent review of CAMHS identifies children experiencing domestic violence as a vulnerable group at whom services should be targeted. However, many of the parenting programmes regularly delivered by CAMHS, such as Incredible Years and Triple P (Jones 2007; Webster-Stratton 2011), are not designed to address the specific needs of families where children are experiencing domestic violence. Increasingly, CAMHS are moving into schools with the Targeted Mental Health in Schools (TaMHS) initiative, which ran from 2008 to 2011, at the forefront of this development. This may contribute to CAMHS taking a broader approach to children's mental health needs which acknowledges the influence of the wider family and community contexts including issues such as domestic violence. It will also be important for CAMHS representatives to be invited to contribute to some of the emerging multi-agency initiatives described below.

Schools play a key role in respect of interventions aimed at preventing domestic violence with the majority of such programmes delivered in educational settings (Stanley *et al.* 2015). However, as the research findings discussed in Chapter 3 of this book indicate, education professionals can struggle to respond to disclosures of domestic violence by children and young people whether these concern abuse in their parents' relationships or in their own intimate relationships. UK evidence concerning education professionals' interventions with children experiencing domestic violence is scarce, although McGee's (2000) study found that some schools and nurseries provided valuable and sensitive support for both children and their mothers. In contrast, some small-scale studies (Byrne and Taylor 2007; Adamson and Deverell 2009) that have addressed education professionals' work in this area tend to emphasise a lack of knowledge and confidence in respect of children living with domestic violence.

Integrated systems for identifying and managing high-risk cases

The high volume of domestic violence incidents reported to both the police and children's social services have resulted in the development of systems that aim to identify those cases where the risks are highest and where multi-agency collaboration is required to inform both assessment and management of risk. These bring professionals from different agencies together to perform risk assessments with the aim of routing children and families to the appropriate level of intervention.

Multi-Agency Risk Assessment Conferences (MARACs) have been introduced in England and Wales as a means of improving interagency risk assessment and risk management for victims of domestic violence. Led by the police, they bring representatives from the police, probation, housing, health, children's social services and domestic violence services together to pool information and to produce a multi-agency plan to ensure the victim's safety. MARACs appear to have been successful in achieving information sharing but the focus is on the safety of high-risk adult victims rather than their children (Steel, Blakeborough and Nicholas 2011). However, they have provided a multi-agency forum where information about children living with domestic violence can be shared and discussed (Robinson 2004). Inevitably, a focus on high-risk victims means that those who are assessed as below the high-risk threshold may not receive a service that could conceivably prevent them becoming high-risk victims. Another criticism of the MARAC approach is that victims themselves do not attend the meetings, but are instead represented by independent domestic violence advisers (IDVAs).

Multi-Agency Safeguarding Hubs (MASH) offer a new approach to screening referrals to children's social services and they are currently being rolled out in local authorities across England. Their introduction has been fuelled in part by the difficulties experienced by children's social services in managing the growing mountain of police notifications of children involved in domestic violence incidents. The MASH model involves the establishment of a multi-agency team usually involving practitioners and administrative staff from children's social services, the police and health services, although other agencies such as housing and youth offending services may also contribute staff (King 2012). Team members have the capacity to collate information from their respective agencies to inform the screening of all referrals from professionals and the public, thus replacing children's social services' previous mono-agency intake systems. Interagency information sharing is freed from concerns about confidentiality and data protection by designating the multi-agency team as a 'sealed intelligence hub' (Golden, Aston and Durbin 2011, p.2) where information can be released from different agencies' databases and used to inform risk assessment with protocols covering its dissemination outside the hub. An initial traffic-light rating determines the speed at which a referral will be processed. An early process evaluation of MASH implementation in London (Crockett *et al.* 2013) suggested that the introduction of the MASH had contributed to sensitive and dynamic risk assessment, with decisions based on information that was extensive and timely. However, some professionals felt excluded from the MASH process and both MASH practitioners and those referring to the MASH reported that they would value receiving information about the outcome of referrals.

Whilst the MASH system only addresses information sharing at the front door of children's social services, it appears to be having wider effects in freeing up information exchange from restrictions concerning confidentiality and data protection. However, when domestic violence is an issue in families, confidentiality concerns can also be a means of ensuring the safety of victims, and further research on the outcomes of MASH assessments would be valuable in this respect. We need to understand whether concentrating multi-agency efforts at the threshold of children's social services increases the likelihood of all children and families receiving appropriate levels of support or whether it serves to focus resources on a few families. Does the emphasis on multi-agency information sharing and decision making at the outset of a referral increase multi-agency communication thereafter or does multi-agency collaboration drop away as the findings from the evaluation of MASH in London (Crockett *et al.* 2013) reported above suggest? The MASH system is in the early stages of implementation in England and there is as yet limited evidence of its effectiveness. However, the speed with which the model has been adopted is indicative of an enthusiasm for finding new ways to share information and strengthen risk assessments systems.

One-stop shops

Co-location is a key feature of the MASH system and the one-stop shop is the model that aims to co-locate the fullest range of agencies. Aimed at providing all the services that victims of domestic violence might need in one central location, the one-stop shop originated in San Diego, California, where they are known as Family Justice Centers and the model has been replicated in the US, Canada and the UK. Multi-agency teams provide a wide range of services which vary from one centre to another. However, the full range of services offered can include: support through the criminal justice system; legal and housing services; advice on finances, benefits, employment and immigration issues; advocacy, counselling and safety planning; interventions for mothers and children; medical examinations; adult education; substance misuse services; and (in one centre in East London) a forced marriage unit. An evaluation of eight Family Justice Centers in California (EMT Associates 2013) found that women came with multiple needs and the vast majority used more than one type of service offered at the centres, receiving between 1.3 and 4.4 different services. The two services most commonly used were legal assistance and advocacy/support.

One-stop shops are well established in Wales, and Berry *et al.*'s (2014) study indicated that one-stop shops may be particularly appropriate for families in rural areas who can access a range of services in one journey to their nearest large town. They also can offer an opportunity to provide responsive attitudes and sensitivity to the language and cultural needs of minority ethnic victims who may have a range of complex needs. Women using the Californian Family Justice Centers, for example, described receiving immigration advice and services as one of the most important benefits they experienced (EMT Associates 2013). However, whilst one-stop shops would seem an ideal setting in which to provide services and support for children and young people alongside those for adult victims, the model does not guarantee this focus on children.

Parallel interventions for children and mothers

North American evidence (Sudermann, Marshall and Loosely 2000; Graham-Bermann *et al.* 2007) on the effectiveness of programmes that provide parallel groups for mothers and children recovering from domestic violence has influenced the development of these interventions in the UK. Although such interventions are not yet widely available, they appear to be proliferating and recent guidance from the National Institute for Health and Care Excellence (NICE) (2014) recommending these programmes may boost this form of provision further. The majority of such programmes are provided through partnerships between domestic violence organisations and other agencies which may second staff to work alongside specialist domestic violence practitioners. Together, they deliver concurrent groups for mothers and children, most of which adopt a psychoeducational approach. For example, the NSPCC's Domestic Abuse Recovery Together (DART) programme has been delivered by social workers and specialist domestic violence practitioners across a number of sites in the UK. The evaluation (McManus *et al.* 2013), which used a comparison group, showed that children had significantly reduced behavioural difficulties following the programme. AVA's Community Group Programme adopts a similar model of intervention and is delivered in a large number of London boroughs by practitioners drawn from a range of agencies in both the voluntary and statutory sectors (Nolas, Neville and Sanders-McDonagh 2012).

The extent of interaction and integration between the two arms of these interventions varies from one programme to another. The DART programme brings children and parents together at the beginning of a session, then separates them into two groups and brings them together again at the close of a session. The Community Group Programme does not appear to involve much in the way of interaction between the two sets of groups. The Australian PARKAS intervention uses the same facilitators for both children's and parents' groups, so what is learnt in one setting can inform work in the other (Bunston 2008).

Three-in-one services

A number of UK initiatives have built on the Duluth model of delivering separate services for different family members affected by domestic violence within one locality and these have delivered separate services for victims, perpetrators and children from the same organisational base. Two domestic violence projects in northern England provide an example of this approach. Both projects were delivered by multi-agency partnerships with the aim of ensuring that a full range of services was available to families. Each project included three arms which provided separate services for mothers and children and a perpetrator programme. The evaluation (Donovan *et al.* 2010) reported success in reducing reported incidents and repeat referrals and the group and individual interventions provided for children appeared to be filling a gap in provision, although the impact of this service was not measured. However, the projects struggled to recruit participants to their perpetrator programmes and the researchers found that frontline practitioners in other agencies did not generally consider it part of their remit to motivate abusive men to attend such programmes. There were other challenges encountered with respect to multi-agency engagement which fell away over time leaving only a small core of committed agencies. The projects struggled to establish credibility with other agencies and to attract sufficient engagement from senior managers.

As Alderson, Kelly and Westmarland note in Chapter 11 in this book, perpetrator interventions in the UK are increasingly offering support services for children who have experienced domestic violence alongside a perpetrator programme and a support service for perpetrators' partners. This has resulted in a new approach to three-in-one services, one that starts from an intervention for perpetrators rather than one premised on a service for victims. The Caledonian system in Scotland (Scottish Government 2015) is probably the best established example of this approach but as yet there is no available evaluation of this three-pronged initiative. Caring Dads, an NSPCC intervention based on a Canadian model (Scott and Lishak 2012), is delivered in five UK sites (see also Chapter 12 for a discussion of this programme). The intervention comprises a programme for abusive men which aims to improve their parenting and to change abusive behaviour as well as delivering support services for men's partners and children. The programme is mainly delivered by NSPCC staff with some staff seconded from other agencies. The evaluation (McConnell *et al.* 2014) reported mixed evidence of effectiveness for fathers participating in the programme as well as difficulties in recruiting partners and children to the service – the programme did not have the capacity to work with very young children. Interestingly, the evaluation of Caring Dads in Wales (this particular service did not appear to include any support for children) argued for more involvement from other agencies, particularly statutory services, in the process of risk assessment (McCracken and Deave 2012).

Whole family approaches

Three-in-one services can suffer from fragmentation within the project (see Bell and Stanley 2005) or one arm of the service can come to dominate the work of the others. Kelly and Westmarland's (2015) evaluation of UK perpetrator programmes found that these programmes often struggled to fund and maintain a parallel women's support service and only three of the 12 Respect accredited programmes included in their study incorporated a support service for children. An alternative approach is to target a single integrated service on all members of a family experiencing domestic violence and whilst this remains a controversial approach, there is increasing evidence of services adopting a whole family approach for families living with domestic violence.

The Daybreak programme which has been implemented in several sites in England draws on Pennell and Burford's (2000) Canadian work which uses family group decision making (FGDM) as an intervention for families experiencing domestic violence. The Canadian evaluation utilised a comparison group selected from child protection case files and found that maltreatment reduced among children in the FGDM group and abusive events declined for mothers in the FGDM group whilst they rose for mothers in the comparison group (Pennell and Burford 2000). Daybreak accepts referrals from statutory and voluntary agencies, with some programmes also accepting self-referrals from families. Programme staff suggest that the use of family group conferences (FGCs), where all family members, including children, meet together with a facilitator to identify their problems and find appropriate solutions, acts to erode the secrecy that traditionally surrounds domestic violence. Internal evaluations indicate that the programme has had some success in reducing families' contact with the local police subsequent to the intervention (Hampshire Constabulary 2007, 2010). However, there are concerns about the extent to which FGCs can expose and address power and control dynamics in families and whether the safety of all family members can be protected in the context of an FGC approach.

Also in England, the Stefanou Foundation has recently launched the Healthy Relationships, Healthy Baby initiative (The Stefanou Foundation 2015) which aims to protect babies from the impact of domestic violence by working with both parents. The intervention begins in pregnancy and combines parenting support with interventions that address the perpetrator's behaviour and provide support for the victim. At the time of writing, this initiative is in the early stages of development but it represents a growth of interest in whole family interventions.

The Oranje Huis (Orange House) approach in the Netherlands provides an example of a well-developed intervention for the whole family that has its origins in the domestic violence sector. The approach, which is described as rooted in the recognition that many women wish to continue their relationship with their abusive partner (Blijf Groep 2011), involves contacting the partners of female victims whilst the victims are utilising the service's refuge accommodation and offering them an opportunity to also receive the Oranje Huis service following a risk assessment. One worker works with each family delivering an intervention that aims to promote change and resilience and which focuses heavily on parenting and child safety. Victims and perpetrators are seen individually and together and an additional support service is provided for children in the refuge. Another key feature of the Oranje Huis approach is the emphasis on transparency and visibility. Whilst security measures are in place in the refuge, the location and function of the Oranje Huis are not hidden or secret: openness about its location and role is argued to be a means of acknowledging that domestic violence is a feature of community life and that other members of the community have a social responsibility for tackling it (Blijf Groep 2011).

Project data from 2010 showed that work with partners was undertaken in 40 per cent of cases and that following the shift to a whole family approach, fewer women returned to live with their abusive partners (Blijf Groep 2011). A process evaluation (Lünnemann, Smit and Drost 2010) found that clients and staff were satisfied with the approach but recommended that services for children should be strengthened.

Towards greater collaboration and integration

Some key themes emerge from this account. Institutional empathy has been identified as a central feature of successful multi-agency communication. Collaboration and the importance of understanding how other professionals function and think and in what context they do so is also evident in Blacklock and Phillips' account of the collaboration between DVIP and Hackney children's services in Chapter 12 of this book. This apprehension of other agencies' functions and remits can be developed through multi-agency training that, in addition to raising knowledge and awareness of domestic violence and its impact on children, can educate practitioners about the roles, tasks and responsibilities of other professionals. Co-location also has a key role to play in promoting institutional empathy and this can take many forms and shapes. It may involve different services sharing premises but can also involve individual practitioners spending part of their working week or short periods working alongside other professionals with the aim of sharing skills and expertise.

This chapter has noted a move towards increased information sharing between agencies and this is generally to be welcomed as more information is likely to deliver better informed risk assessments and can be a means of increasing the resources available to contribute to plans and interventions. We have yet to see whether structures such as the MASH can improve outcomes for children experiencing domestic violence. There are some risks attached to the growing enthusiasm for these multi-agency meeting or panels. These include the possibility that staff outside the MARAC or MASH feel excluded from decision making and plans; that a focus on identifying high-risk cases excludes the possibility of early intervention for other children and families; and that concentrating multi-agency collaboration at the front door of children's social work means that there is little activity beyond the threshold.

Some agencies are still less active than others in these multi-agency partnerships. The NICE Guidance (2014) represents a clarion call for health services in England and Wales to engage with the issue of domestic violence and children feature prominently in the agenda set by the guidance. An increasing pressure on schools to engage in work aimed at preventing domestic abuse in young people's relationships is likely to result in stronger links between schools services that can deliver support to children and young people who do disclose domestic abuse in their own or their parents' relationships. One of the themes addressed in this chapter concerns a fuller integration of specialist domestic violence services with other community services – a movement away from secrecy into visibility. If such a move becomes more pronounced, the challenge for specialist domestic violence services will be to retain their own specific identify and expertise.

This chapter has also discerned a trend towards developing integrated services that work with the whole family experiencing domestic violence. This is a challenging but exciting direction which builds on the recognitions that men need to be fully engaged in the task of protecting children from the harm inflicted by domestic violence, that separation does not always signal an end to abuse and violence, and that families will choose to remain together despite the damage inflicted by domestic violence. There are risks for children, victims and for practitioners in pursuing these new models of intervention but it is apparent that there are a number of models emerging that need to be fully tested and compared.

The research evidence for the effectiveness of multi-agency collaboration is still surprisingly slight. This absence of evidence leaves us overly reliant on the findings of inquiries and on enthusiasm for change and innovation. We need to increase our understanding about which models and configurations of collaboration are effective and why. The various contexts in which new forms of interagency work are developed also need to be taken into account as local histories and established patterns of communication and joint work are likely to be influential. This means that our historic reliance on North American research may not be the best base on which to build multi-agency collaboration in the UK and Australia. We need to generate evidence which is grounded in the service context and history of multi-agency communication and coordination we have inherited and which identifies solutions and structures which are responsive to the gaps and challenges reported by those with first-hand experience of local services: children, families and practitioners.

References

Adamson, S. and Deverell, C. (2009) 'CAF in the country: implementing the Common Assessment Framework in a rural area.' *Child and Family Social Work 14*, 4, 400–409.

Banks, D., Dutch, N. and Wang, K. (2008) 'Collaborative efforts to improve system response to families who are experiencing child maltreatment and domestic violence.' *Journal of Interpersonal Violence 23*, 7, 876–902.

Bell, J. and Stanley, N. (2005) *Tackling Domestic Violence at the Local Level: An Evaluation of the Preston Road Domestic Violence Project*. Hull: University of Hull.

Berry, V., Stanley, N., Radford, L., McCarry, M. and Larkins, C. (2014) *Building Effective Responses: An Independent Review of Violence against Women, Domestic Abuse and Sexual Violence Services in Wales*. Cardiff: Welsh Government. Available at http://wales. gov.uk/statistics-and-research/building-effective-responses-independent-review-violence-against-women/?lang=en, accessed on 12 February 2015.

Blijf Groep (2011) *The Oranje Huis Approach: A New Style Women's Shelter in the Netherlands*. Amsterdam: Stichting Blijf Groep.

Bradford Safeguarding Children Board (2013) *A Serious Case Review, Hamzah Khan: The Overview Report*. Bradford: Bradford Safeguarding Children Board.

Bunston, W. (2008) 'Baby lead the way: mental health group work for infants, children and mothers affected by family violence.' *Journal of Family Studies 14*, 2–3, 334–341.

Byrne, D. and Taylor, B. (2007) 'Children at risk from domestic violence and their educational attainment: perspectives of education welfare officers, social workers and teachers.' *Child Care in Practice 13*, 3, 185–201.

Cleaver, H., Unell, I. and Aldgate, J. (2010) *The Impact of Parental Mental Illness, Learning Disability, Problem Alcohol and Drug Use and Domestic Violence on Children's Safety and Development, 2nd Edition.* London: TSO.

Coventry Safeguarding Children Board (2013) *Serious Case Review Re. Daniel Pelka, Born 15th July 2007, Died 3rd March 2012: Overview Report.* Coventry: Coventry Safeguarding Children Board.

Crockett, R., Gilchrist, G., Davies, J., Henshall, A. *et al.* (2013) *Assessing the Early Impact of Multi Agency Safeguarding Hubs (MASH) in London: Final Report.* London: London Councils, University of Greenwich.

Donovan, C., Griffiths, S., Groves, N., Johnson, H. and Douglass, J. (2010) *Evaluation of Early Intervention Models for Change in Domestic Violence: Northern Rock Foundation Domestic Abuse Intervention Project, 2004–2009.* Newcastle upon Tyne: Northern Rock Foundation.

EMT Associates (2013) *Final Evaluation Results: Phase II California Family Justice Initiative Statewide Evaluation.* Burbank, CA: EMT. Available at www.familyjusticecenter. org/index.php/jdownloads/finish/41-evaluation-a-outcomes/728-evaluation-a-outcomes-full-report-of-california-family-justice-initiative-statewide-evaluation-july-2013.html, accessed on 12 February 2015.

Department for Children, Schools and Families/Department of Health (2010) *Keeping Children and Young People in Mind: The Government's Full Response to the Independent Review of CAMHS.* Nottingham: DCSF.

Golden, S., Aston, H. and Durbin, B. (2011) *Devon Multi-Agency Safeguarding Hub: Case-Study Report.* Slough: National Foundation for Educational Research.

Graham-Bermann, S. A., Lynch, S. A., Banyard, V., DeVoe, E. R. and Halabu, H. (2007) 'Community-based intervention for children exposed to intimate partner violence: an efficacy trial.' *Journal of Consulting and Clinical Psychology 75*, 2, 199–209.

Hamby, S. and Grych, J. (2013) *The Web of Violence: Exploring Connections among Different Forms of Interpersonal Violence and Abuse.* New York, NY: Springer.

Hampshire Constabulary (2007) *North and East OCU Analyst Report* (unpublished report). Winchester: Hampshire Constabulary.

Hester, M. (2011) 'The three planet model: towards an understanding of contradictions in approaches to women and children's safety in contexts of domestic violence.' *British Journal of Social Work 41*, 837–853.

Holt, S., Buckley, H. and Whelan, S. (2008) 'The impact of exposure to domestic violence on children and young people: a review of the literature.' *Child Abuse and Neglect 32*, 8, 797–810.

Jones, J. (2007) *The Three P's of Parenting.* LearnGarden Press.

Kelly, L. and Westmarland, N. (2015) *Domestic Violence Perpetrator Programmes: Steps to Change. Executive Summary.* Available at www.dur.ac.uk/resources/criva/ProjectMirabalexecutivesummary.pdf, accessed on 30 January 2015.

King, J. (2012) *Local Authority Readiness Assessment for MASH.* London: London MASH Project Board.

Lünnemann, K. D., Smit, W. and Drost, L. F. (2010) *De Methodiek Oranje Huis in Uitvoering.* Utrecht: Verwey-Jonker Instituut.

McConnell, N., Barnard, M., Holdsworth, T. and Taylor, J. (2014) *Caring Dads: Safer Children. Interim Evaluation Report.* London: NSPCC.

McCracken, K. and Deave, T. (2012) *Evaluation of the Caring Dads Cymru Programme. Report No. 18/2012.* Cardiff: Welsh Assembly Government. Available at http://wales. gov.uk/docs/caecd/research/120706caringdadsen.pdf, accessed on 30 January 2015.

McManus, E., Belton, E., Barnard, M., Cotmore, R. and Taylor, J. (2013) 'Recovering from domestic abuse, strengthening the mother–child relationship: mothers' and children's perspectives of a new intervention.' *Child Care in Practice 19*, 291–310.

National Institute for Health and Care Excellence (NICE) (2014) *Domestic Violence and Abuse: How Health Service, Social Care, and the Organisations They Work with Can Respond Effectively.* London: NICE.

Nolas, S. M., Neville, L. and Sanders-McDonagh, E. (2012) *Evaluation of the Community Group Programme for Children and Young People: Final Report.* Middlesex University, University of Sussex and AVA.

Överlien, C. (2011) 'Abused women with children or children of abused women? A study of conflicting perspectives at women's refuges in Norway.' *Child & Family Social Work 16*, 1, 71–80.

Penell, J. and Burford, G. (2000) 'Family group decision making: protecting children and women'. *Child Welfare: Journal of Policy, Practice and Program 9*, 2, 131–158.

Radford, L., Aitken, R., Miller, P., Ellis, J., Roberts, J. and Firkic, A. (2011) *Meeting the Needs of Children Living with Domestic Violence in London: Research Report.* London: Refuge/NSPCC.

Richardson Foster, H., Stanley, N., Miller, P. and Thomson, G. (2012) 'Police intervention in domestic violence incidents where children are present: police and children's perspectives.' *Policing and Society 22*, 2, 220–234.

Robinson, A. (2004) *Domestic Violence MARACs (Multi-Agency Risk Assessment Conferences) for Very High-Risk Victims in Cardiff, Wales: A Process and Outcome Evaluation.* Cardiff: Cardiff University.

Scottish Government (2010) *The Caledonian System.* Available at www.scotland.gov. uk/Topics/People/Equality/violence-women/CaledonianSystem, accessed on 30 January 2015.

Scott, K. L. and Lishak, V. (2012) 'Intervention for maltreating fathers: statistically and clinically significant change.' *Child Abuse and Neglect 36*, 9, 680–684.

Stafford, A., Stead, J. and Grimes, M. (2007) *The Support Needs of Children and Young People Who Have to Move Home Because of Domestic Abuse.* Edinburgh: Scottish Women's Aid.

Stanley, N. (2011) *Children Experiencing Domestic Violence: A Research Review.* Dartington: Research in Practice.

Stanley, N., Ellis, J., Farrelly, N., Hollinghurst, S., Bailey, S. and Downe, S. (2015, in press) 'Preventing Domestic Abuse for Children and Young People (PEACH): A Mixed Knowledge Scoping Review.' *Public Health Research.*

Stanley, N., Miller, P., Richardson Foster, H. and Thomson, G. (2011) 'Children's experiences of domestic violence: developing an integrated response from police and child protection services.' *Journal of Interpersonal Violence 26*, 12, 2372–2391.

Stanley, N., Miller, P., Richardson Foster, H. and Thomson, G. (2010) *Children and Families Experiencing Domestic Violence: Police and Children's Services' Responses.* London: NSPCC. Available at www.nspcc.org.uk/Inform/research/Findings/children_experiencing_ domestic_violence_wda68549.html, accessed on 30 January 2015.

Steel, N., Blakeborough, L. and Nicholas, S. (2011) *Supporting High-Risk Victims of Domestic Violence: A Review of Multi-Agency Risk Assessment Conferences (MARACs), Research Report 55.* London: The Home Office.

Sudermann, M., Marshall, L. and Loosely, S. (2000) 'Evaluation of the London (Ontario) community group treatment programme for children who have witnessed woman abuse.' *Journal of Aggression, Maltreatment & Trauma 31*, 127–146.

The Stefanou Foundation (2015) Available at www.stefanoufoundation.org/core-programmes.pl, accessed on 30 January 2015.

Webster-Stratton, C. (2011) *The Incredible Years Parents, Teachers, and Children Training Series: Program Content, Methods, Research and Dissemination, 1980–2011.* Seattle, WA: Incredible Years Inc.

CONCLUSION

New Challenges and Developments in Responding to Children Experiencing Domestic Violence

Cathy Humphreys and Nicky Stanley

The authors and researchers who have contributed to this book provide testimony to both the challenges and the new developments in protecting children exposed to domestic violence. The recognition that everyone has a responsibility to ensure the safety and well-being of children is a glib phrase which can obfuscate the importance of this statement. Certainly, the contributors to this book have demonstrated that practice aimed at safeguarding children and preventing domestic violence is not restricted to statutory child protection services. The voices of children and young people are telling in this regard, emphasising the importance of a 'web of safety' which includes both their informal relationships (friends and family) as well as the potential significance of formal organisations in relation to schooling, health care, advocacy and youth services.

It is clear that we are not going to 'treat' our way out of this destructive social problem and that we require a multi-faceted approach to domestic violence. Desmond (2011) helpfully identifies four levels of domestic violence intervention: primary prevention, secondary prevention, crisis intervention and post-crisis intervention. Currently, crisis intervention tends to absorb a disproportionate amount of resources. Child protection and refuge and outreach services are responsible for much of this crisis work and have traditionally been charged with providing the frontline response to women and children.

However, both these sectors are undergoing profound change. As noted in the discussion of the Multi-Agency Safeguarding Hubs (MASH) in Chapter 14, child protection services are seeking to develop a differential response to families experiencing domestic violence. This should ensure that more families receive community-based support with the more intrusive child protection intervention targeted on those who need it. However, there is a risk that the investigative function of statutory child protection services will be unavailable for many families along with the evidence generated by those investigations which can be used to promote change for victims and children.

At the same time, the independent domestic violence sector is diversifying and is moving beyond the delivery of crisis services to deliver a range of post-crisis interventions such as the KIDVA advocacy services for children described by Joanne Westwood and Cath Larkins in Chapter 4, or the interventions aimed at promoting the recovery of mothers and children discussed by Cathy Humphreys and colleagues in Chapters 8 and by Wendy Bunston in Chapter 9.

The voluntary sector has also been prepared to grasp the nettle of work with perpetrators, and Chapter 11 by Sue Alderson and colleagues and Chapter 12 by Ruth Phillips and Neil Blacklock have provided examples of some of the forms that work is assuming as well as its impact on children. Chapter 12 identified some of the gains and challenges involved in sharing expertise and knowledge in work with perpetrators across the independent and statutory sectors, and initiatives of this sort may proliferate as both sectors become increasingly open to collaboration.

The domestic violence sector is also creating new partnerships with statutory services in the field of prevention. In Chapter 3, Jane Ellis and colleagues highlighted the partnerships between schools and domestic violence organisations forged to deliver preventive domestic violence programmes in schools. Chapter 6 by Zahra Alijah and Khatidja Chantler provided an example of collaboration between education and a specialist service in Manchester aimed at raising awareness and addressing the issue of forced marriage at an early stage.

However, some parts of the system appear to have resisted change. In Chapter 7, Lorraine Radford and Marianne Hester noted children's continued exposure to domestic abuse in the context of contact. This argument is reinforced by research reported by Anita Morris and colleagues in Chapter 1 and by Stephanie Holt in Chapter 10 which provide vivid illustrations of the myriad ways in which contact continues to be unsafe for children and young people. The failure to address this issue can be attributed to the priority given to fathers' rights in legislation and in the courts and the lack of weight given to children's perspectives and safety.

There are other arenas where change is required. Eszter Szilassy and colleagues' account in Chapter 13 of general practice professionals' interventions with children and families depicts them as isolated from both domestic violence services and children's social services. Whilst GPs appeared to have some awareness of the harm domestic violence represented for children, they had little knowledge of what interventions were appropriate or available beyond the crisis response represented by a child protection referral.

Increased understanding of the diverse ways in which violence and abuse within the family are perpetrated brings new challenges for both identification and intervention systems. Child to parent violence (see Chapter 5 by Wilcox and Pooley) and forced marriage (see Chapter 6) are cases in point. As both Chapters 5 and 6 emphasise, professional awareness is undeveloped and both victims and perpetrators involved in these forms of abuse often fall through the gaps in the intervention system. They fit poorly into the traditional service system which clings to fixed ideas about who are victims and perpetrators (Hunter, Nixon and Parr 2010). Similarly, as we learn more about abuse and violence in young people's relationships, we recognise how rarely young people disclose this type of harm and how unprepared services are to respond to it. The young people participating in Per Hellevik and colleagues' European study reported in Chapter 2 were unlikely to confide in adults although they thought that both schools and parents should do more to prevent interpersonal violence and abuse.

As awareness of domestic violence and the harm it inflicts on children and young people grows, both the definition and the service response are acknowledging new forms of harm. This broadening of the remit is balanced by the fact that a wider range of practitioners from varying backgrounds and settings are contributing to interventions aimed at children and families. The sense that we are not alone in our efforts but connected through a wider social movement to address violence towards women and children adds to the sustainability of this work. Increasingly, domestic violence is found to be implicated in the deaths of women and children, and this amplifies the call to action. These deaths represent the tragic end point of violence, but they are only the tip of the iceberg of this widespread social problem.

This book points to new directions that provide optimism and hope in the face of challenges that are both familiar and changing. Policy, practice and research need to be inclusive, open and responsive to innovation, particularly that which draws on the depth of experience which has been accumulated in this field. Domestic violence is a social and individual scourge which impacts on children's lives both in the present and in their future. The chapters in this book provide testimony to the energy and the creative responses that are required to combat this 'wicked' social problem.

References

Desmond, K. (2011) *Filling the Gap: Integrated Post-Crisis Response for Women and Children Who Have Experienced Family Violence.* Melbourne: Good Shepherd Youth and Family Services. Available at www.goodshepvic.org.au/Assets/Files/Filling_The_Gap_Service_Model_April_2011.pdf, accessed on 23 February 2015.
Hunter, C., Nixon, J. and Parr, S. (2010) 'Mother abuse: a matter of youth justice, child welfare and domestic violence?' *Journal of Law and Society 37,* 264–284.

CONTRIBUTOR PROFILES

NADIA AGHTAIE

Nadia Aghtaie is a lecturer in gender-based violence at the School for Policy Studies, University of Bristol. She is an active member of the Centre for Gender Violence and Research. She has researched and published within the field of gender violence in national and international contexts. Her recent work has focused on structural and cultural gender violence within the Muslim context.

SUE ALDERSON

Sue Alderson is a senior lecturer in social work at the University of Seychelles. Prior to taking up this post, she was a doctoral researcher at Durham University and a research associate undertaking various research projects focusing on domestic violence, early child development, children's services and rape crisis interventions.

ZAHRA ALIJAH

Zahra Alijah is a lecturer in education at the University of Manchester specialising in teacher training. Her research interest is sex and relationship education in schools and informal education contexts, with a focus on gender, body image and relationships. Zahra has also worked on forced marriage awareness raising in schools and has been a schoolteacher and an adviser working with schools in diverse ethnic and socioeconomic contexts.

CHRISTINE BARTER

Dr Christine Barter is an NSPCC senior research fellow at the School for Policy Studies, University of Bristol. She has published widely on a range of children's welfare issues. Her most recent work has focused on violence and control in young people's intimate relationships, the first European study in this area.

NEIL BLACKLOCK

Neil Blacklock is development director at Respect, the UK lead for organisations working with perpetrators of intimate partner violence, male victims and young people using violence and abuse in close relationships. He founded the Domestic Violence Intervention Project in 1991, moved to Respect in 2006 and is the current chair of the European network Work With Perpetrators (www.workwithperpetrators.eu).

WENDY BUNSTON

Wendy Bunston is a senior clinical consultant and trainer specialising in working with infants, children and their mothers impacted by family violence. She has developed award-winning therapeutic programmes and published widely in this area. She is currently a PhD candidate and associate lecturer at La Trobe University, Melbourne, Australia.

KHATIDJA CHANTLER

Khatidja Chantler is a reader in the School of Social Work, University of Central Lancashire, and founder member of the Connect Centre for International Research on Interpersonal Violence and Harm. She has extensive experience of researching gender-based violence, particularly in minoritised communities. Her publications include British, European and international journal articles, book chapters and co-authored and co-edited works.

SOO DOWNE

Soo Downe is professor of midwifery studies at the University of Central Lancashire. Her primary research area is the nature and consequences of normal birth, including for marginalised women. She is interested in developing new approaches to systematic reviews and she worked on the PEACH study on preventing domestic abuse for children.

JESSICA DRINKWATER

Jessica Drinkwater is an academic general practitioner at the University of Leeds. She has an interest in how general practice can support families experiencing domestic violence.

JANE ELLIS

Jane Ellis is senior lecturer in social policy at Anglia Ruskin University. Her main interests are gendered violence, childhood and children's participation. She has conducted research and consultancy on prevention work in schools. Before undertaking her PhD she worked with children, young people and their families in formal and informal educational settings as a teacher and community education worker.

NICOLA FARRELLY

Nicola Farrelly was formerly a residential social worker supporting adolescents and subsequently carried out research on issues affecting young people in care. As a research fellow at the School of Social Work, University of Central Lancashire, she worked on a study of interventions aimed at preventing domestic violence for children.

GENE FEDER

Gene Feder is professor of primary care at the University of Bristol and a GP. He led the first European epidemiological study of domestic violence and abuse (DVA) in primary care, landmark systematic reviews on DVA screening and survivors' expectations of clinicians and trials of DVA interventions. He also chaired the development of the 2013 WHO intimate partner violence guidelines and the 2014 UK National Institute for Clinical Excellence DVA guidelines.

KELSEY HEGARTY

Professor Kelsey Hegarty is a general practitioner and director of the abuse and violence research programme in the Primary Care Research Unit at the University of Melbourne. She leads a programme of research developing and testing interventions for women, men and children delivered through primary care and technology.

PER MOUM HELLEVIK

Per Moum Hellevik is a PhD candidate at the Norwegian Centre for Violence and Traumatic Stress Studies and the Institute for Media and Communication at the University of Oslo. He is a sociologist specialising in the internet and social media.

MARIANNE HESTER

Professor Marianne Hester OBE holds the chair in gender, violence and international policy at the University of Bristol and heads the Centre for Gender and Violence Research. She is a leading researcher of gender-based violence internationally and has directed research in the UK, Europe, China and Scandinavia.

SANDRA HOLLINGHURST

Sandra Hollinghurst is a senior lecturer in health economics at the University of Bristol. Based at the Centre for Academic Primary Care, her research focuses on using economics to inform decision making in primary healthcare practice. Recent work includes the evaluation of a psychological intervention for survivors of domestic abuse.

STEPHANIE HOLT

Stephanie Holt is an academic in social work at the School of Social Work and Social Policy, Trinity College, Dublin. Prior to her current academic post she worked as a child and family social worker and coordinated a family support service in Dublin. Her academic and research interests include domestic violence, intimate partner homicide, post-separation child contact, child care and family support.

CATHY HUMPHREYS (EDITOR)

Cathy Humphreys is professor of social work at the University of Melbourne. She specialises in research in domestic violence as well as vulnerable children in the care system. For 12 years she worked in the UK at the University of Warwick. She worked as a social work practitioner for 16 years prior to becoming an academic.

JOCELYN JONES

Dr Jocelyn Jones is director of Mindful Practice Ltd (www.mindfulpractice. co.uk), a company which specialises in child-centred leadership coaching and the professional development of child protection managers across the UK. Jocelyn holds an honorary research fellowship at Royal Holloway, University of London, and a visiting fellowship at Bournemouth University.

LIZ KELLY

Professor Liz Kelly is director of the Child and Woman Abuse Studies Unit at the London Metropolitan University. In 2000 Liz was appointed professor of sexualised violence and was awarded a CBE for services combating violence against women and children. In 2006 she was appointed Roddick chair of violence against women.

CATH LARKINS

Dr Cath Larkins is co-director of the Centre for Children's and Young People's Participation, University of Central Lancashire. She facilitates co-research with children and young people across Europe, focused on challenging discrimination and improving services. She writes on citizenship theory and participation, and co-chairs Eurochild's advisory group on participatory methods.

ANITA MORRIS

Anita Morris is manager of social work at Western Health, a large teaching hospital in Melbourne, Australia. She is also a trainee representative on the committee of PreVAiL, a Canadian international research consortium. Anita completed her PhD in 2015 and has published in the area of research ethics.

CAROLINA ÖVERLIEN

Carolina Överlien is an assistant professor at Stockholm University, Sweden and a researcher at the Norwegian Centre for Violence and Traumatic Stress Studies in Oslo. Her main research has focused on children experiencing domestic violence and teenage girls in juvenile care.

RUTH PHILLIPS

Ruth Phillips is a doctoral candidate examining programme integrity for British domestic violence perpetrator programmes at the Child and Woman Abuse Studies Unit, London Metropolitan University. She was recently appointed as a principal risk assessor at the Domestic Violence Intervention Project, London, providing expert witness reports for the family courts.

MICHELLE POOLEY

Michelle Pooley is a community engagement and domestic violence practitioner at Brighton and Hove City Council. She was the Brighton and Hove coordinator of the EU 'Responding to Child to Parent Violence 2013–2015' project funded by the Daphne Programme. She coordinates the multi-agency Break4change programme.

LORRAINE RADFORD

Lorraine Radford is professor of social policy and social work at the University of Central Lancashire and co-director of the Connect Centre for International Research on Interpersonal Violence and Harm. She is currently researching early help for women and children living with domestic violence and cross-national responses to child sexual exploitation and abuse.

CATHY SHARP

Cathy Sharp is the director of Research for Real, an Edinburgh-based action research consultancy. She was responsible for the evaluation of the Cedar National Pilot (2011) with Jocelyn Jones, Gina Netto and Cathy Humphreys. She continues to work alongside the Scottish Women's Aid Cedar national development team.

NICKY STANLEY (EDITOR)

Nicky Stanley is professor of social work and co-director of the Connect Centre for International Research on Interpersonal Violence and Harm at the University of Central Lancashire. She researches on domestic violence, child protection, parental mental health and young people's mental health. She is currently working on a number of studies examining services for children and families experiencing domestic violence.

ESZTER SZILASSY

Dr Eszter Szilassy is a research associate at the University of Bristol. She has worked as a researcher on various projects on DVA, health and child protection. She manages the domestic violence and health research group at the Centre for Academic Primary Care at the School of Social and Community Medicine at the University of Bristol.

RAVI K. THIARA

Dr Ravi K. Thiara is a principal research fellow and director of the Centre for the Study of Safety and Well-Being, University of Warwick, UK. She has been involved in research on violence against women and children for the last 25 years and has carried out this work at a national and international level.

WILLIAM TURNER

William Turner is a senior lecturer at the School for Policy Studies at the University of Bristol. His research interests include the application of quantitative methods, particularly randomised controlled trial and systematic reviews, child mental health and the evaluation of psychotherapeutic interventions aimed at children and young people.

NICOLE WESTMARLAND

Nicole Westmarland is a professor of criminology at Durham University and co-director of the Durham Centre for Research into Violence and Abuse. She led the Durham part of Project Mirabal and has published a range of books and articles on male violence against women.

JOANNE WESTWOOD

Joanne Westwood is a senior lecturer in the School of Applied Social Science at the University of Stirling. Her research draws on qualitative participatory methodologies and focuses on the exclusion and marginalisation of children and young people, including unaccompanied minors and trafficked young people in the UK and Roma young people in the EU.

PAULA WILCOX

Paula Wilcox is a reader in criminology at the University of Brighton and principle investigator of the EU 'Responding to Child to Parent Violence 2013–2015' project funded by the Daphne Programme. She has published over 20 journal articles and published the book *Surviving Domestic Violence: Gender, Poverty and Agency* in 2006.

MARSHA WOOD

Marsha Wood is a research associate at the School for Policy Studies, University of Bristol. She has worked on numerous studies exploring in particular young people's experiences of intimate partner violence and issues faced by looked-after children. Marsha has published articles in journals such as *Child and Family Social Work* and *Children and Society.*

SUBJECT INDEX

absent presence 31
abuse, new forms 15
abusive fathers, engaging
    with 15
Abusive Household Gender
    Regime (AHGR) 131
academies and free schools
    programme 50–1
access, safety of 24
action research 133–4, 139
adolescence, autonomy in 37
adolescent violence in
    the home 84
adolescents, intimate
    relationships see
    Safeguarding
    Teenage Intimate
    Relationships (STIR)
Adoption and Children
    Act 2002 197–8
advertising, of services 234
advocacy 64, 65, 78
    see also KIDVA
affection 175
age 15
agency 24–31
agency responses, three planets
    model 115–16, 117
Anti-Social Behaviour,
    Crime and Policing
    Act, 2014 99
anti-social behaviour
    orders 199
antisocial behaviour 199
approachability 45
arranged marriages 97
Australia, recognition of
    domestic violence 120–1
autonomy, in adolescence 37
AVA Community Group
    Programme 240

being there 173
being with 151–2, 153
blame 197
book
    aims 13–14
    changing context of 14–15
    content and scope 14
    overview 249
    structure 16
    summary and conclusions
        249–52
boundaries 55
BuBs on Board 154

CAFCASS 114, 125
Caledonian system 241
capacity, children 170, 179
Caring Dads 201, 241
Caring Dads in Wales 125, 241
case studies
    Benny 158–9
    Darcy 154–6
    Pia 156–8
    Tina 76–7
Casey, Louise 184, 200
Cedar (Children Experiencing
    Domestic Abuse
    Recovery) 130, 138–44
    assessment process 139–40
    children's and young
        people's experiences
        142, 144
    concurrent groups 142
    curriculum 140
    development of 138
    iceberg exercise 141
    influence on mother–child
        relationship 143–4
    nature of project 138–9
    participants' starting
        points 144
    partnership working 139
    peer learning 142–3
    research method 139

strengthening
    mother–child
    relationship 139–43
strengths-based
    approach 140
change, resistance to 250–1
child and adolescent mental
    health services
    (CAMHS) 235–6
child arrangement orders 116
child-centred approach 20
child contact, as context
    of violence 15
child development, influence
    of fathers 166–7
child protection
    differential responding 250
    effects of service
        fragmentation 232–3
    forced marriage 99–100
    responding to families 15
child protection plans 198
Child to Parent Violence and
    Abuse (CPV) 15, 81
    awareness of 251
    criminalisation of
        children 90–2
    deficit model 90–2
    defining 83–6
    disclosure and
        discussion 87–8
    as domestic violence 85
    interventions 92
    and IPV 85–6
    practitioner awareness 92
    prevalence 86–7
    recognition 87–8
    research 82
    stigma 89
    summary and conclusions
        93–4
    see also Responding to
        Child to Parent
        Violence (RCPV)

children
  activities with fathers 193
  agency 24, 25–31
  appropriate approaches
    to 124
  availability of mother 132
  burden of secrecy 123
  within contact debate
    169–70
  feelings before DVPP 191
  feelings of safety 193–4
  feelings towards
    fathers 192–3
  as intrinsic motivation
    for change 190
  lack of autonomy and
    control 13
  manipulation 121, 122
  outcome of preventive
    intervention 58
  positioning 123–4
  protection from
    harassment 124
  role in decision making
    169–70, 176–7
  as social agents 19–20
  strategies in father–child
    relationship 167
  as vulnerable or capable
    170, 179
Children Act 1989 99
Children and Adoption
  Act 2006 114
Children and Families
  Act 2014 114
children's and young
  people's experiences
  Amelia 23
  Andrea 41–2
  Cathy 173
  Cedar (Children
    Experiencing
    Domestic Abuse
    Recovery) 142, 144
  Ciara 172, 175, 176
  of CPV 91
  Davide 41
  Elena 38
  Eva 173, 176, 177
  Giorgos 38–9
  Kate 175
  Kevin 192
  Kyrenia, 40
  Leah 173
  Lily 42
  Linda 23–4
  Lise 40
  Maria 43
  Max 26–8

  Michelle 18
  Molly 44
  Nikolaj 43
  Nina 38
  Pernille 44
  Peter 26–8
  Petra 40
  post-separation fathering
    172–4
  Rachel 172, 174
  Robert 172
  Sally and Sam 192–3
  Sara 176
  Sofie 42
  Sophia 37
  Tahlia 21–3
  Talking to My Mum
    project 135, 136
  Tina 76–7
  Todd 177
  Tone 41
  Zoe 28–31
children's rights 170
children's views see
  SARAH project
Civil Protection Act (Forced
  Marriage) 2007 98
co-construction
  family resiliency 31
  family units 31
co-delivery 60
co-location
  collaborative working
    203–4, 210
  Domestic Violence
    Perpetrator
    Programmes
    (DVPPs) 204–6
  institutional empathy 244
  of services 130, 239
Coaching Boys into Men 45
coercive behaviour 120, 121
coercive control
  enlisting agencies in 122
  and mothering 122
  resistance 122–3
collaborative working
  challenges for DVPPs
    208–9
  challenges for statutory
    services 209–10
  co-location 203–6
  context and overview
    196–7
  Domestic Violence
    Perpetrator
    Programmes
    (DVPPs) 202–3

  engagement with fathers
    199–200
  fathers as resource 200–2
  moving forward 210
  The Safe and Together
    Model™ 207–8
  see also integrated services;
    multi-agency work
communication
  barriers 233–6
  difficulties 232–3
  between professionals 228
Community Groupwork
  Treatment Programme
  (CGP) 138
confidentiality 38–9, 55,
  66, 71, 233–4
connection 168, 173
consent, SARAH project 20
contact centres 118–19
contemplative practice
  151–2, 153
controlling behaviour 120, 121
coordinated community
  response model 202
coordinated community
  responses 197
courts 114
criminal justice system 90–2
crisis intervention 249
critical pedagogy 105
cross-agency working 115

danger, and vulnerability 21–5
DASH (domestic abuse,
  stalking and harassment
  risk assessment)
  tool 113, 119–20
Daybreak programme 242
deaths 251–2
deficit model, of CPV 90–2
dialogical ethics 20, 28
digital media, intimate partner
  violence (IPV) 34
disability 15
disclosure
  confidentiality 55
  of CPV 87–8
  fear of 51, 54
  level of 53–4
  managing 56–7, 60
  process of 55
  summary and
    conclusions 60
  and trust 55, 58
Domestic Abuse Recovery
  Together (DART) 240

domestic violence
    as attack on mother–child
        relationship 131
    conceptualisations 14
    defining 85, 120, 121
    increased focus on 197–9
Domestic Violence Awareness
    Raising 54, 58
Domestic Violence Intervention
    Project (DVIP)
    (Hackney) 205, 206
Domestic Violence Perpetrator
    Programmes (DVPPs)
    availability 202–3
    challenges for 208–9
    challenges for statutory
        services 209–10
    children's feelings before
        intervention 191
    children's feelings towards
        fathers 192–3
    co-location 204–6
    collaborative working see
        collaborative working
    context and overview
        182–3
    fathers' activities with
        children 193
    feelings of safety 193–4
    group work 188–90
    infrequency of
        intervention 183
    summary and
        conclusions 194
    understandings of
        success 185–8
double disappearing act
    114–19, 125
Duluth model 240

education, for protection 45
emotional literacy 144
emotional regulation,
    infants 150
emotions 22–3
empathy 41–2
EMT Associates 239
ethics 19–20, 28
ethnicity 15
Every Child Matters 60, 70

Facebook 44
failure to protect 131
failure to understand 131
Family Court 114
family experiences, Talking to
    My Mum project 138

family group conferences
    (FGCs) 242
family group decision
    making (FGDM) 242
family intervention
    projects (FIPs) 86
Family Justice Centers 239
Family Law Act (1996) (Forced
    Marriage) (Relevant
    Third Party) 98–9
family resiliency,
    co-construction
    26, 27–8, 31
family units, co-construction
    31
Family Violence
    Committee 119
father–child relationship
    children's strategies 167
    post-separation contact 168
    psychological presence 168
    quality of 173
    see also fathering
Fatherhood Institute 201
fathering
    and childhood
        experience 175
    children's and young
        people's experiences
        172–4
    children's role in
        decision making
        169–70, 176–7
    children's views on
        contact 169–70
    contact experience 171–2
    context and overview
        166–7
    discussion of findings
        171–4
    domestically abusive
        men 167–9
    dual-lens perspective 169
    fathers' perspectives 174–5
    perpetrator programmes
        169
    provider role 174–5
    research methods 170–1
    summary and conclusions
        178–9
    and violence 125
    see also Domestic Violence
        Perpetrator
        Programmes
        (DVPPs); father–child
        relationship

fathers
    activities with children 193
    engagement with 15,
        199–200
    infant-led practice 158–60
    influence on child
        development 166–7
    invisible 183–4
    relationships with 27
    as resource 200–2
    risk 179
fathers' experiences 174
    Brendan 189
    Brian 175
    Desmond 189–90
    Matthew 184
    Max 184
    Steve 173, 175
    Tom 175
Fathers Matters 3 review 183
feminist discourse 15
forced marriage 15
    awareness of 251
    child protection and
        schools 99–100
    context and overview 97–8
    Free2Choose 105–7, 108
    legal framework 98–9
    Manchester as research
        context 100–4
    prevalence 97–8, 101
    recognition of problem 107
    removing children from
        school 103
    review, Manchester 102
    school attendance 100,
        102–3, 108
    school safeguarding
        leads 103–4
    staff training 102,
        103–4, 107
    statutory guidance 99
    summary and conclusions
        107–8
    triggering safeguarding
        100
Forced Marriage Protection
    Order (FMPO) 98–9, 101
Forced Marriage Unit
    (FMU) 97–8
four levels of intervention 249
fragmentation 232–3, 242
framework analysis 35–6
Free2Choose 105–8
friends, support from
    30, 36, 44
friendships, KIDVA 73–4
future developments 252

gender equality 42, 45
gendered analysis 15
gendered inequalities 201
general practice
    barriers to multi-agency
        work 227–8
    child protection and
        domestic violence
        219–21
    context and overview
        214–16
    diverse perspectives 228
    duties and role 215
    focus of 227
    guidance 215, 227
    intervention potential
        214–15
    isolation 251
    joint working 214
    referrals and feedback
        222–4
    relationships with
        children's social
        services 219–24
    relationships with
        other health care
        professionals 225–6
    relationships with specialist
        services 217–19
    social work processes and
        procedures 221–2
    strengths and weaknesses
        226–8
    summary and conclusions
        228–9
    understanding roles of
        other agencies 224
ghost fathers 183
government guidance 64
Greenbook initiative 119
group work 188–90
guidance 64, 99, 216,
    227, 240, 244

Hampshire Constabulary 242
harm, new forms 15
Healthy Relationships, Healthy
    Baby initiative 242–3
hermeneutic phenomenological
    approach 21
home, preventive role 42, 45
Hyndburn and Ribble Valley
    (HARV) 64–5
    see also KIDVA

iceberg exercise 141
immigration rules, and
    forced marriage 98

Independent Domestic
    Violence Advisors
    (IDVAs) 65–6, 204, 237
independent sector 250
infant development 150–1
infant-led practice
    application of theory and
        knowledge 154–9
    attuning to signals 152
    being with 151
    case study: Benny 158–9
    case study: Darcy 154–6
    case study: Pia 156–8
    context and overview
        148–9
    in context of family
        violence 149–50
    interactions 149
    neuro-biology of
        trauma 150–1
    physical care and
        treatment 153
    practice implications 151–3
    pre-verbal 149
    safety 149–50, 152
    summary and
        conclusions 160
    working with fathers
        158–60
infants
    personality development
        151
    routine 152–3
    stress 150, 152
    vulnerability 153
informal communication 228
information, availability 234
institutional empathy 221–2,
    224, 234–5, 244
integrated services
    barriers to coordination
        and communication
        233–6
    co-location 239, 244
    context and overview 232
    difficulties 232–3
    effects of secrecy 233–4
    fragmentation 242
    institutional empathy
        234–5, 244
    knowledge gaps 235–6
    parallel interventions
        239–40
    research evidence 245
    risk assessment and
        management 237–8
    summary and conclusions
        244–5

three-in-one services
    240–1
whole family approaches
    242–3
see also multi-agency work
interagency collaboration see
    multi-agency work
intersectionality 15
intervention, four levels 249
intimate partner violence (IPV)
    and CPV 85–6
    digital media 34
    teenage IPV see
        Safeguarding
        Teenage Intimate
        Relationships (STIR)
intimate relationships,
    attitudes to 28
    see also Safeguarding
        Teenage Intimate
        Relationships (STIR)
intrinsic motivation 190
invisible fathers 183
isolation 122

Jay Review 228
joint working 214

KIDVA 63, 250
    accessibility 71
    activities 74
    case closures 77–8
    case study: Tina 76–7
    children's and young
        people's experiences
        70–8
    choice of services 67–8
    confidentiality 66, 71
    consent 66, 69
    contact frequency, methods
        and duration 75–8
    context and overview 63
    discussion 78–9
    eligibility 66
    ethics 69
    evaluation participants
        68–9
    focus groups 69–70, 73–4
    friendships 73–4
    funding 78
    Independent Domestic
        Violence Advisor
        (IDVA) as
        model 65–6
    initial contact 66–7
    interviews 70
    listening 71–2
    methods 69–70
    nature of service 65–7

non-participant
observation 70
policy context 63–5
referrals 66, 67–8
relationships 73–4
respect 71–2
safety 71, 74–5
security 74–5
skills 72
trust 71
well-being 74–5
see also advocacy
knowledge base,
expanding 15–16
knowledge gaps 235–6

Laming Report 223
legal aid 117
Legal Aid, Sentencing and
Punishment of Offenders
Act 2012 (LASPO) 117
legal obligations, for
protection 45
listening to the voice of
the child 167, 170,
177, 179, 190, 249
local authorities, relationships
with schools 50–1
long-term school absences,
and risk of forced
marriage 100

Manchester
ethnic diversity 100–1
Forced Marriage Protection
Order (FMPO) 101
forced marriage review 102
prevalence of forced
marriage 101
response to forced
marriage 107–8
safeguarding and forced
marriage strategy 101
safeguarding policy 101–2
Manchester Domestic
Violence Forum 101
Manchester Forced Marriage
Safeguarding
Standard 101
marginalisation, of children 14
marriage, arranged
marriages 97
see also forced marriage
mediation information and
assessment meetings
(MIAMs) 116
mediation, separation 116–17
mental health, and
support 36–7, 39

Mentors in Violence
Prevention 45
modelling
safety 25–6, 27, 29–30
violent behaviour 23–4
moral reasoning 28
mother–child psychotherapy
132–3
mother–child relationship
background to study 131–3
barriers to supporting 132
Cedar (Children
Experiencing
Domestic Abuse
Recovery) 138–44
context and overview
130–1
customising approaches
145
as foundation for safety 14
group support
programmes 133
resilience 132
Talking to My Mum
project 133–8
undermining 131–2
Mothering through Domestic
Violence (Radford
and Hester) 121–2
mothers
agency 24
availability to children 132
as focus of interventions
183
mothers' experiences
Cedar (Children
Experiencing
Domestic Abuse
Recovery) 140,
142, 143–4
Joyce 24–5
Lorraine 27
Opal 22
Penelope 29–30
Talking to My Mum
project 135, 136
multi-agency interventions,
development of 14–15
Multi-Agency Risk Assessment
Conferences (MARACs)
66, 113, 237, 244
Multi-Agency Safeguarding
Hubs (MASHs) 204,
237–9, 244, 250
multi-agency work
barriers to 227–8
Home Office report 205–6
role of GPs 215–16
see also integrated services
Munro Review 202

National Advocacy
Standards 66, 70
National Society for
Prevention of Cruelty
to Children (NSPCC)
calls regarding forced
marriage 101
Caring Dads 201, 241
Domestic Abuse Recovery
Together (DART)
programme 240
neuro-biology, of
trauma 150–1
NICE guidance 240, 244

one-stop shops 239
online abuse 15
Oranje Huis (Orange
House) 243
outcomes, preventive
interventions 58–9

parallel interventions 239–40
parent experiences, Child to
Parent Violence and
Abuse (CPV) 89, 92
parenting, compensating
for violence 132
parenting interventions
199–200
parenting orders 199
PARKAS (Parents Accepting
Responsibility Kids
Are Safe) 154, 240
participatory action learning
approach 130–1
partnership working 250
PEACH (Preventing Domestic
Abuse for Children) study
aims and content of
programmes 51–3
context and overview 50–1
education consultation
groups 54,
56–7, 58–9
level of disclosure 53–4
managing disclosures 56–7
outcomes of preventive
interventions 58–9
process of disclosure 55
staff training 57–8
summary and
conclusions 60
teacher's role 57
young people's consultation
group 52–3

Peek-A-Boo Club 154
peer attitudes, teenage
    IPV 44, 45
perpetrator programmes
    fathering 169
    three-in-one services 241
    see also Domestic Violence
        Perpetrator
        Programmes (DVPPs)
perpetrators, accountability
    and responsibility 197
personal responsibility,
    teenage IPV 43–4
Personal, Social and Health
    Education (PSHE) 50
physical effects 24–5
post-separation
    child-care 113–14
post-separation contact
    children's role in
        decision making
        169–70, 176–7
    children's wishes 117–18
    contact centres 118–19
    as default option 124–5
    experiences of 171
    father–child relationship
        168
    safety 250–1
    services for 119
post-separation violence
    agency attitudes 115–16
    and child-care 113–14
    children's status 123–4
    coercive control and
        mothering 122
    context and overview 112
    developing shared
        understanding
        119–23
    double disappearing act
        114–19, 125
    indirect 122
    integrated programmes 119
    legal framework 116
    manipulation of children
        121, 122
    policy context 113–14
    risk assessment 113,
        119–20
    summary and
        conclusions 125
post-traumatic stress
    reactions 36
poverty 15
practitioner wisdom 139
praxis 106

prevalence 13, 18
prevention
    aims and content of
        programmes 51–3
    staff training 57–8
preventive interventions
    co-delivery 60
    outcomes of interventions
        58–9
    summary and
        conclusions 60
primary prevention 50
professionals
    awareness of issues 251–2
    disconnections 227
    powerlessness 197
    vulnerability 152
professionals' experiences
    Child to Parent Violence
        and Abuse (CPV) 83,
        87, 88, 89, 91, 92
    Domestic Violence
        Intervention Project
        (DVIP) (Hackney)
        206, 209
    Domestic Violence
        Perpetrator
        Programmes (DVPPs)
        188, 208–9
    police 235
    primary care workers 218–
        19, 220–3, 225–6
    Talking to My Mum
        project 136
progress 16
Project Mirabal
    children's feelings before
        intervention 191
    children's feelings towards
        fathers 192–3
    context and overview
        182–3
    fathers' activities with
        children 193
    feelings of safety 193–4
    group work 188–90
    listening to the voice of
        the child 190
    pilot study 185
    summary and
        conclusions 194
    understandings of
        success 185–8
protecting relationships 39–40
protection 13
    legal obligations 45
    understanding of 14

provider role 174–5
psychological presence
    168, 173
public services, role of 44
publicity, for services 234

qualitative research 20
Quila case 98
Qvortrup, J. 20

R (Quila and another) v Sec of
    State for the Home Dept 98
race 15
reactive practice 151–2
recognition
    Australia 120–1
    England 124
    Sweden 124
    of trauma 131
referrals and feedback, from
    general practice 222–4
refuges, secrecy 234
regulation theory 153
relationships
    KIDVA 73–4
    learning about 30
    protecting 39–40
    staying in 40
research practice 20
research programmes 15–16
resignation 43–4
resilience, mother–child
    relationship 132
resiliency, co-construction
    26, 27–8
resistance, of coercion 122–3
resource allocation 249
Respect 202
Respect accredited
    programmes 242
Respect programme 57
Responding to Child to Parent
    Violence (RCPV)
    abusive behaviours 85
    context and overview 81–2
    disclosure and
        discussion 87–8
    prevalence of CPV
        reported 86
    research methods 82–3
    working with children
        90–2
    see also Child to Parent
        Violence and
        Abuse (CPV)

RESPONDS study
    barriers to multi-agency
        work 227–8
    child protection and
        domestic violence
        219–21
    context and overview
        214–16
    diverse perspectives 228
    methods 216–17
    participants 216
    referrals and feedback
        222–4
    relationships with
        children's social
        services 219–24
    relationships with
        other health care
        professionals 225–6
    relationships with specialist
        services 217–19
    social work processes and
        procedures 221–2
    strengths and weaknesses
        of general
        practice 226–8
    summary and conclusions
        228–9
risk assessment 21,
        113, 119–20
    differing approaches 224
    fathering 179
    and management 237–8
role models 42
routine, infants 152–3

safeguarding, responsibility
        for 60
Safeguarding Teenage Intimate
        Relationships (STIR)
    barriers to seeking
        support 37–40
    context and overview 34–5
    IPV as private issue 37–8
    lack of trust 38–9
    peer attitudes 44, 45
    personal responsibility
        43–4
    potential long-term
        effects 46
    prevention 40–4
    protecting relationships
        39–40
    research method 35–6
    resignation 43–4
    role of public services 44

    role of school and
        home 40–2, 45
    staying in relationship 40
    summary and
        conclusions 46
    support sources 36–7
Safer Families Project
        (Edinburgh) 205
safety 13
    of access 24
    discussion 44–5
    feelings of 193–4
    infant-led practice
        149–50, 152
    modelling 25–6, 27, 29–30
    negotiating 25–31
    post-separation contact
        250–1
    as right and priority 124
SARAH project 18
    background 19–20
    children's agency 25–31
    consent 20
    context and overview
        18–19
    implications for
        practice 31–2
    negotiating safety 25–31
    research method 20–1
    research protocols 21
    vulnerability and
        danger 21–5
school attendance, and risk
        of forced marriage
        100, 102–3, 108
school-based prevention see
    PEACH (Preventing
        Domestic Abuse for
        Children) study
School Model Safeguarding
        Policy, Manchester 101–2
school, preventive role 45
school safeguarding
        leads 103–4
schools
    fears of disclosure 51, 54
    forced marriage 99–100
    knowledge gaps 236–7
    preventive role 40–2, 244
    recording absences 100
    relationships with local
        authorities 50–1
    removing children 103
    safeguarding policy,
        Manchester 101–2
secrecy 123, 233–4

self blame 90
separation, mediation 116–17
service fragmentation
        232–3, 241
shame, CPV 90
Shifting Boundaries
        programme 55
social work responses
    challenges for DVPPs
        208–9
    challenges for statutory
        services 209–10
    co-location 203–6
    context and overview
        196–7
    Domestic Violence
        Perpetrator
        Programmes
        (DVPPs) 202–3
    engagement with fathers
        199–200
    fathers as resource 200–2
    increased focus on domestic
        violence 197–9
    moving forward 210
    The Safe and Together
        Model™ 207–8
social work support 64
social workers, turnover 102
sociology of childhood 19
staff training 121
    collaborative working 210
    forced marriage 102,
        103, 107
    interagency collaboration
        229
    preventive programmes
        57–8
    supporting mother–child
        relationship 132
staying in relationships 40
stigma, of CPV 89
stress
    effects on infants 150
    recognition and
        understanding 152
support
    approachability 45
    barriers to seeking 37–40
    from friends 30, 36, 44
    and mental health 36–7, 39
    teenage IPV 36–7
Sweden, recognition of
        domestic violence 124

Talking to My Mum
project 130
children's and young
people's experiences
135, 136
communication in
context of domestic
violence 134–5
family experiences 138
impact 137–8
methodology 133
mothers' experiences
135, 136
participants 133–4
professionals'
experiences 136
value of talking 136–7
Targeted Mental Health
in Schools (TaMHS)
initiative 236
teachers 57, 58
teenage IPV 251
barriers to seeking
support 37–40
disclosure 36–7
discussion 44–5
lack of trust 38–9
peer attitudes 44, 45
personal responsibility
43–4
potential long-term
effects 46
prevalence 36
prevention 40–4
preventive role of school
and home 40–2
as private issue 37–8
protecting relationships
39–40
resignation 43–4
role of public services 44
staying in relationship 40
summary and
conclusions 46
teenagers, intimate
relationships see
Safeguarding
Teenage Intimate
Relationships (STIR)
The Safe and Together
Model™ 207–8
The Stefanou Foundation
242–3
Theatre of the Oppressed
105, 106
Think Families (Social Exclusion
Taskforce) 199–200
three-in-one services 240–1

three planets model
115–16, 117
transparency 243
trauma
infants and mothers 151
neuro-biology 150–1
recognition 131
Triple P 92
Troubled Families programme
183–4, 200
trust
and disclosure 55, 58
in GPs 214
KIDVA 71
lack of 38–9
learning about 30

undermining 122
United Nations Convention
on the Rights of the
Child 19, 45, 64, 170

victim blame 197
violence
compensating for 132
effects on infants 150–1
and fathering 125
violent men, as parents 124–5
visibility 243
voluntary sector 250
vulnerability 31
children 170, 179
and danger 21–5
infants 153
professionals 152

WEAVE study 20
well-being 13
whole family approaches
242–3
whole system working see
integrated services

Young People and Children's
Scrutiny Committee 101

Zero Tolerance project 54

AUTHOR INDEX

Abramsky, T. 34
Adams. Jr, C. N. 105
Adamson, G. 58
Adamson, S. 236
Agnew, R. 86
AIHW 153
Alba, R. J. L. 84
Alderson, P. 20, 169, 191, 241
Aldgate, J. 233
Alexander, H. 53, 168
Allen, R. 102
Allnock, D. 55
Alvarez, A. R. G. 34
Amato, P. R. 166–7
AMICA 168
Anderson, L. 82, 88, 94
Andrews, B. 36
Aris, R. 114
Aroca, M. C. 84
Arvidson, J. 151, 152
Ashley, C. 198–9
Asthana, S. 227
Aston, H. 238
Atkinson, M. 203

Baginsky, M. 60
Bailey, S. 112
Baker, H. 89
Bala, N. 168
Bancroft, L. 125, 167, 173
Banks, D. 221, 235
Barlow, A. 116
Barnett, A. 112, 117, 119
Barron, J. 168
Barry, M. 51
Barter, C. 34, 36, 41, 64
Baynes, P. 200
Beek, M. 168
Belknap, R. A. 55
Bell, J. 45, 55, 242
Bellver, M. M. C. 84
Benson, M. L. 167
Berry, V. 234, 239
Birchall, E. 215
Black, B. M. 56

Blacklock, N. 243
Blakeborough, L. 237
Blijf Groep 243
Bloch, A. 117
Boal, A. 105, 106
Borelli, J. L. 150
Borthwich, R. 190
Boylan, J. 65
Bradbury, H. 130
Bradford Safeguarding
    Children Board 232
Bradley, R. H. 132
Brady, L. 64
Brandon, M. 112, 153
Break4Change 92
Brewin, C. R. 36
Britton, A. 214
Brown, L. 183
Brown, T. 168
Browne, K. D. 84
Bruce, C. 168
Buchbinder, E. 169, 174
Buckley, H. 31, 70,
    131, 171, 233
Bunston, W. 138, 148, 149,
    152, 154, 158, 240
Burford, G. 242
Burgess, A. 199, 201
Burgess, B. 102
Burke, S.C. 34
Burton, S. 202
Butler, I. 176, 179
Byrne, D. 236

CAADA 66
CAFCASS 117, 119
Calvete, E. 91
Campbell, R. 132
Carbin, M. 15
Carpenter, J. 229
Carrion, V. 148
Carter, Y. 227
Casanueva, C. 131, 132
Cashmore, J. 119, 121
Cassidy, D. 113, 117

Chalder-Mills, J. 185
Chau, S. 119
Chief Secretary to the
    Treasury 60
Children's Act Sub-
    Committee 114
Children's Commissioner
    for Wales 78
Cleaver, H. 233
Cohen, N. J. 152
Cohen, S. 36
Condry, R. 86
Conger, R. D. 34
Connolly, J. 168
Coogan, D. 84
Cook, D. 204
Coombs, R. H. 84
Cornell, C. P. 86
Cottrell, B. 84, 89–90, 91
Coventry Safeguarding
    Children Board 232
Coy, M. 112, 204, 205
Cozolino, L. 153
Cram, F. 36
Crockett, R. 238
Crook, W. 118, 168
Crossley, S. 184

Dalrymple, J. 65
Daly, K. 91
Dank, M. 34
Datta, J. 58
Davey, S. 113, 117
Davies, C. 215, 223
Day Sclater, S. 170
DCFS 236
De Koker, P. 34, 45
Deane, F. P. 37
Deave, T. 201, 241
Debbonaire, T. 138
Department for Communities
    and Local Government
    183–4
Derry, A. 86
Desmond, K. 249

Devaney, J. 222
Deverell, C. 236
DfE 99, 117, 215
DMSS 58
DOH 66, 70, 215, 236
Donovan, C. 125, 241
Draucker, C. B. 34
Drost, L. F. 243
Durbin, B. 238
Dutch, N. 221, 235

Edleson, J. 20, 119, 183
Edwards, K. M. 39
Eisikovits, Z. 169, 174
Ellis, J. 45, 50, 51, 52,
    54, 55, 58
Endenheim, S. 15
Enlow, M. B. 150
Eriksson, M. 20, 113,
    119, 123, 124
Evans, S. F. 150
EVAW 51

Family Court 120
Family Lives 86
Farmer, E. 118
Fatherhood Institute 200, 201
Featherstone, B. 200
Feder, G. 215
Ferguson, H. 201, 201–2
Firth, A. 117
Fisher, J. L. 86
Fleming, W. M. 45
Flowerdew, J. 25
Follingstad, D. 132
Fortin, J. 112, 118
Fox, C. 57
Fox, G. L. 167, 168, 178
Fraser, C. 200
Free2Choose 106–7
Freire, P. 105, 106
Friend, P. 50
Furman, W. 34

Gadd, D. 57
Gallagher, E. 85, 86
Gangoli, G. 97
Gelles, R. J. 86
Ghate, D. 199
Gilbreth, J. G. 166–7
Gill, A. 112, 118
Glaser, D. 169, 178
Glennen, K. 154
Goddard, C. 20, 21
Golden, S. 238
Gondolf, E. W. 90
Gosley, J. 112

Graham-Bermann, S. A.
    19, 130, 133, 239
Graham-Kevan, N. 190
Griffiths, S. 125
Grimes, M. 234
Groenhout, R. 20, 28
Grych, J. 233
Guille, L. 167

Haddon, A. 58
Hale, B. 57
Hallett, C. 215, 227
Hamby, S. 233
Hamilton, C. E. 84
Harbin, H. 84
Harne, L. 169
Harrison, C. 114
Hegarty, K. 20, 69, 214
Heide, K. M. 148
Heisterkamp, H. A. 45
Hendrick, H. 90
Hester, M. 58, 97, 112, 117,
    119, 121, 121–2, 131,
    201, 227, 232, 233
HM Government 70, 97
HMIC 116, 197
Holden, G. W. 167, 175
Holland, S. 200
Holt, A. 90
Holt, S. 70, 82, 131, 168,
    170, 171, 233
Home Affairs Committee
    99–100
Home Office 120, 204, 205–6
Honjo, S. 86
Hopwood, N. 35
House of Commons Education
    Committee 51
Howard, J. 84, 86
Howarth, E. 112
Hughes, J. 119
Huguley, S. 86
Humphreys, C. 15, 20, 31,
    69, 116, 124, 130,
    131, 132, 134, 196
Hunt, J. 112, 117
Hunter, C. 86, 251
Hunter, R. 89, 94, 112,
    116, 117, 119

Indermaur, D. 18
Ippen, C. G. 130

Jackson, S. 36, 38
Jaffe, P. 19, 52, 113, 168
Jay, A. 215, 228
Jaye, C. 215

Jenks, C. 117
Johnson, K. 18
Johnson, M. 113
Jones, J. 130, 139, 236
Jones, M. 203
Jones, S. 160
Jordan, B. 149
Jordan, C. 132

Kaganas, F. 170
Kanow, C. 198–9
Katz, J. 45
Kazimirski, A. 97
Kelle, U. 70
Kelly, J. 113
Kelly, L. 19, 169, 183, 185, 191,
    202, 204, 205, 241, 242
Kennair, N. 82
Kernic, M. A. 168
Khan, P. 215
Kidwell, J. S. 86
Kilkelly, U. 170
King, J. 237
Kishor, S. 18
Kitzmann, K. 13, 131, 196
Kletter, H. 148
Knight, A. 65
Koehn, D. 20, 28
Krampe, E. M. 168
Krug, E. G. 34

Laing, K. 170, 177
Laing, L. 15, 124, 131
Lamb, M. E. 166
Laming, J. A. 215, 223
Lamont, E. 203
Landsverk, J. 84
Larkins, C. 65
Laurent, A. 86
Laverty, S. 21
Leavey, G. 38
Leen, E. 34
Legal Aid Agency 117
Lemon, N 113
Levendosky, A. 19, 167
Lewis, C. 81
Leyden, P. 154
Lieberman, A. F. 130, 132
Lieten, G. 25
Lishak, V. 241
Loosely, S. 139, 239
Lord Chancellor's
    Department 114
Lünnemann, K. D. 243
Lupton, 226
Lupton, C. 215
Lutman, E. 118

McAllister, F. 199
McCarry, M. 64, 97
McConnell, M. 125
McConnell, N. 241
McCracken, K. 201, 241
Macdonald, E. 53
McElearney, A. 58
McGee, C. 236
Mackaskill, C. 118
McKibbin, G. 15
Mcleod, A. 112, 117
McLoed, R. 117
McManus, E. 240
Macpherson, P. 60
Madden, D. 84
Malik, N. 119
Manchester City Council
    100, 101, 103
Manchester Safeguarding
    Adults Board 101
Manchester Safeguarding
    Children Board
    (MSCB) 101–2
Mandel, D. 167
Manship, S. 55, 57
Mantle, G. 170, 179
Marshall, L. 138, 239
Martsolf, D. S. 34
Matey, P. 86
Maxwell, N. 201
Mayo, A. 102
Melander, L. A. 34
Mellor, D. 82
Miles, C. 86
Miller, D. 215
Miller, E. 45
Miller, P. 55
MoJ 99, 117
Monk, P. 91
Moore, K. 119
Morgan, A. 149–50
Morley, R. 19
Morris, A. 20, 21, 69, 131
Morrow, V. 20
Mudaly, N. 20, 21
Mullender, A. 19, 178, 196
Mullins, A. 196
Murray, S. 18

Nancarrow, H. 91
Näsman, E. 20, 123
Neale, B. 25, 170
Neville, L. 138, 240
NICE 217, 218, 227, 240, 244
Nicholas, S. 237
Nixon, J. 86, 251
Nixon, K. 131
Nolas, S. M. 138, 240
North, N. 215

Oehme, K. 118
Oliver, C. 65
Osborn, M. 199, 201
Överlien, C. 20, 234

Pagelow, M. 86
Parentline Plus 86
Parker, T. 112, 118
Parkinson, P. 119, 121
Parr, S. 86, 251
Paterson, R. 84
Paton, S. 53
Paul, C. 148, 149
Paul, R. 38
Paulson, M. J. 84, 86
Pavlidis, T. 154
Peacey, V. 113
Pearce, J. 51
Peek, C. W. 86
Peled, E. 19, 167, 168,
    169, 172, 173–4
Pence, E. 197, 202
Pennell, J. 242
Pepler, D. 44
Perel, G. 168, 169
Perry, B. 151
Perry, R. 55, 57
Phillips, R. 201, 202, 205, 243
Poisson, S. 113
Pooley, M. 94
Powell, A. 18
Practice Direction 114
Pryor, J. 169, 170, 178
Pufall, P. 25

Quinlivan, J. A. 150

Radford, L. 13, 18, 54, 64,
    112, 113, 114, 115–16,
    116, 117, 118, 121,
    121–2, 123, 131,
    168, 171, 217, 236
Ramella, M. 199
Razak, A. 97
Reason, P. 130
Reece, H. 168
Regan, L. 202
Registrados 200 casos de
    maltrato familiar por
    parte de menores 86
Reid Howie Associates
    54, 57, 58
Richardson-Foster, H. 235
Richardson, S. 227
Richie, K. L. 167, 175
Rifkin-Graboi, A. 150
Ritchie, J. 35, 217
Rivara, P. 131

Riviara, F.P. 13
Robinson, A. 237
Robinson, P. 102
Roche, J. 170, 179
Rodgers, B. 169, 170, 178
Romito, P. 184
Rosewater, A. 119
Roskill, C. 183
Rothi, D. 38
Rothman, E. F. 167, 174
Routt, G. 82, 88, 94
Royal College of General
    Practitioners (RCGP) 215

Sanders-McDonagh,
    E. 138, 240
Sarkar, N. N. 150
Saunders, H. 112, 168
Savage, E. 170
Sayer, S. 168, 171
Sayers, J. 168
Scanlon, S. 112
Schechter, D. S. 148
Schore, A. 148, 150, 151, 153
Scott, K. L. 241
Scottish Government 241
Scourfield, J. 200
Seymour, F. 36
Shaffer, L. 34
Sharp, C. 130, 139
Shaw, C. 58
Shepard, M. 197, 202
Shonkoff, J. P. 148
Sidebotham, P. 112
Siegel, D. J. 148, 150, 151
Silverman, J. 125, 167, 173
Skamballis, A. 131
Sketchley, R. 152
Smart, C. 168, 172, 173
Smit, W. 243
Smith, S. 86
Smithers, A. 102
Smithson, J. 116
Social Exclusion Taskforce
    199–200
Solomon, E. P. 148
Spencer, L. 35, 217
Srivastava, P. 35
Stafford, A. 234
Stanley, N. 45, 51, 55, 64, 112,
    113, 166, 183, 190, 196,
    202, 232, 234, 235, 236
Stark, E. 120, 186
Stead, J. 234
Steel, N. 237
Stephenson, P. 58
Stern, D. N. 148
Sturge, C. 169, 178
Sudermann, M. 239

Sylaska, K. M. 39
Szilassy, E. 229

Taylor, B. G. 55, 236
Teicher, M. H. 148
Thatcher, M. 199
The Stefanou Foundation
    242–3
Thiara, R. K. 31, 58, 112,
    116, 118, 131
Thoburn, J 112
Thoits, P. A. 36
Thomson Salo, F. 148, 149
Thoresen, S. 38
Timms, J. 112
Tompsett, H. 215, 219
Toombs, B. 117
Trinder, L. 117, 118, 168, 173
Tronick, E. Z. 153

Unell, I. 233
Unsworth, R. 25

Valentine, J. D. 37
Van Horn, P. 130
Vincent, S. 112

Wakabayashi, S. 86
Walby, S. 19
Wang, K. 221, 235
Ward, H. 215, 223
Webster-Stratton, C. 236
Weisz, A. N. 56
Wekerle, C. 44
Westmarland, N. 58, 169, 183,
    185, 191, 202, 241, 242
Whelan, S. 70, 131, 171, 233
Wicks, P. 130, 133
Wilcox, K. 18
Wilcox, P. 86, 89, 94
Wile, I. 18
Willheim, E. 148
Wills, T. A. 36
Wilson, C. J. 37
Wilson, S. 19, 52
Winnicott, D. W. 153
Winter, V. 112
Wolfe, D. 19, 44, 52
Women's Aid 217
Wong, S. 148
Woodman, J. 215, 219
Woods, P. 50, 51

Zweig, J. 34